The It Girls

The It Girls

Glamor, Celebrity, and Scandal

Caroline Young

ROWMAN & LITTLEFIELD
Lanham • Boulder • New York • London

Published by Rowman & Littlefield
An imprint of The Rowman & Littlefield Publishing Group, Inc.
4501 Forbes Boulevard, Suite 200, Lanham, Maryland 20706
www.rowman.com

86-90 Paul Street, London EC2A 4NE, United Kingdom

British Library Cataloguing in Publication Information Available

Library of Congress Cataloging-in-Publication Data

Names: Young, Caroline, 1979- author.
Title: The It girls : glamor, celebrity, and scandal / Caroline Young.
Description: Lanham : Rowman & Littlefield, 2025. | Includes
  bibliographical references and index. | Summary: "From bohemian artists'
  muses to today's socialites, including Nell Gwyn, Clara Bow, Josephine
  Baker, Marilyn Monroe, Britney Spears, the Kardashians, and more, The It
  Girls delves into the history and lives of these explosive,
  trend-setting women, whose much-disseminated images came to define
  notions of beauty, celebrity, sex, and scandal"—Provided by publisher.
Identifiers: LCCN 2024031126 (print) | LCCN 2024031127 (ebook) | ISBN
  9781538186213 (cloth) | ISBN 9781538186220 (epub)
Subjects: LCSH: Celebrities. | Women in mass media. | Women in popular
  culture. | Fame—Social aspects.
Classification: LCC HM621 .Y68 2025 (print) | LCC HM621 (ebook) | DDC
  306—dc23/eng/20240911
LC record available at https://lccn.loc.gov/2024031126
LC ebook record available at https://lccn.loc.gov/2024031127

∞™ The paper used in this publication meets the minimum requirements of American National Standard for Information Sciences—Permanence of Paper for Printed Library Materials, ANSI/NISO Z39.48-1992.

Contents

Contents

Introduction

The Evolution of the "It" Girl

Clara Bow, the first official "It" girl, in 1929. *The Legacy Collection/THA/Shutterstock.*

In 1927, cinema audiences were captivated by a girl with large, earnest eyes, who romped and flitted on screen as if it was impossible for her to keep still. They had been told authoritatively by writer Elinor Glyn that she possessed "It"—a magnetic charisma which made all men want to be with her, and other women want to *be* her.

The girl was Clara Bow, and in the movie *It*, based on a story by Glyn, she captured the frenetic, fizzing energy of the Jazz Age. It sold a message to its majority-female audience that they could act with the same impudence as Clara if they were similarly "It."

Glyn had first used this enigmatic word to denote sex appeal in her 1914 novel *The Man and the Moment*, although she wasn't the first to use the same two letters to define a woman with that magic spark. In his 1904 short story "Mrs. Bathurst," Rudyard Kipling struggled to find the words to describe the charms of a barmaid. "T'isn't beauty, so to speak, nor good talk necessarily," he wrote. "It's just It. Some women'll stay in a man's memory if they once walk down a street."[1]

Despite these early mentions, the term wasn't formalized until Elinor Glyn sailed into Hollywood as the commanding voice on good taste. She wasn't from a wealthy background; rather, she had been instructed by her grandmother on how to mimic upper-class society. She had also made a name for herself as a proponent of rather scandalous erotic fiction for female readers, on a par with the *Fifty Shades of Grey* phenomenon, as she encouraged women to find pleasure in sex.

Throughout her marriage to a barrister, she had affairs with aristocrats, including Lord Curzon, the former Viceroy of India, and these illicit moments would be inspiration for her writings, including *Three Weeks*, later adapted into a 1928 vehicle for Clara Bow and infamous for a torrid love scene on a tiger-skin rug.

Glyn had initially considered movies cheap and vulgar, but when she came to California in her mid-fifties she was seduced by the languorous lifestyle with the boulevards lined with palm trees and the pool-side cocktail parties. As she told actress Gloria Swanson, whom she had helped to hone her million-dollar glamor, "Motion pictures are going to change everything. They are the most important thing that's come along since the printing press. . . . People don't care about royalty anymore. They're much more interested in queens of the screen like you, dear."[2]

In turn, the film community was impressed by her dignified faux British aristocratic air, and they listened to her proclamations of what was hot and what was not. In her 1927 novella, *It*, serialized in *Cosmopolitan* magazine, she compared this certain type of sexual power to that of a cat or a tiger (hence that tiger-skin rug), where the possessor, as she noted in her cameo in the *It* movie, had "self-confidence and indifference as to whether you are pleasing or not."

When Paramount Pictures planned to adapt this story into a film for Clara Bow, they offered Glyn $50,000 to promote their star as the very first "It" girl. Whether or not Glyn had been paid for her endorsement, Clara came to exemplify the premise that would thereafter refer to a woman with looks that defined an era, bewitching charisma and a restless, sparkling energy that soaked up all the attention.

It's a quality sometimes known as "X," an expression coined in 1933 by writer Hilary Lynn to replace the now passé "It," and its flapper connotations, to describe an allure "which illuminates a woman until she appears to both sexes a goddess to be worshiped."[3] In 1930s Hollywood there was also "Oomph" to describe a sexually attractive woman; actress Ann Sheridan was voted the "Oomph girl" in 1939, where it was explained as "a certain indefinable something that commands male interest."[4] By the 1950s, "oomph" was often attached to mentions of Marilyn Monroe and other blonde starlets like Jayne Mansfield whose fame was cemented by the sheer number of column inches they claimed.

While Edie Sedgwick and Twiggy were named as "Girl of the Year" in the sixties, the notion of an "It" girl didn't fully make a return to the scene until the 1990s, when British socialite Tara Palmer-Tomkinson was splashed on the cover of *Tatler* with the new "It" girl tag.

By the 2000s she was everywhere. Young female celebrities like Paris Hilton, Nicole Richie, and Britney Spears were captured by paparazzi slurping a Frappuccino in a trucker cap, shopping in their Juicy Couture tracksuits, or with a flip-phone pinned to their ear and the latest "It" bag dangling from their arms. Ruthless, money-hungry snappers prowled outside nightclubs into the early hours, counting on a famous hot mess to spill out in disheveled clothes. If they didn't accidentally flash their underwear, then the paparazzi positioned their camera to ensure they got that upskirt shot. To see "It" girls like Paris come undone was the end goal. It was a means of humiliating and punishing them for being too pretty, popular, and successful.

Long before "It" there was also "star." Hollywood studios had been using this galactic symbolism to describe their top actors and actresses since the 1910s, with MGM going by the tagline, "More stars than there are in heaven." It had also been applied to actors on stage since a century before, with historian Clara Tuite noting that the first time "star" was used in this context coincided with the visibility of the great comets of 1811 and 1819, when the public were encouraged by astronomers to gaze up to the night sky. In this way celebrities replaced gods, as it was they who now blazed like a natural wonder.

The "It" girl also taps into the notion of "famous for being famous." This phrase, believed to have first been used by Malcolm Muggeridge, the British journalist, in his 1967 autobiography, owes a debt to the line "I awoke one morning and found myself famous," which was attributed to Lord Byron by his contemporary biographer Thomas Moore in 1830.[5]

On news of Jayne Mansfield's death in June 1967, the Indianapolis news columnist Fremont Power, while acknowledging her lack of talent as an actress, credited her with excelling in her special field. She was "the creation, pure and simple, of a particular kind of publicity and promotion which can make a person famous for being famous. Zsa Zsa Gabor is an example. Does anybody know what Zsa Zsa is famous for except being famous."[6]

The concept of "famous for being famous" could also be applied to the British courtesans of the Georgian era who became fashion icons and gossip queens thanks to the thriving print industry of the late eighteenth-century. They were arguably the first celebrities, a term which comes from the Latin "celebritatum" and was adapted into use in English in the fifteenth-century.

The "It" girl is a particular type of celebrity with that indefinable quality that makes her stand out, and whose fame is created through the buzz of the media, while her talents are sometimes dismissed. She possesses a daring fashion sense, a charming personality that draws people in, and her need for fun often makes her the last girl standing at the party.

Many of the women featured in this book were talented actresses, singers, and models, but having a job isn't a requirement to be an "It" girl. What she excels at is the approach to being famous. She is seen at events in attention-grabbing clothing, she is interviewed in magazines, and she hits the headlines with her romances and feuds.

Coming from relative obscurity (although some were born into it) their fame was shaped by the way their beauty and their persona was captured in mass media, whether that was through portrait painters, satirical cartoonists, gossip pamphlets, newspaper columnists, photographers, and social media feeds.

The flicker of cinema democratized celebrity in the 1920s, but from the 1600s developments in print brought new ways of disseminating images of glamorous women. The invention of photography in the mid-1800s also significantly shaped celebrity culture as it meant that their image was accessible and available, and photos of actresses and society beauties were regularly sold and collected as postcards. By the late 1800s actresses and models were also being offered sponsorship deals, with Lillie Langtry advertising Pears Soap, and in the 1910s, silent star Mabel Normand as the face of Coca-Cola. With the magazine business booming in the 1900s, celebrity photographs provided an access point to wish fulfillment and enviable lifestyles. Alongside it, gossip columnists fed the demand from the public to find out everything there was to know about these glamorous beings.

Fame may have been the endgame for "It" girls, perceived to be as fun as the flowing champagne, the top designers at their service, and travel on private railway carriages and jets, but there was an intense pressure as their lives were scrutinized by the media. There are three tenets to fame—the celebrity, the media, and the public—and their relationship can shift from worshipful to combative. They all work together to create the star, or the "It" girl, but they can shift in their dominance.[7]

The media can attack a star, with the public coming to their defense, or the star can do something controversial to provoke anger from the public, which is then played out on the pages of newspapers of gossip sites. Clara Bow, for example, was considered both a flirt and a tomboy on screen and off, and her penchant for gambling, drinking, and illicit affairs led to her being dragged through the media. Nell Gwyn was a seventeenth-century celebrity who was publicly discussed, adored, and hated in equal measures. Because she had lifted herself out of an impoverished background to become King Charles II's mistress, she was a popular target for misogynist satires. Her body was scrutinized in the nude portraits that circulated as prints, and there was much gossip and inuendo about how she seduced and performed for the king.

Nell and Clara were both a reflection of the hedonistic times they lived in, which is true of "It" girls as a rule. They represent and set the beauty aesthetic of the day, from their body shape to hair style. They also reveal long-held prejudices in society, which is why the majority of "It" girls are white, thin, and straight, given that the media has traditionally been controlled by white men.

Even though the original definition of an "It" girl as set by Glyn was that men wanted to be with them, their charisma is not just reflected in the male gaze. In the twenty-first century, it's women and gay men who determine who the latest "It" girl is. After all, it wasn't straight men who bought the tabloid magazines to read about Britney and Paris Hilton. K-pop's female idols are fashion icons rather than sex symbols, as their unique style is coveted by their female fans, leading to major endorsement deals with luxury brands.

The "It" girl's life is often described as a Cinderella story, but she can also be the Poor Little Rich Girl archetype. Edie Sedgwick and Paris Hilton were socialites from wealthy families who appeared to have it all, yet their privilege masked childhood trauma. In 1928, Clara Bow told reporter Adela Rogers St. Johns: "I think that wildly gay people are usually hiding from something in themselves. They dare not be quiet, for there is no peace nor serenity in their souls. The best life has taught them is to snatch at every moment of fun and excitement, because they feel sure that fate is going to hit them over the head with a club at the first opportunity."[8]

Some of the stories in this book are gut-wrenchingly tragic. They are laced with childhood trauma, misogyny, gaslighting, media intrusion, and exploitation. Sometimes the pain in their early years manifested a desire to seek approval from others. And as they wore their heart on their sleeves and revealed the intimate details of their lives, it opened an "It" girl up to further scrutiny. Popular culture places a woman's sexuality on a pedestal, but with double standards and hypocrisy, society has continually punished women for dating too much, for revealing too much of their bodies, for being an attention-seeker or a "publicity whore."

"It" girls have been blamed for the ills of the world; Kate Moss was accused of encouraging anorexia, Mabel Normand for negatively influencing young people when she was involved in two shooting scandals, and Kim Kardashian has been blamed by medical professionals for encouraging cosmetic surgery. Some had the strength to play the game, but others crumbled under the pressure and were pushed aside for the next hot thing.

Clara Bow's reputation would far outlive the movie *It*, as it was her own experience, that she was the hottest thing one minute, and then pariah the next, that would come to define the phenomenon. Her struggles with mental illness were exacerbated by the stress and the excesses of working in the film industry, until she was considered washed-up at the ripe age of twenty-six. In the way she described her own experience, Clara Bow's perception of herself as a flapper, and equally, an "It" girl, was incredibly insightful. "All the time the flapper is laughing and dancing, there's a feeling of tragedy underneath. She's kind of unhappy and disillusioned, and that's what people sense. They can't analyze it, but it's what makes her different from other whoopee girls."[9]

Clara's story is universal, as the way she was described in the press during her reign could easily be applied to the "It" girls of the 1950s or the 2000s. If there was one person who could be the modern incarnation of Clara, it was Britney Spears, who generated similar headlines around her love life, who was dismissed as trashy, and who was pushed to a mental breaking-point by the sheer weight of fame. As I explore a range of stories from across history, from Georgian courtesans to sixties youthquakes and the paparazzi targets of the noughties, there are several rules that are equated with being an "It" girl—although not all apply at the same time to the women featured in this book.

Rule Number One: Overcome a tough background using sheer grit and charm.
While this rule applies to many of the "It" girls that will be explored in this book, it's not necessarily universal. British socialite Tara Palmer-Tomkinson

detailed her frantic social life in her society column for the *Sunday Times*, while Brenda Frazier was dubbed a "Poor Little Rich Girl" for failing to find happiness despite her multimillion-dollar trust fund.

Rule Number Two: Stand out by being different, but ultimately be true to yourself.
Clara found fame by showcasing her own personality; amping up the energy and excitement in her performances. Audiences may have loved her, but she was rejected by the movie colony for her completely liberated, unselfconscious way of being, which was at odds with their ethos of maintaining a sense of control. "I'm a curiosity in Hollywood," Clara once said. "I'm a big freak, because I'm myself!"[10]

Rule Number Three: Become the ultimate example of beauty and spirit of the day.
Clara Bow possessed the wild, reckless live-for-the-moment spirit of the 1920s flapper. Similarly, Paris Hilton's arrival as a "celebutante" coincided with a new desire for precocious femininity for the 2000s with her straight, blonde hair, midriff-revealing clothes, and a love of girlish pink. Marilyn Monroe and Jayne Mansfield were representatives of the mammary-fixated fifties, where women were expected to be soft and submissive, while Edie Sedgwick and Jane Birkin were hip, sexually charged symbols of the sixties. Kate Moss in the 1990s reflected the grunge and Britpop movements and Kim Kardashian's meteoric rise in the 2010s coincided with a cultural shift away from the size-zero beauty ideal toward one that celebrated curves.

Rule Number Four: Hit the headlines and become the center of a media storm.
Being an "It" girl goes hand in hand with a certain amount of chaos, and Clara became a morbid curiosity, with audiences admiring her beauty while relishing the way she lived her life on the edge. Often the "It" girl is celebrated for her unconventional behavior, but those very qualities that made her so famous will be used against her.

And Rule Number Five: Eventually they'll tear you down.
Inevitably, success and adoration come with a price, and as Clara Bow discovered, when she reached the height of fame, the backlash began, and there was nothing she could do to stop the exposés. Many of these "It" girls became embroiled in their own media storms. Paris Hilton and Kim Kardashian had sex tape scandals, Kate Moss was secretly recorded doing cocaine, Mabel Normand and Evelyn Nesbit were caught up in murder trials.

These rules are a guide to the way that the lives of an "It" girl are played out in the media. But to tell the full story of the "It" girl, we need to go way back to before Clara Bow, before the development of cinema, radio, and photography. It begins in the 1660s, at the dawn of the invention of the printing press, and at the birth of a new hedonistic age in Britain, when women were only just being permitted to perform on the stage.

1

Nell Gwyn

From Orange Seller to Actress and Royal Mistress

Nell Gwyn as Venus, and her son as Cupid, in a portrait by Sir Peter Lely. *Sotheby's.*

If the flicker of the cinema screen was the way that "It" girls were introduced to the masses in the first decades of the twentieth century, then over three hundred years before, it was risqué portraits and satirical pamphlets. With the invention of the printing press under the reign of Charles II, it was as easy for a tavern dweller as a lord to salivate over the erotic nude portraits of an actress-turned-mistress of a king.

Like the "It" girls that came after her, Nell Gwyn's celebrity status triggered strong reactions in the Restoration-era London of the 1660s and 1670s.

Because her life story was so fascinating, because she was the "Protestant whore" who had fought her own way out of the London slums, and because she was so brazen and unapologetic about it, she was loved and hated in equal measure.

Discovered selling oranges in the pits of the London stage, she was bound for stardom because she possessed the golden triumvirate of beauty, brains, and wit. With her peachy-toned soft flesh and hair that was given a blazing chestnut tint in her portraits, Nell Gwyn had the appearance of a seventeenth-century Joan from *Mad Men* and the brazen, bawdy attitude of Mae West. She was praised by the most famous writers of the period, including diarist Samuel Pepys, who named her affectionately as "pretty witty Nell."

As one of the first women to be allowed to act on a British stage, she took advantage of the increasing freedoms for her sex under the reign of Charles II, "the Merry Monarch," despite having been born dirt poor. Before Nell, celebrity was just for royals and aristocrats—well-connected women whose fathers were prominent courtiers or heads of state. It was the Anne Boleyns and Catherine de' Medicis whose fashion whims were copied in court. Nell Gwyn circumvented these social hierarchies to show that a girl with nothing could be just as charming, beautiful, and influential.

She may not have been the most important of the king's lovers (he had over a dozen recognized mistresses), but her legendary status as a romantic heroine was amplified after her death at thirty-seven, a relatively young age for the times. Decades, and then centuries, later, Nell's name conjured up the glamor of a mythical age of debauchery and excess. Throughout the nineteenth century her life was mined for stage comedies and operettas, and in the early days of cinema there were silent movies—the 1911 Australian-produced *Sweet Nell of Old Drury*, and the 1915 Hollywood version which starred Mary Pickford as the titular *Mistress Nell*.

Like the much-romanticized Hollywood biographies of Pickford and Clara Bow, Nell's was likened to a Cinderella tale, where a sparky young beauty raised in the soot and dust of poverty found fame and great riches, yet was never able to achieve that much-desired happy-ever-after.

In fact, in her lifetime, Nell was often lampooned as "Cinder Nell," at a time when the fairy tale was much in its infancy. It was only fourteen years before Nell came into the world that the folk story of Cinderella was recorded on paper—with Giambattista Basile's *The Cat Cinderella* in 1634.

In *A Panegyrick on Nelly* (1679) which served as a satirical and sarcastic biography of Nell, the alleged author, the rakish alcoholic John Wilmot, second Earl of Rochester, wrote, "Ev'n while she cinders rak'd her swelling breast with thoughts of glorious whoredom was possess'd."[1]

Cinderella slept in the hearth, and Nell's place of birth was similarly grubby. As first recounted by Captain Alexander Smith in his 1715 book, *The Secret History of the Lives of the Most Celebrated Beauties*, she was born Eleanor, or Ellen, Gwyn, in 1650 in Coal Yard, Drury Lane, and was described by other biographers as "a plebeian of the lowest rank."[2] Charles Beauclerk, Nell's biographer and descendent of her oldest son by King Charles II, suggests Oxford as her likely birthplace, as it was her father, Captain Thomas Gwyn, who lived and died there in a debtors' jail in the early 1650s.[3]

After his death, Nell's mother, Ellen, or "Old Madam" Gwyn as she would be known, returned to Covent Garden, her place of birth, with her two daughters, Nell and Rose. Nell was born less than a year after King Charles I's execution following a tumultuous civil war. His death lurched Britain into a dark period of religious persecution under Lord Protector of the Commonwealth Oliver Cromwell. He was a dour, fervent Puritan, and under his control, theatres closed and public entertainments were banned. Despite this, London's medieval network of narrow streets and crooked, timber-framed buildings housed many taverns and "bawdy houses," which were rowdy brothels awash with booze.

In a diary entry for October 1667, Samuel Pepys wrote of a conversation he'd heard, where "Nelly" claimed she was "brought up in a bawdy house to fill strong waters to the guests."[4] Nell's mother worked as a prostitute here, while her daughters were tasked with serving drinks. Given they were surrounded by lecherous patrons, it was likely that they were exploited while barely in their teens. As one of just a few options for poor and uneducated young women to make money, Nell also sold herrings and oysters from a barrow stall, developing a powerful voice as she cried out her wares to draw customers in.

From a young age she possessed a magnetic allure, as if she was almost too beautiful for the fish markets and sleazy taverns. One story, recounted in an early eighteenth-century text, was that a homeless torchbearer named Poor Dick was so enchanted by her that he saved up his meagre wages to pay for a pair of worsted stockings to protect her feet from chilblains.[5] As her biographer Charles Beauclerk wrote: "She was an urchin queen in the grimy little alleys off Drury Lane, fantasizing about a regal life and commanding the allegiance of a troop of spirited waifs and ragamuffins."[6]

Cromwell died in 1658 and King Charles II returned to England after many years living in exile to claim the throne on his thirtieth birthday: May 29, 1660. His arrival marked the dawn of the Restoration period, and as he set up home in the royal residence at Whitehall, he ushered in a colorful new era of entertainment and debauchery after years of bleak Puritanism.

Under the influence of the "merry monarch," as John Wilmot, second Earl of Rochester branded him, culture flourished, with theatres reopening after twelve years of closure, and new innovations in arts and sciences, sport and trade. Having spent much of his exile in the French court of Louis XIV, he introduced Paris fashions and court etiquette to the English courts, as well as a proclivity for sexual experimentation with his bevy of mistresses. As Linda Porter writes in *Mistresses: Sex and Scandal at the Court of Charles II*: "Clever, urbane and handsome, Charles presided over a hedonistic court, in which licence and licentiousness prevailed."[7]

He was, to many, a benevolent, yet roguish, monarch, softening his sins with his buckets of charm and good humor. Charles had a weakness, and some would say an addiction, for women, and his first night at Whitehall was spent in bed with his prime mistress, Barbara Villiers, who was married to one of his ardent supporters, Roger Palmer. Barbara hadn't let Cromwell's regime hamper her sexual appetites, and she defied puritanism with her brazen affairs before and after marriage. When she gave birth to the king's daughter nine months later in February 1661, her husband was given the title first Earl of Castlemaine, as a reward for "loyalty," given the awkwardness of the situation.

At a time when women had very little rights in society, becoming a mistress to a wealthy gentleman was one of the few options for success, and to be a king's mistress was the biggest prize of all. It brought with it many advantages and rewards, including a dukedom for their children, political influence, and the gift of jewels and a lavish home.

Barbara was considered one of the most beautiful women of her day, with her tall and voluptuous figure framed by thick dark hair, and her heavy-lidded eyes and pouting mouth the ultimate in desirability. But her haughty, sly manner didn't endear her to people—John Evelyn described her as "the curse of the nation."[8]

With her steadfast loyalty to the king, she was one of the most powerful royal mistresses, and her relationship with the king ruined her marriage, but it didn't matter—she wanted great wealth and fame. Like the influencers of today, she exploited her image to achieve this ambition, ensuring she was at peak desirability while on the arm of the king at court balls and in the royal box at the theatre.[9]

She also commissioned painters to depict her as a goddess in a mythical realm. One of the most important court artists of the day, Peter Lely, treated her as his muse in his lavish works. She was Minerva, Roman goddess of wisdom and warfare with a feathered headdress and staff in hand; Mary Magdalene in a gold satin gown, and, most audacious of all, as the Madonna and Child, where she posed with Charles Fitzroy, her illegitimate son with the king. These paintings were a defiant answer to the nasty pamphlets and satirical verses that dismissed her as a whore.[10]

Skilled printmakers from France and Italy had arrived in London under Charles II, and they developed new production processes such as mezzotints, a monochrome printmaking process. It allowed for portraits by Peter Lely to be reproduced on a mass scale, and these could be pinned to the walls of coffeehouses and taverns, so everyone could see the king's mistresses for themselves.[11]

Now that his crown had been restored, Charles was the most eligible bachelor in Europe, and shortly before Barbara gave birth to their second child, he married the Portuguese Catherine of Braganza in May 1662. Charles didn't feel the same passion for the plainer Catherine, whereas Barbara just radiated sexual power in her silks and jewels. Catherine also struggled with the one job she was expected to do as queen—to get pregnant and produce a royal heir.[12]

Charles adored the theatre as much as he adored collecting mistresses, and in April 1662 he passed an official decree to lift the ban on women appearing on stage. For centuries prior, men had performed the feminine roles, and this cultural shift ushered in a new liberty. Women may have been allowed to tread the boards, but they were still reduced to eye candy, their primary purpose being to entice the audience with a saucy flash of their petticoats and a bawdy joke, and to offer certain favors after the show.

Still, the Restoration-era proved to be a positive change for women, who could now run businesses, write plays, and take part in politics. Aphra Behn was the first woman in England to earn a living from writing, and her plays and poetry offered a lyricism to her sexual frankness that wouldn't be seen again for centuries. In *A Room of One's Own*, Virginia Woolf would praise Behn as a trailblazer. "All women together ought to let flowers fall on the tomb of Aphra Behn," she wrote. "For it was she who earned them the right to speak their minds."[13]

Their talents may have been encouraged to thrive, but they were still treated as sex objects, and were very much second-class citizens. Men may have liked the sexual liberation of women—it took carnal activities out of the brothels—but still, it wouldn't do for them to be too independent.

One of the most important figures in London theatre was Thomas Killigrew. Having followed the king into exile on the outbreak of civil war, he was rewarded with a royal warrant to form a theatre company. It was his name that was on the pledge to allow women on stage, and when he opened the Theatre Royal on Drury Lane in May 1663, as part of the entertainments, he hired young women as orange vendors. Oranges were considered a sweet delicacy for enjoying during entertainments—the Restoration version of a

Cornetto or a bag of Maltesers—and were sold for sixpence each. Having arrived in Europe from China in the fifteenth century, they became fashionable under the influence of Catherine de' Medici. After Sir Walter Raleigh planted orange seeds in a field in Surrey, the trees were producing regular crops by 1595.[14]

A friend of Madam Gwyn's, Mary Meggs, also known as Orange Moll, was given the license to sell oranges, lemons, sweetmeats, and other confectionery, and she hired Nell and her sister Rose to work as her assistants. In the pit of the theatre, between each act, they held baskets of oranges covered in vine leaves, and called out, "Oranges! Will you have any oranges?"

It was pertinent for Nell to be hawking oranges; in Charles Perrault's 1697 version, Cinderella gives her ugly sisters a gift of oranges and lemons, as she transforms from servant to princess. There was also the link with fertility—Renaissance paintings such as Botticelli's "Primavera" (late 1470s to early 1480s) depicted a red-haired goddess surrounded by fertile orange trees. For Nell, the money she made from selling oranges allowed her to leave Coal Yard Alley and move into a room above the Cock and Pie tavern on Maypole Alley.

Charles was the first monarch who visited a public theatre—before him, entertainments were delivered privately—and he created a huge spectacle whenever he swept into view with his entourage and mistress by his side. It's likely that he met Nell on occasion, perhaps when she was selling oranges below, as in her short time she had developed a reputation as a girl to watch. The comic writer John Seymour, in his 1752 *Memoirs of the Life of Eleanor Gwinn*, set the scene: "No sooner had she appeared in the Pit and behind the Scenes with her Oranges, than the Eyes of the Players, and those sparkish Gentlemen who frequent the Theatres were fixed upon her, all anxious to know the Story and Birth of the handsome Orange Wench."[15]

Seymour conceded that "Beauty in high Life may charm, but at the same time it awes; while Beauty in Low Life charms and invites"—in other words, her common background made her more accessible—and Nell had charm galore. Killigrew couldn't help but be impressed by her boldness, and he introduced her to his most celebrated actors, John Lacy and Charles Hart. They took the fourteen-year-old under their wings and while Lacy taught her how to dance, Hart taught her the skills to be a successful comedian—the art of ad-lib, slapstick, and of how to draw in, and then interact with the audience.

By November 1664 Killigrew had put her on the stage, and she built up a reputation among the Theatre Royal's patrons as a quick wit. She was completely herself, free and natural on stage, and it didn't hurt that she often gave the audience a flash of her legs.

Her talents earned her a mention in Samuel Pepys diary for the first time when, in an entry on April 3, 1665, he described seeing "pretty, witty Nell," while the king and Lady Castlemaine were watching from the royal box.

Nell's first years on the stage coincided with the outbreak of the Second Anglo-Dutch War, followed by a devastating bubonic plague pandemic, and in June 1665, all theatres in London were closed. Bustling London was now desolate as residents were confined indoors, with the infected dying around them and with surgeons patrolling the area in intimidating beaked masks. Nell escaped the plague by going to Oxford with her mother, where she was hired to work for the king's theatre company.

It took another disaster, the Great Fire of London on September 2, 1666, to wipe out the plague that had spread through the overcrowded Tudor slums. The Theatre Royal, Drury Lane survived the fire, and by March 1667 Nell was the star performer in Dryden's tragicomedy *Secret Love*, also known as *The Maiden Queen*, where she played the comical heroine Florimel. The play had been written especially for Nell and Charles Hart, and as well as living together, the two were, for a time, theatre's comedy couple.

After seeing the play with his wife, Pepys was full of admiration for Nell, writing in his diary that it was a performance "that I never can hope ever to see the like done again, by man or woman . . . both as a mad girle, then most and best of all when she comes in like a young gallant."[16]

Pepys hinted at Nell's cross-dressing when she appeared on stage in breeches, and that year, in 1667, when the king requested Nell as his personal entertainer, she teased and titillated him in court performances by dressing up in male clothing and calling herself "William Nell." These "in breeches" were considered particularly erotic, as it was the only time that the outline of a woman's legs and buttocks was visible in public.

As Lady Castlemaine was losing her influence, Nell competed for the king's affections with another actress, Mary (Moll) Davis, who, like Nell, appealed to the king's affection for underdogs because of her impoverished background and rough tongue. There were rumors that the rivalry went so deep that Nell, with the help of Aphra Behn, spiked Moll's sweetmeats with laxatives before she was due to meet the king for a tryst, leading to a very embarrassing moment for Moll.[17]

Nell wasn't going to be a pushover when it came to being a royal mistress—and after she demanded a pension of £500 a year to leave the stage for the royal court, the king decided to bat for Moll instead. But by the summer of 1668 Nell was an important part of the king's household, stepping into the place of Barbara as the mistress on his arm at the theatre. Audiences would scramble to catch a glimpse of this glittering celebrity couple; the dashing king and his beautiful but bawdy lover.

Charles provided her with a house at Bagnigge Wells, near King's Cross, and for their clandestine meetings at Whitehall, she would arrive by boat to access the back Privy Stairs, which backed onto the Thames. Her voice, loud and sweary, was an unmistakable marker of her presence in the corridors of the royal residence, and like Cinderella, she would be sent back to her lodgings at the metaphorical stroke of midnight.

The beauty standard for the Restoration-era was to be pale and plump, with rounded limbs and bellies, and Nell's topless body was flaunted in portraits by the most famous painters of the day, including Peter Lely. His series of Windsor Beauties, painted in the early 1660s, immortalized some of the most alluring women in the court of Charles II, including Barbara, Lady Castlemaine. The virtuous but sexy look, of long, flowing, and wavy hair, and large, languorous eyes, referred to as "grace," was one that Lely specialized in. Being part of this prestigious series of portraits was the equivalent of being a pin-up girl, as engraved prints, or mezzotints, of the paintings were bought by influencers like Pepys, sold by printers, and circulated in public houses.

Nell Gwyn was not included as a Windsor Beauty, yet her celebrity eclipsed the others. In her portraits she was often nude, to reflect her status as wanton mistress, and was depicted as enticing and goddess-like as Venus, with lustrous, flowing hair, rouged cheeks to indicate her blushing modesty, and a coquettish tilt of the head. One mezzotint of Nell as a topless cupid, with a bow and arrow in her hand, was said to be a favorite of Pepys, who kept it on his desk as a reminder of the woman he described as "a bold merry slut."

King Charles also kept a nude portrait of her in his bedchamber—a Lely titled "Portrait of a Young Lady and Child as Venus and Cupid"—in which she poses on a divan with her eldest son with Charles.

Nell was such a celebrity that there was merchandise sold, including a series of costumes painted on translucent paper, which could then be placed over a miniature portrait of her. Her mother was proud of the success of her daughter, and in the local taverns that she frequented, her fellow drinkers would jokingly toast her as "the Queen Mother."

At the same time as Nell was lauded in portraiture, she was ridiculed by misogynist writers. In a similar way that gossip websites like Perez Hilton slut-shamed young female celebrities in the 2000s, satirical pamphlets targeted and shamed her as a "royal whore." These pamphlets, like early newspapers, allowed the middle classes to read about life in court, while also fulfilling a public desire to consume gossip about the king's many mistresses.

Restoration satire was moralistic in nature, using ridicule to guide the public to be more virtuous. For the writers of the day, Nell's stage success and her role as mistress was counter to how women were expected to behave.

In 1669, the year after she and the king began their relationship, there was a popular, and unattributed, rhyme called *Nell Gwynne*, that went: "Hard by Pall Mall lives a wench call'd Nell. King Charles the Second he kept her. She hath got a trick to handle his prick. But never lays hands on his sceptre."

Similar to other satires of her, it depicts her as a promiscuous woman who is skilled in seduction, but who lacks the political ambition (keeping her hand off his scepter) of Barbara, who used her fiery temper and strong will to hold sway, and was known to take money from ambitious courtiers to sell an audience to the king. Nell did wield some influence over the king, and not just in how she was able to secure a long lease on 79 Pall Mall and a title for her son. A long-held rumor was that she persuaded him to establish the Royal Hospital Chelsea for war veterans.[18]

In 1670 Nell gave birth to her first child, Charles, the king's seventh son. Nell took to addressing him as the "little bastard" in front of the king, and this shamed him into bestowing the child with the title of Charles Beauclerk, first Duke of St. Albans. She gave birth to another son on Christmas Day 1671 and he would be given the name James Beauclerk.

Her Pall Mall home became a gathering place for artists and politicians, actors, writers, and courtiers, where they danced, flirted, and tucked into a huge ten-course buffet serving all sorts of delicacies—herring, salmon, meats, wine, cider and beer, and oranges, which was understandably her good luck charm.

Nell's childhood had been desperate, and now that she had a generous allowance from the king, she spent extravagantly. She adored beautiful fashions, purchasing red satin gowns, scented gloves, pearl necklaces, and delicate satin shoes for her dainty feet. When it came to decorating her home, she spared no expense, and as proof she had really made it, her initials "EG" (for Eleanor Gwyn) were embossed or engraved on the fine silks and silverware. She bought three barrels of oysters a week for her raucous parties, she traveled by private sedan chair, and slept on a £1,000 silver bedstead which featured a baroque design of eagles, crowns, and cherubs, and as a centerpiece, a likeness of Nell and the king. If other mistresses posed a threat, at least she could sleep with a form of him every night.

She was such a star in London that admiring members of the public left flowers at her door, and she drew a crowd of curious onlookers whenever she was spotted. She visited the theatre several times a week, often in a mask to disguise her now recognizable features, but she would always buy oranges from a new generation of sellers who must have felt awe and admiration at how far she'd come.

Nell may have eclipsed Barbara, but another important mistress was slipping into the king's affections. Louise de Kérouaille was a French courtier whom Charles nicknamed "Fubbs," for her short, chubby stature. Nell had some other choice names for her rival—"Squintabella," because of a squint in her eye and "Weeping Willow" for her tendency to cry. Louise in turn, looked down on Nell for her coarseness—"Anybody may know she has been an orange wench by her swearing"—and for her extravagance when it came to lavish dress.[19]

When she provided false flattery one day, "Nelly, you are grown rich, I see, by your dress; why, woman, you are fine enough to be a queen," Nell replied: "Quite right, madam. And you are whore enough to be duchess."[20]

Another reason for Nell's popularity was that she was a Protestant, while Louise was a Catholic. England continued to be fraught by its religious divide, with suspicion that there was a "Popish plot" of Catholics aiming to take over the Whig government, who believed that the monarchy and the church should not have absolute power over parliament.

Riding through Oxford one day, Nell's coach was mistaken for Louise's, and she was surrounded by a mob of Whig sympathizers who were hurling abuse at her and calling her a French whore. She popped her head out the window to calm them: "Pray, good people, be civil, I am the Protestant whore!" The abuse turned to cheers and claps, and she waved to them as the coach was allowed to pass.[21]

The year 1678 proved to be a traumatic one for Nell. In January, on Twelfth Night, her Pal Mall home was broken into, and much of her engraved silverware was stolen. It was a symbol of her success, and to lose it was devastating. But worse was to come. She sent her younger son, James, to Paris for school, and he died a few years later from an infection. Her mother also died in the summer of 1679, when she accidentally drowned in the river near her Chelsea home.

She was only thirty, but Nell was already facing mockery for her middle-aged looks. Rather than Pepys's "pretty witty Nelly" she was called "old Nelly," "ugly fac'd Nelly," the "wither'd Whore."[22]

The king was increasingly suffering from ill health, and Nell was all too aware that without his support, her future, as a mistress without the security of marriage, would be in peril. Following a sudden apoplectic fit, the king died on February 2, 1685. In his last moments he still thought of Nell, pleading to his brother, James II, "let not poor Nelly starve." Despite the new king's piety, he kept to his word and granted her a £1,500 pension.[23]

Nell was bereft at the loss of her social standing, and she also suffered from poor circulation, high blood pressure caused by a possible syphilis infection, which in March 1687 led to a stroke. A second stroke affected her speech and movement and left her confined to her silver bed. She died from apoplexy on November 14, 1687, at the age of just thirty-seven. On the day of her funeral, a huge crowd gathered on the streets to say goodbye, made up of people from all ranks of society, including street-sweepers and orange sellers, who saw themselves reflected in her rags-to-riches story.

Nell's celebrity lived on after her death, and not just in the eighteenth-century biographies that explored her life. She made an appearance in Henry Fielding's 1749 novel *Tom Jones* and in Virginia Woolf's *Orlando: A Biography* (1928), and on stage, first with 1799 comedy by Edward Jerningham, titled *The Peckham Frolic, or Nell Gwyn*, and a 1924 West End musical, *Our Nell*, with songs by Ivor Novello. In 1884, the operetta *Nell Gwynne* transferred to New York's Casino Theater, where the bawdy star once again flashed her pantaloons for the king.

The year before, in 1883, another king's mistress had swept the New York stage, finding favor among its gilded age denizens. If Nell had been the first "It" girl with a royal patron, then Lillie Langtry, the "Jersey Lily," would once again demonstrate the fickleness of fame for celebrated beauties and royal mistresses, as we'll see in a later chapter.

The Georgian Celebrity Age

From Courtesans to Queens

Kitty Fisher as Cleopatra dropping a pearl into her wine, in a portrait by Joshua Reynolds (1759). *Yale Center for British Art.*

In March 1759, a nineteen-year-old woman went for a ride in Hyde Park, London's bustling green space where the great and the fashionable expected to be seen. In a fleeting moment, she slipped and fell from her horse, and as she landed on her posterior, her skirts flew overhead. Given women in the eighteenth-century went without underwear, she revealed all. She was whisked away in a sedan chair, just as curious onlookers began to murmur that this young woman looked like Kitty Fisher, the courtesan.

This was a perfect publicity coup for Kitty, perhaps as titillating as Marilyn's nude calendar or Kim Kardashian's "breaking the internet" photo-spread. Whether it was by well-engineered design, she was now literally the "fallen woman" as she became the talk of the "ton." Derived from "bon ton," the French for good taste, in London, the "ton" was a collective name for the top people in the city who led on mode and manners. Under the reign of George III (1760 to 1811) and his wife Queen Charlotte, a consumerist culture thrived, where fashion was everything. While aristocrats like Georgiana Cavendish, Duchess of Devonshire were incredibly influential on shaping what society wore, it was the courtesans who could be considered original street style influencers.

After her fall, there was a huge appetite to read the latest gossip about Kitty Fisher in the press, and to cash in on her sudden fame, a brief biography, *The Juvenile Adventures of Miss Kitty Fisher*, was rushed into print. Without any perceived talents except for an ability to display herself, she was now famous for being famous, and three weeks after falling from the horse, she arrived at Joshua Reynolds's studio to have her portrait painted. As one of the leading portrait painters of the day, and the Royal Academy of Arts's first president, he achieved his own level of fame for his portraits of infamous beauties. He was the equivalent of a celebrity photographer—the Herb Ritts, Mario Testino, or Annie Leibovitz of the eighteenth century.

In Reynolds's 1759 portrait of Kitty, she gazes directly at the viewer, her arms crossed in front of her on a desk as her voluminous lace sleeves, and a letter, spill around her. Engraver Edward Fisher quickly knocked up his own mezzotint of the painting, which circulated in July of that year. The rich and influential used portraiture to demonstrate their power, and the public wanted to own these images, particularly if they were as intriguing as Kitty, whose print was snapped up in the thousands.

High-class courtesans like Kitty Fisher—the "It" girls of the Georgian era—were sometimes referred to as "the Cyprian Corps" and "the Cytherians"; the most successful were labeled as the "Toast of the Town."[1] They were bejeweled and upholstered in pearls and diamonds, silk and lace, they reserved the most prominent boxes at the theatre for the season, and their benefactors were some of the most powerful men in London. The city's lively social scene played out in the taverns and coffeehouses, with flowing gin and the pungent smell of tobacco, as gentlemen dealt cards and flirted with their courtesan companions and the prostitutes of the local bawdy houses, and where the whispers of gossip would filter into the printed press.

Like Nell Gwyn as a royal mistress, the high-class courtesans used their sexual power to achieve success, playing the game to lift themselves from humble beginnings to a fashionable status that was on a par with that of a duchess. The game involved being seen in all the right public spaces, including in the best boxes at the theatre, at Ranelagh pleasure gardens, and at the Pantheon, a domed entertainment center with masquerades and concerts. And it also meant dazzling the public with their portraits and prints, and ensuring their names were in the scandal sheets for every discretion and affair.[2]

Celebrity as a concept blossomed in Britain in the 1700s. This was due to several dynamics coming together to create an aspirational society driven by the burgeoning middle classes. It thrived on the chatter spread by a new generation of print media, and a public sphere where the latest political news and gossip could be debated in the coffeehouses and salons.[3]

When the Licensing Act expired in 1695, it ended censorship and libel laws, so that writers and artists were now free to say whatever they wanted. There was also an increasingly educated public, with literacy opening up a new world of books, newspapers, and pamphlets which thrived under the new technologies that made printing much more affordable.

Britain's first daily newspaper, the *Daily Courant*, was launched in 1702, and by the mid-1700s around 100,000 newspapers were sold in London every week, out of a population of 750,000 people. While they were only affordable to the affluent, copies could be circulated around taverns and coffeehouses for a wider readership.[4]

Weekly periodicals were introduced, first with *Tatler* in 1709, which printed the gossip heard around London coffeehouses, while also offering instructions on manners to the middle-class readership. When the *Town & Country Magazine* was first published in 1769, it attracted curious readership for its Tête-à-Tête series, which showed oval portraits of two lovers side by side, and with thinly veiled clues to their identities.

Satirical prints also boomed under the Georgians, with artists like Thomas Rowlandson and James Gillray setting tongues wagging with their on-point caricatures of politicians and courtesans, rakes and macaronis, the young Englishmen who returned from their Grand Tour having adopted a lavish and colorful style of dress. As Alice Loxton writes in *Uproar!: Satire, Scandal and Printmakers in Georgian London*, these prints "were so acerbic, so insightful, that every Londoner's folly and foible was fair game." Copies were shared in the stately homes and "even had a place at the breakfast table of Queen Charlotte."[5]

Joshua Reynolds worked closely with mezzotint engravers so that his paintings could quickly be mass-produced, purchased, and hung on walls. The mezzotint process was upgraded to aquatints in the 1770s, where a touch of Egyptian blue or Venetian red could be applied after the print had dried. The ready availability of mezzotints and aquatints sparked a craze for collecting pictures of the glitterati. There was even a crafting boom among young ladies who collected prints and pasted them into books or on the walls of their dressing rooms.

In 1771 Joshua Reynolds completed one of his most famous portraits of a courtesan, that of actress Frances "Fanny" Abington, whose legacy included setting a trend for the "Abington Cap." Posing as Miss Prue in William Congreve's *Love for Love*, she looks directly at the viewer, as her thumb sensationally brushes her lip to hint at her role as mistress.

Joshua Reynold's 1771 portrait of Fanny Abington as Miss Prue in *Love for Love* depicts her as a fashion icon and courtesan with the wrist bands and controversial gaze. *Yale Center for British Art.*

Art was now in the public realm, moving from private palaces into public galleries, and theatres thrived. Courtesans often treaded the boards as a means of advertising their services—a member of the audience could go home with them that night—but Sarah Siddons, a young mother who was definitely not a courtesan, sparked what became known as "Siddonsmania" for her stage performances.

Sarah, an actress from Wales, appeared on the stage on December 29, 1776, at London's Drury Lane theatre, to play Portia in *The Merchant of Venice*. Her poorly received performance led to her being cast out from the theatre. Yet she fought back, and after touring the provinces, by 1786 she was a sensation, and the "Queen of Drury Lane" was now a tragedienne, as she took to the stage as Lady Macbeth and Desdemona. Her abundant dark hair and regal stature separated her from the courtesan actresses who used the theatre as their calling card. Because Sarah was a young mother of three children, the audiences felt protective of her, and regularly flocked to her dressing room to show their support. Potter Josiah Wedgwood also cashed in on her celebrity by creating a chess set with Sarah as queen, and thus giving the middle classes a piece of her to play with.[6]

Despite Sarah Siddons's respectability, Covent Gardens was home to the prostitutes of London, not only displaying themselves at the theatre, but also in the bawdy houses that surrounded them. Harris's *List of Covent Garden Ladies* was a directory of whores, with details of their looks, their price, and their specialties. According to Gretchen Gerzina in *Black England: A Forgotten Georgian History*, there were also Black sex workers operating here, with at least one all-Black brothel in the area.[7]

It's believed that one in five women in eighteenth-century London took part in sex work. The vast majority lived a life of poverty and degradation, where they were blighted by sexually transmitted infections and struggled as they aged. It was only the few who rose to the top to become the "Toast of the Town" as they worked society's drawing rooms. There was an endless public fascination with these high-class courtesans, and this demand was fulfilled by the publication of their memoirs, with several being released in the Georgian era; the equivalent of the British model Jordan (aka Katie Price) who had several bestselling biographies in the 2000s, while still only in her twenties. Kitty Fisher and Fanny Murray rose up from the lowliest position to becoming top, glittering celebrities, before marrying and dying young.

A mezzotint by Henry Robert Morland of Fanny Murray with an enormous pearl earring sold thousands of copies for her elegance and aspirational style. Men also wanted these images to lust after, and so a miniature of her face was created and designed for inserting into a watch case or to hang from a gold chain.[8]

The mezzotints of these glamorous women were aspirational to working-class shopgirls who looked up to the courtesans in the same way the Kardashians inspire young women on social media. Fanny Murray was such a fashion leader that she was honored with gin cocktails, ships, racehorses, and a style of cap being named after her. Born in Bath in 1729, she had been orphaned as a child and after being seduced by politician John Spencer, at fourteen she entered the murky world of London prostitution. As mistress of John Montagu, fourth Earl of Sandwich, she became the "reigning Toast of the Town" as every whim set a trend.

She eventually left the demimonde for marriage in 1757 and just two years later it was Kitty Fisher who was the most celebrated courtesan in London. Born in London's Soho in 1741 as Catherine Maria, Kitty is believed to have worked as a milliner, one of the lowest of professions and often linked with prostitution. All the descriptions of Kitty are that she was vivacious, flirtatious, and with a sparkling wit, and it's believed that she was a regular escort at Arthur's club, a spin-off from the famous gentlemen's club and chocolate house, White's. As the mistress of influential army officers, she was taken to all the right places to be seen—to the theatre and for supper in Ranelagh Gardens, where visitors displayed themselves under the glow of lanterns and to the strains of music.[9]

Just months after her fortunate fall in Hyde Park, she had sparked a "Fishermania," as her style was pored over and the gossip around her latest conquests were readily discussed. Kitty dripped in pearls and diamonds, she wore fine silk gowns and entered a room in a cloud of feathers and frou-frou. The poem "The Hundred Pound Miss" was a reference to the price for her company, and there was a famous story that she placed a hundred-pound note between two slices of bread and ate it, although this was also attributed to Fanny Murray and several other Georgian courtesans.

This notion of a powerful woman who is so successful that she can consume her own wealth was further reinforced with another portrait of Kitty by Reynolds, in which she poses as Cleopatra dropping a large pearl into a glass of wine, having won a wager against Mark Antony. As well as Joshua Reynolds, she was also painted by Nathaniel Hone, who symbolically placed her next to a kitten scrambling by a goldfish bowl, and with the mezzotints that were purchased in their thousands, she became one of the most recognizable faces in London.

When the notorious Venetian lover Giacomo Casanova met "the celebrated Kitty Fisher" in London in 1763, as she was on her way to a ball, he wrote down his impressions. "She had on over a hundred thousand crowns' worth of diamonds. [Author Ange] Goudar told me I could seize the opportunity to have her for ten guineas, but I did not want to do so. She was charming, but she spoke only English. Accustomed to loving with all my senses, I could not indulge in love without including my sense of hearing." He also recounted in these memoirs the buttered bread and hundred-pound note story which was circulating about her at the time.[10]

By 1764 Kitty was tiring of fleeting encounters, and after marrying a man called John Norris, they spent a blissful extended honeymoon riding on his Kent estate. When Kitty fell ill with pneumonia or tuberculosis, she sought a cure at a hot springs near Bristol, but at a carriage stop near Bath she rapidly deteriorated and died on March 10, 1767, at just twenty-six years old. Her death was a shock and tributes sprung up after her death, including poems and songs, and a mention in the famous nursery rhyme "Lucy Locket."[11]

After Kitty's death, the celebrity baton switched to Mary Robinson, a mistress of George, the Prince of Wales, later George IV, who was dubbed "the most beautiful woman in England." Known for her beauty and style, whatever she wore was faithfully copied, with the "Robinson" cap, muffs, and gold stockings all replicated and advertised under her name. After a visit to Paris, she introduced to London Marie Antoinette's controversial pastoral "la chemise à la Reine," which influenced an entire era of dress.

Born Mary Darby in Bristol in 1757 to a naval captain and his wife, her early start was much more comfortable than that of Kitty Fisher and Fanny Murray. She was tall and striking by the time she was a teenager. She adored fashion but she also had a melancholy air as she enjoyed "morbid poetry," and "sombre music and being left in solitary contemplation." Mary liked to dress simply, as if she was a Quaker in light brown silk; an example of her individual style that drew attention to her.[12]

Taking advantage of the new educational opportunities for women, she attended a series of schools. While studying at Oxford House in Marylebone, the school's dancing master introduced her to the deputy manager of Covent Garden Theatre, and she successfully auditioned to go on the stage. For one of her first outings in society, she spent hours dressing herself for a visit to the Pantheon, a large pleasure venue on Oxford Street which was famed for its huge dome. Having chosen a pink satin gown trimmed with sable, she relished the chatter and admiring glances of all the other visitors who wondered who she was. As she wrote in her memoirs, "I looked forward with delight both to celebrity and to fortune."[13]

With her mother having been abandoned by her father, Mary was encouraged to give up acting and marry a clerk, Thomas Robinson, but she soon learned that his promise of possessing an inheritance was a lie. He spent heavily to fund an elaborate lifestyle, and after being sent to prison for his debts, Mary and their baby daughter were forced to live in the prison for a time too. She wrote poetry as a respite, and her first collection, *Poems by Mrs*

Robinson, published in 1775, came to the attention of Georgiana, Duchess of Devonshire, who was so moved by both her talents and her unfortunate circumstances that she acted as her patron.[14]

In December 1776 Mary made a return to the stage in Theatre Royal, Drury Lane's production of *Romeo and Juliet*. She drew good reviews, and theatre audiences were drawn to her striking style, with actresses at the time typically choosing their own fashions to wear on stage. Particularly popular were her "in breeches" roles as Viola in *Twelfth Night* and Rosalind in *As You Like It*, because they offered the tantalizing glimpse of the outline on her legs. But it was as Perdita in *The Winter's Tale*, performed on December 3, 1779, that would forever be entwined with her persona. In the royal boxes that evening was King George III, Queen Charlotte, and the seventeen-year-old George, Prince of Wales, who was completely transfixed as she appeared to utter her lines directly to him. After months of exchanging letters, she visited him at his palace at Kew and by 1781 was appearing in public with him. According to an introduction of a reprint of her memoirs, she was now, thanks to the prince, "magnificently dressed, driving a splendid equipage which had cost him nine hundred guineas, and surrounded by his friends."[15]

While she relished her new status, the affair exposed her to the press, where every move was documented. She was featured in *Town and Country Magazine*'s Tête-à-Tête column, where she was referred to as "Perdita," and the prince as "Florizel." A 1783 satirical print depicted a bust divided in two, with one half as the prince and the other as Perdita, and with Thomas Robinson as a stag's head mounted on a wall with the words "King of Cuckolds."

In Mary's salacious unauthorized memoirs, published in 1784, designed to undermine her, she was depicted as a nymphomaniac with an uncontrollable sexual drive. In one anecdote she seduced a stranger in a long-distanced coach, while her husband was sitting on the roof, further placing him in the role of cuckold. She then used sex to achieve all the trappings of her luxury lifestyle. Mary was proud that she wasn't a courtesan, yet she would be lambasted for years in satirical prints and vicious commentary.[16]

The prince's jealousies had forced her to abandon the stage, and when he tired of her, she pressured him to provide her with a lifetime annuity. Once the contract was signed, she left for Paris in October 1781, where she made an impression as the notorious "La Belle Anglaise." She was invited as a guest to the opera and to fashionable parties, and even received a prestigious invitation for an audience with Marie Antoinette. She needed a suitable gown to meet the queen and was granted time with Rose Bertin, the royal modiste, where she ordered a pale green gown decorated with bunches of lilac, and with plumes of white feathers in her hair.[17]

In Paris, courtiers would visit Paris's influential *La Marchande de modes* to buy gowns that followed the latest fashion whimsy of the queen, from towering headdresses to gowns covered in ribbons and feathers. These fashions would also be used as illustrations in fashion magazines, setting trends for the latest styles that were straight out of Versailles. In a world where men ruled, Marie Antoinette's image was set by women. Not only were her gowns devised by her dressmaker Rose Bertin, but also her portrait was painted by the female artist Élisabeth Louise Vigée Le Brun.[18]

In the 1780s, Marie Antoinette wished to be free from the stuffy restrictions of Versailles, and as she escaped to her country retreat, the Petit Trianon, she chose to dress in informal white muslin gowns, which were similar to the type of dress worn by Creole women in the West Indies. Controversially, she chose to wear one of these informal white gowns by Rose Bertin in a royal portrait by Vigée Le Brun. When it was put on public display, she was accused of mocking the crown. By choosing cotton muslin for these gowns, she was also widely criticized for damaging France's important silk industry. Marie Antoinette was now developing a negative reputation for how she conducted herself. She racked up obscene debts on the gambling table, she went to the theatre in disguise, and while the French people struggled to survive under crippling taxes, she was falsely accused of uttering the dismissive words, "Let them eat cake." She was really a victim of a bad press campaign which generated rumors of lesbian affairs and exposed a scandal over the ownership of a very expensive necklace. Satirical cartoons depicted her as an extravagant, complacent queen nicknamed "Madame Deficit," she was hissed at the opera, and her lavish spending, vanity, and public display finally led her to lose her head in the French Revolution.[19] In the 2006 movie of her life, director Sofia Coppola places Marie Antoinette as a modern "It" girl like Paris Hilton, who lusts over pretty shoes and delectable cakes, and who was built up as a fashion icon to be destroyed by the press.

Mary arrived back in London at Christmas 1781, and, showcasing her new French style, she caused jams on the thoroughfares whenever she went shopping. In the December 1783 edition of the fashion periodical *The Lady's Magazine* she was praised for "The Robinson hat," and the airy, pale *chemise à la Reine* was rebranded "The Perdita chemise." Georgiana, Duchess of Devonshire had also favored this freeing form of dress, but it was Mary, as an actress, who made it accessible. As fashion moved toward a more natural look, in part inspired by the French Revolution, the chemise represented new liberties, and because it could be worn for all classes, it was considered much more democratic. It was also a style that was ripe for satire due to its flimsiness. Gillray's *The Graces in a High Wind* (1810) depicted this new trend for un-dress as three ladies are exposed in the wind and rain by the revealing nature of their muslin gowns. It's important to note that this fashion was steeped in brutality. The overwhelming demand for fine muslin cotton led to mass exploitation and cruel practices first in India, and then on the slave plantations in North America.

Mary could never shake off the "Perdita" persona, and after an affair with politician Charles James Fox, she settled down with celebrated commander Banastre Tarleton, who her biographer Sarah Gristwood said, "gave muscle to her glitzy, slightly showbiz fame" and placed them as "the Posh and Becks of their day."[20] At the age of twenty-five she was struck down by rheumatoid arthritis after a reckless overnight carriage ride while trying to locate the philandering and often absent Tarleton. The illness drained her vitality as the debilitating pain rendered her unable to walk, and which meant she had to be carried into and out of carriages. Yet her disability didn't save her from the vicious attacks on her reputation in the press as a former royal mistress and lover of politician Fox. She was mercilessly mocked in satirical cartoons and pamphlets, including one in the August 1784 edition of *The Rambler's Magazine* titled "Perdita upon her last legs," which depicted her as a ragged street prostitute.

The relationship with Tarleton lasted fifteen volatile years until he finally abandoned her for good.

Devastated and in pain, she came to rely on morphine while still building a career as an incredibly successful author of novels, poetry, and feminist essays on a par with Mary Wollstonecraft.

As her biographer Paula Byrne wrote: "Actress, entertainer, author, provoker of scandal, fashion icon, sex object, darling of the gossip columns, self-promoter: one can see why she has been described as the Madonna of the eighteenth century."[21]

Her celebrity is a ready comparison to the "It" girls of the paparazzi age who were subjects of "get the look" features and unauthorized biographies, and who were so often slut-shamed for their sexual appetites. Yet when Mary aged out of it, she established herself as a great intellect and social commentator, becoming a true survivor of the fickle nature of fame.

3

The Pre-Raphaelite Muses

Lizzie Siddal in Rossetti's *Beata Beatrix* (1877), painted after her death. *Tate*.

It was after midnight in London's Highgate Cemetery, and a group of gentlemen gathered around the burial place of Elizabeth "Lizzie" Siddal, as gravediggers, guided by the eerie flicker of candlelight and bonfire, dug their spade into the earth. The well-dressed gentlemen, wrapped for the October chill—a doctor, a lawyer, and the agent of the artist Dante Gabriel Rossetti—watched grimly as the spades scraped across the coffin, anticipating the moment when its lid would be prized open.

They were here for one purpose—to retrieve a book of poetry that Rossetti had nestled beside the body of his wife when he buried her. Seven years after Lizzie's tragic death from a laudanum overdose in 1862, he regretted having sacrificed the only copy of what he considered his best works. Once the now soggy and rotting book was plucked from the coffin, she was sealed up and buried once more, and the men traipsed from the graveside, haunted by the smell and the sight of a decaying corpse.

That night, Rossetti's agent, Charles Augustus Howell, went to the artist's home to deliver the poetry book. Rossetti was tortured at the thought of his wife and muse in death, and couldn't bring himself to be there, but Howell, looking into his friend's anxious eyes, had a story to tell him—that when they had opened the coffin, Lizzie's body was perfectly preserved, almost glowing in its translucence, and because her celebrated hair had continued to grow, the coffin was now filled with mounds of copper curls.

It was a fantastical tale that would be repeated for many years after, placing Lizzie into the same mythical realm as Ophelia, the most famous character she posed as. "Alive," biographer Lucinda Hawksley wrote, "she had often not been appreciated, but in death Lizzie apparently remained a thing of extraordinary beauty."[1]

When John Everett Millais's *Ophelia* was displayed at the Royal Academy in 1852, viewers lined up from morning to evening to view it, and then jostled with one another to get a closer look. Most curious of all was the dead woman centered in the painting, who was floating in a stream strewn with flowers, moss, and reeds that were so naturalistic it could be a photograph. Her red hair was spread out in the water like a halo, and with her hands and face turning up to the sky, blue eyes open and lips parted, her expression was almost close to ecstasy. As Franny Moyle writes in *Desperate Romantics*, Millais could see real Lizzie's tragedy. "All he had to do was paint around it. No subject could have been better designed for this girl, and no girl could have posed better for the subject."[2]

Lizzie would become the face of an art movement, and the painting appeared to prophesize her early death; the blaze of an "It" girl extinguished too soon. And like those who came after her, the fame she had so desired didn't bring her the happiness she sought.

She was one of the most vital muses of the group of artists known as the Pre-Raphaelite Brotherhood, which included Dante Gabriel Rossetti, John Everett Millais, William Holman Hunt, and later members Edward Burne-Jones, and William Morris, the original interior design influencer.

They may not have used the expression "It," but artists' models Lizzie Siddal, Jane Morris, and Alexa Wilding were just as influential in London as Twiggy would be a century later. The artists used a different word—"Stunners"—to describe their elusive beauty. These muses were pulled from very humble backgrounds, but they were elevated to supermodel status as the focus of sensual, tragic works. "Stunners" was a term coined by Rossetti and as his biographer Henrietta Garnett describes: "She might be propriety personified, but she is the kind of woman, from any social class, who turns the heads of complete strangers wherever she goes. She is, in fact, a star."[3]

The Pre-Raphaelite Brotherhood was formed in 1848 by seven young art students at the Royal Academy who bonded over their struggles with money, or "tin," as their de facto leader Rossetti referred to it. They believed art was at its purest before the advent of the painter Raphael, and they took medieval legends and ballads as their inspiration. They drew up a list of "Immortals," with Jesus at the top, followed by Geoffrey Chaucer, William Shakespeare, and romantic poets John Keats, William Blake, and Alfred Tennyson. They were young and idealistic bohemians with a dedication to the arts and a sense of sexual exploration, and who, like the foppish 1960s countercultural spiritualists with a taste for Art Nouveau, wore their hair long and draped themselves in velvet suits.

Signing their paintings with the initials "PRB," they preferred to paint "en plein air" to capture a naturalistic world as true to life as possible, often trekking across fields and rivers to find the perfect position. They then applied layers of rich, vivid paint, such as gamboge, cobalt, and viridian, to fire the imagination with an enhanced reality in a literary or medieval legend setting. It was a worship of beauty, and the female form, naked or barely clothed, was vital to their vision. They depicted women as sensual goddesses and fallen women who hold the viewer's gaze, as if challenging them to see who she really is. Critics and the public at first found the heightened naturalism obscene as they eulogized womanhood in mythical settings, while expressing their real anxieties around love, marriage, and motherhood.

The respectable women of their class would never agree to be an artist's model as it was tainted with disrepute. Instead, the artists would flirt with girls working in the fields or they picked them out from the audience in the theatre or while window-shopping. Just as they worshipped myth, they had a Pygmalion attitude in the way they wished to transform a poor, unrefined girl into a lady to uncover the swan inside the rough exterior. It was the classic savior complex, combined with a bit of pre-Hollywood wish fulfillment—of taking an ordinary girl and turning her into a goddess.

In the winter of 1849, Walter Howell Deverell was searching for the perfect model for Viola in his painting of a scene from Shakespeare's *Twelfth Night*. Because she would be dressed as a boy, he was after a thin redhead, but had so far failed to find her.

One day his friend, Irish poet William Allingham, spotted a young woman through the window of Mrs. Tozer's hat shop in Cranbourne Alley, a narrow passage off Leicester Square which was crammed with milliners and dressmakers. With her pale face, mass of red hair, and thin limbs, she was the exact fit.

The nineteen-year-old Elizabeth Siddall (as was the original spelling of her surname) was striking in her uniqueness. By the beauty standards of the time, she was considered too tall and thin, when women were celebrated for being curvaceous. With her full lips and heavy eyes, and her mane of copper red hair, she appeared as if she was from another realm. According to medieval superstitions which still lingered in Victorian Britain, red hair was linked with black magic and witches. There was a superstition that if the first person you saw on New Year's Day was a redhead, then they would bring you bad luck. Lizzie's hair had up to this point been a cursed chalice, as she had been teased throughout her childhood for it.

She was born in 1829 in Hatton Garden, later renowned as the jewelry center of London. Her Sheffield-born father, Charles Siddall, owned his own cutlery-making business, and while they could have been comfortable, he spent much of the family finances trying to prove he was descended from landed gentry.[4] Much like the D'Urbervilles in Thomas Hardy's novel, her parents had a sense of grandeur, and like the fictional Tess, Lizzie's fortunes would be changed by her beauty. After meeting the pre-Raphaelites, Lizzie chose to exaggerate her background by claiming she grew up in a slum; a story which made it into Rossetti's early biographies. Lizzie had discovered the works of Tennyson when she found a poem on a piece of newspaper that had been wrapped around butter, and his words inspired her to create a more romantic life for herself. Exhausted by the long hours spent hunched over a desk in dim light in the milliners' workroom, she realized that modeling would not only pay double the salary, but would be her entry into a more exciting, glamorous world.

Given the common assumptions that modeling was akin to prostitution (with many tales of an artist seducing his muse from across the canvas), Deverell felt it wouldn't be proper for him to approach her with his proposition, so he sent his mother to ask instead. The rather grand lady arrived outside the Siddall home in a carriage and convinced her mother of the merits of being a model.

Deverell was impressed by her ease in front of the canvas, and as he painted her in the shed of his garden, he couldn't wait to tell the brotherhood about the discovery. He rushed into William Holman Hunt's studio, where he found Hunt and Rossetti peacefully working on their art. "What a stupendously beautiful creature I have found," he told them. "By Jove! She's like a queen, magnificently tall, with a lovely figure, a stately neck, and a face of the most delicate and finished modelling."[5]

He invited his friends to call into his makeshift studio the next day to see her "wonder"[6] and Hunt was quick to snap her up as a model for his work in progress, *A Converted British Family Sheltering a Christian Priest from the Persecution of the Druids* (1850) and as Sylvia in *Valentine Rescuing Sylvia from Proteus* (1851), from Shakespeare's *The Two Gentlemen of Verona*.[7]

Lizzie enjoyed the relaxed studio life; she didn't mind having to sit still for long periods of time and imagined that this experience might help her become a proper lady. Her father appreciated the steady income for the household, but he couldn't understand why the men wanted to paint his gaunt and pale daughter with the "social suicide" red hair. But she didn't care, as she loved being the focus of attention among these painters who worshipped her rare beauty, when she had been used to being treated as a common shopgirl.[8] She became their mascot, they nicknamed her "The Sid," and created within her a sense of belonging among this bohemian group.[9]

In 1851, Lizzie agreed to sit for Millais as Ophelia in a painting of a scene from Shakespeare's *Hamlet* that he had been researching for months. Rather than as a seductive figure, he wanted his Ophelia to be a tragedy; rejected by her love, Hamlet, she sinks into despair and destroys herself by drowning.

After exploring the banks of the Hogsmill River in Surrey, he discovered the perfect stretch of water to form the background of his painting. The light on the water was shaded by the overhanging willow, and the river was bogged with daisies, forget-me-nots, and meadowsweet. Lizzie wouldn't be posing in this river though; she would lie in a bathtub in the artist's home, with the water heated by candles placed underneath the tub by Millais's mother. Millais found an old brocade costume for Ophelia in a junk shop, and when she submerged herself in the water, the full skirt spread around her, as if she was uncorseted and unrestricted.

Lizzie was so patient and still, and he was so engrossed in his work, that he didn't notice the candles had snuffed out, and that Lizzie was shivering and almost blue from being submerged in freezing water. By the end of the sitting, she was suffering from a severe cold, and her father, angered at Millais's carelessness, insisted the artist pay her doctor's bills, and she was sent to the spa town of Hastings to recover.

By 1851 Rossetti had become obsessed with her, and he asked that she only sit for him. From muse to lover, she practically moved into his residence on Chatham Place, where he tirelessly sketched her. They were so wrapped up in one another that they isolated themselves from the other artists and gave each other pet names. He called her "Dove," often sketching the bird in place of her name, and insisted she drop the extra "L" from her surname, as he thought "Siddal" was so much more refined. Lizzie had found a new celebrity as Ophelia, and she gave up her millinery work to exclusively sit for Rossetti. He inspired and encouraged her to write her own poetry and to paint and illustrate Arthurian legends and ballads. When he saw how talented she was in her poetry and art, he decided to be her teacher, providing her with his expensive painting supplies.

Now that Lizzie's time was taken up first by Millais, and then by Rossetti, William Holman Hunt sourced his own working-class Stunners.

He encountered another redhead, Annie Miller, a slum girl who was serving beers in the Cross Keys pubs in Chelsea, and despite her bawdiness, the swear words spitting out of her sharp features, she quickly replaced Lizzie as his favorite model, as well as becoming his lover. In *The Awakening Conscience* (1853), she is a mistress, or "fallen woman" who is rising from her position on a louche man's lap, as if the light from outside the window has triggered feelings of guilt.

Having grown up in extreme poverty following the death of her mother, Annie Miller's newfound celebrity allowed her to escape a grim fate, and she was determined to enjoy it. She ambitiously eyed up the possibilities of a new life—that by embracing Hunt's desire to be Pygmalion, he would transfer her into a lady fit for marriage. When Hunt embarked on a journey to the Holy Land, he placed her in the care of a local boardinghouse and hired a teacher to guide her in social etiquette. Rossetti was enamored by Lizzie, but he couldn't help but be attracted to Annie too, given his fetish for wild, abundant, red hair. When novelist Elizabeth Gaskell met Rosetti in London, she observed that his head was always turned by women with beautiful hair. As she wrote, "if a particular kind of reddish brown, crepe wavy hair came in, he was away in a moment struggling for an introduction to the owner of said head of hair. He is not as mad as a March hare, but hair-mad."[10]

Lizzie was not only jealous of Rossetti's womanizing, but she hated to see another woman worshipped by her band of artists. Annie, in turn, enjoyed seeing her in misery. When Hunt returned from overseas in January 1856, he discovered Annie's affair with Rossetti, and she faded out of their world. The fallen woman was only lauded in painting—not in real life.

Everyone who met Lizzie was struck by her unique style. Her homemade gowns harked back to a medieval silhouette and were the antithesis of the corsets and crinolines of the 1850s. Georgiana Burne-Jones, wife of later pre-Raphaelite Edward Burne-Jones, adoringly described her as a "slender, elegant figure—tall for those days," and dressed in a "graceful and simple dress, the incarnate opposite of the 'tailor-made' young lady."[11]

The discovery of the first synthetic dye, mauveine, in 1856 by William Henry Perkin encouraged other chemists to rush out their own aniline dyes to transform dull cloth into vibrant rainbow colors. City streets and salons were soon swamped by a glaring sea of brilliant silks, as crinolines became a canvas and women were transformed into birds of paradise. But Lizzie, and the artist's models in her circle, chose to wear earthy colors—sage, brown, or a pearl gray known as "moon"—which fell into the mode of aesthetic dress as championed by the pre-Raphaelites in their works, and decades later, in the Art Nouveau, freedom-giving designs of Liberty.

Lizzie's dark and brooding poems explored her inner fears of unrequited love and death. Even though Rossetti loved her, and they were described by a friend as being like Adam and Eve in paradise when in his studio together, he insisted he had no desire to marry.

In the poem *Fragment of a Ballad*, she referred to her heroine's status as mistress as like "a living death," and she provided illustrations to doomed romantic Border Ballads such as Tennyson's *The Lady of Shalott* in 1853 and Sir Walter Scott's *Clerk Saunders* in 1856. She also illustrated Tennyson's *St. Agnes' Eve*, a poem about the night before St. Agnes's Day on January 21, where unmarried women must fast before they go to sleep, so that they can dream of the man they'll marry. It was a prescient story as Lizzie, when she despaired at Rossetti being with other models, fell into sickness and nausea, and refused to eat.

For much of Lizzie's adult life she suffered acute illness, which has latterly been diagnosed as tuberculosis, anorexia, or neuroticism. But what ailed her the most, and was responsible for the sickness, the loss of appetite, dizziness, and breathlessness, was her addiction to laudanum, which she consumed in excessive amounts as an escape from the pain of Rossetti's refusal to make her respectable. The heady and addictive mix of opium and alcohol was available over the counter, and she developed a dangerous dependency. She worried that as she got older, who would want her? With the success of *Ophelia*, her reputation as a model and mistress would repel other gentlemen.

It was much harder for female artists to achieve their own success and independence, unless she had a patron, and so, in March 1855 Rossetti showed Lizzie's paintings and sketches to the pre-Raphaelite champion and benefactor John Ruskin. He was so impressed that he bought all of them.

Ruskin finally met her in person that April, describing her as a "a noble, glorious creature,"[12] and bestowing on her a nickname, "Ida," from a Tennyson poem, *The Princess*. He agreed to fund her art with an annual income of £150. Women were still not allowed to join the Royal Academy, but Rossetti and Ruskin helped place Lizzie's work in exhibitions.

Rossetti's friends couldn't understand why he didn't marry her, particularly as they saw the spark fade with every anxious year that passed. Ford Madox Brown wrote in his diary in October 1854, that Lizzie was looking "thinner and more deathlike and more beautiful and more ragged than ever, a real artist." In a March 1855 entry, he described Lizzie as "a stunner and no mistake. Rossetti once told me that, when he first saw her, he felt his destiny was defined. Why does he not marry her?"[13]

In 1856 Rossetti became fixated on a new model—a voluptuous blonde housemaid, Fanny Cornforth (real name Sarah Cox), whom he had spotted at a firework display in Royal Surrey Gardens to celebrate the return of Florence Nightingale from Crimea. As she loosened her wavy hair, Rossetti was immediately captivated and asked if he could paint her. Poet William Bell Scott later described her as cracking nuts with her teeth and then spitting the shells at Rossetti—a story that reflected her low standing among the other pre-Raphaelites, who considered her crude and rough.[14]

The antithesis of Lizzie's wane beauty, she was so curvaceous that she was nicknamed "The Elephant" and was the inspiration for *Bocca Baciata* (1859), the first of Rossetti's paintings featuring just one woman. Based on the Italian proverb, "The mouth that has been kissed does not lose its fortune, rather it renews itself as does the moon," it depicts a liberated princess who sleeps with eight lovers but is still able to secure marriage to a king.

In 1857, John Ruskin commissioned Rosetti to create a series of murals in the Oxford Union library which were based on Arthurian legend, and joining the creative team were two student artists—William Morris and Edward "Ned" Burne-Jones. The two friends had bonded over their worship of medieval aesthetics and their admiration for the pre-Raphaelites, and while both considered entering the church, they were persuaded by Rossetti to pursue their passion for art.

Together with Rossetti, the artists cut loose at Oxford's theatres and concert halls, where they scanned the audience to search for their own Stunner muses. One evening they spotted a girl in the stalls with a thick main of curly hair, a long neck, and the sensuous mouth so beloved by the pre-Raphaelites.

Jane Burden, the seventeen-year-old daughter of a local stable groom, had gone to the theatre with her sister, and as they were heading home, they were approached by Rossetti, who asked her to pose as his Guinevere for his mural, *Sir Lancelot's Vision of the Holy Grail*. Jane was from a poor Oxford family, and at first she was hesitant, as it didn't seem right to be paid to undress for a man, but she softened to the idea.[15]

Lizzie's laudanum addiction tightened its grip, and when her health deteriorated, she was sent to the spa town of Matlock in Derbyshire to recover her health. Hearing that her love was working with a new model sent her into a spiral of suffering, and Rossetti rushed to her side. As her body wasted away, Rossetti, in desperation, finally asked her to marry him. She recovered sufficiently for their wedding in Hastings in May 1860, and they then moved into a home together in Hampstead.

When Lizzie fell pregnant, she continued to take laudanum throughout, and tragically her daughter was stillborn, having died in the womb three weeks earlier. Rossetti had clung to hope that she would find happiness in having a baby, but with the trauma of a lost child, combined with postnatal depression, she sunk further into despair.[16]

Rossetti had enjoyed flirting with Jane while painting her for the mural, but Morris was also captivated by her. He may have been clumsy and less charming than Rossetti, but he was independently wealthy, given his father's investment in copper mines, and sensing the security he could bring her, in April 1859 Jane agreed to marry him. She was able to achieve a comfortable life that she could never have imagined, when otherwise she would have been destined for domestic servitude. It was also pleasing to be appreciated for her unusual looks and the wild mane of hair that she had been teased for at school and likened to a "gypsy."[17] She also became a popular figure on the London social scene, despite a reputation for being aloof and silent, and while this was down to shyness, it fueled an image of her as a curious goddess.

Working with architect Philip Webb, the Morrises built their aesthetic Arts and Crafts sanctuary, Red House, and on its completion in 1860 it became a pre-Raphaelite paradise which Burne-Jones called "the most beautifullest place on earth."[18] Their neighbors may have been shocked by their outlandish dress, by their habit of holding tea parties on Sunday afternoons, but here, in this utopia, the women, Jane Morris and Ned's wife Georgiana Burne-Jones, were liberated. Jane excelled in her skills in embroidered designs for the house, and they indulged in childhood games such as hide-and-seek, blind man's buff, musical chairs.[19]

Lizzie came to Red House in the hope it would help her recover from her trauma but seeing Jane with her healthy newborn just pushed her into greater despair. No one knew what to do about her unpredictable moods. As Georgiana later recalled: "We found her sitting in a low chair with the childless cradle on the floor beside her, and she looked like Gabriel's Ophelia when she cried with a kind of soft wildness as we came in, 'Hush, Ned, you'll wake it!'"[20]

On the evening of February 10, 1862, Lizzie, Rossetti, and their friend Algernon Charles Swinburne went for dinner at a restaurant in Leicester Square. Lizzie had been in a drowsy and irritated mood all evening and she returned to their house for an early night, while Rossetti headed out again. When he returned home after midnight, he discovered her unconscious, with an empty bottle of laudanum beside her and a note pinned to her nightdress, telling him to look after Harry, her younger disabled brother. He immediately sent for several doctors to help, and despite their efforts she was pronounced dead just before daylight. Distraught at the death of his wife, who had been pregnant again, he rushed to Ford Madox Brown's house. His friend had the foresight to burn the note, as suicide was, at that time, illegal and it would have denied her a proper burial.

Her tragic death helped to form her legend as, according to her biographer, "the first supermodel, in a world where the term had not yet been coined."[21] Rossetti had made hundreds of studies of Lizzie's face and hands, and he continued to draw her from memory. He was haunted by the thoughts of her in death and was convinced that he was visited by her spirit. He created her as *Beata Beatrix* (c. 1870) capturing the moment that Dante's great love Beatrice dies, and with the white poppies as a symbol of the laudanum that killed Lizzie.

He may have struggled to get over her, but there were other models who inspired his work. Fanny Eaton was a diverse face among the dominant pale skin and red hair. The Jamaican-born model arrived in Britain and found work as a domestic help, and then signed up as a model for the Royal Academy of Arts School of Painting. She was discovered by Simeon Solomon, who sketched and then painted her for the figures of Jochebed and Miriam in *The Mother of Moses*, which was exhibited at the Royal Academy in 1860. In 1865 she posed for Rossetti as one of the bridesmaids in *The Beloved*. He wanted to use a variety of different skin tones, but the central figure of the bride, wrapped in an emerald coat, has the copper hair of Lizzie.

For *Venus Verticordia*, painted between 1864 and 1868, Rossetti depicts Venus with flowing red hair and an exposed breast, using for his model "a remarkably handsome cook," whom he met on the street. It was loaded with symbolism of a woman's sexuality, with the roses and honeysuckles symbolic of her flesh and sexual organs. In 1867 he changed the face to that of Alexa Wilding, the red-haired model who would become a favorite.

As a dressmaker, she was also a working-class girl, discovered by Rossetti as she walked along the Strand. Dubious about the morality of his offer, she failed to show up at his studio, but when he spotted her again, he offered to pay her a week's salary to sit for him. She grew to respect him and was the figure of some of his most famous works as a dreamy redhead wrapped in green in *Veronica Veronese* (1872) and *La Ghirlandata* (1873), although there was no romance or sexual relationship between the two. Instead, Rossetti was now obsessed by William Morris's wife.

After Lizzie's death Fanny Cornforth had moved into his home as housekeeper, and she would remain a loyal friend until his death, but it would be the quiet, contemplative Jane who would now be the object of obsessions. It was her expressions and figure he continually tried to capture on paper and canvas over and over again. If Lizzie was the unconventional beauty that defined the first years of the pre-Raphaelites, then Jane Morris was forever entwined with the latter half.

They became more and more intimate with one another, as the artist and model relationship crossed the canvas and into real life, and with Rossetti using his art to depict Jane as a trapped woman at the mercy of her husband.

Jane and Gabriel went to the country together, and he painted her and wrote sonnets, while Morris stayed in London; his friends, despite their bohemian tendencies, were shocked at the way Rossetti would feed strawberries to Jane while Morris was in the same room.[22]

In *Persephone*, or (*Proserpine*) one of his most sensual depictions of her brooding eyebrows and full lips, she holds the forbidden pomegranate that has banished her to the underworld, just as Jane was trapped between adulterous love, and the love for her two daughters and husband.

His final portrait of Jane, painted in 1877, was *Astarte Syriaca*, one of the most sexual of his works as her sage robe clings to her body and slips from her shoulders. After this sitting, she chose to end the relationship for the sake of her daughters. Rossetti died five years later, in April 1882, after years of depression and drug abuse, marking the end of the Pre-Raphaelite Brotherhood. Their muses had completely shaken up the beauty standards of the Victorian Era; some critics had dismissed them as ugly, but their thick mass of hair, the bee-stung lips, the willowy figures would dominate the Art Nouveau movement of the late nineteenth century. The influence can be seen today—in the look of the singer Florence Welch, the Biba and Liberty fashion lines, of the dreamy reimagining of the Victorian Era in period dramas where the heroine wears her hair long and lose, and of the elvish queens in *The Lord of the Rings* trilogy.

Lizzie was a talented painter and artist, Jane was a brilliant embroiderer, and their skills were supported by their partners who saw themselves as Pygmalion figures, but above all, they were worshipped for their beauty. In "In an Artist's Studio," Rossetti's poet sister Christina Rossetti wrote of how the male artist objectifies his model, obsessing over her as he projects his fantasies of how she should be; she is an angel, or a whore, the trapped wife or the seductive vixen, or, like Ophelia and Lizzie Siddal, the woman too beautiful to live. Her words could be applied to all of the "It" girls who were captured in different mediums, and of how society "feeds across her face by day and night" as she looks back "joyful as the light"—when it comes to golden beauty, there's a need to possess and control, and then finally destroy.

Lillie Langtry and Sarah Bernhardt

The First Stars of Photography

Lillie Langtry and Sarah Bernhardt, photographed together in New York in 1887. *Library of Congress.*

In 1887 two of the most famous women in the world posed in front of a camera in a New York photographer's studio. They were both considered beautiful in wildly different ways—one was likened to a classical marble statue, the other compared to an eccentric waif. Lillie Langtry, in a heavily corseted, high-necked gown, turns her head and eyes toward the smaller woman, actress Sarah Bernhardt, whose body is engulfed in a fur-lined coat, as she does her customary stare into the camera, with the tiniest smirk on her face. Just before the photographer had pressed the shutter, Sarah had pinched Lillie on the arm, and the result was this moment captured in time.

Sarah Bernhardt was the first global icon who attracted feverish devotion from her spellbound audiences. She wasn't just defined by her hypnotic stage presence. She was a sculptor, a businesswoman, a philanthropist. She was a fashion leader who set trends, and a gothic queen a century before Siouxsie Sioux—known as much for her antics off-stage as she was for her deep, emotional performances. She engineered her own "viral" stunts—the coffin she took everywhere, the menagerie of animals. She also had an impish smile, evident in the photo with Lillie Langtry, slyly hinting that she knew exactly what she was doing as she challenged her viewers to look at her.

We think of celebrity worship as a recent phenomenon, but when Lillie Langtry reflected on her remarkable fame in her memoirs, it was as if her experience was from the mouth of modern "It" girls like Sienna Miller. She was mobbed by fans when spotted in public, and in society drawing rooms, duchesses clambered on chairs to glimpse her over the clusters of people gathered around her. Possessing social magnetism and the business brain of a Victorian Paris Hilton in the way she exploited her own image, Lillie had all the skills of a modern influencer. She was one of the first celebrities to be used in advertising, appearing in illustrations for Pears' soap, Brown's Iron Bitters, and on trading cards for cigarette brands, and her name was splashed in newspaper columns and court circulars—the nineteenth-century equivalent of tabloid gossip.

One of the many trading cards for sale that featured an image of Lillie Langtry, "The Jersey Lily," circa 1880s. *The Jefferson R. Burdick Collection/The Met Collection.*

From the moment she stepped into the bustle of London from the channel island of Jersey, with only one black dress in her possession, Lillie was a sensation. Painters adored her, Oscar Wilde lauded her, and loyal fans brought their camp stools and sandwiches to wait for hours in a line in the hopes of seeing her on stage. She possessed the type of beauty that was lauded at the time—violet eyes, pale skin, gold-flecked hair, the full mouth framed by a strong nose and jaw. Tall and robust, she appeared as if carved from marble, leading Oscar Wilde to compare her to a Roman goddess, arising "from Jersey like Venus from the foam."[1]

As her biographer Laura Beattie wrote: "There was Sarah Bernhardt. There was Oscar Wilde. And there was Lillie. Each in turn was swept up by Society, fêted and adored and then cast aside like flotsam in favour of some new attraction."[2]

As the mistress of the future King Edward VII, Lillie was the most famous courtesan-slash-actress since Nell Gwyn, and with her humble background, she was also adored and ridiculed in equal measures. She was only too willing to take on the role of love goddess, to be worshipped even if that meant sacrificing her husband and her reputation.

Sarah, like Lillie, was an unmarried mother who refused to be shamed for going against the morality of the day. She captivated audiences with her depictions of passionate, dangerous women—mistresses, murderers, consumptive courtesans—who were also as transgressive as she was.

Sarah, born Henriette-Rosine Bernard in 1844, was the illegitimate daughter of a wealthy attorney and a Belgian Jewish courtesan, Julie Bernard, whose blonde beauty made her one of the most desirable in Paris. Julie devoted her time to her wealthy protectors who took her on luxury wellness tours around Europe but gave little attention to her three daughters. Sarah, in particular, was neglected, spending her early years in the care of a Breton foster family.

Lillie's true name was Emilie Charlotte Le Breton. She earned her nickname for her pale skin, which would remind besotted artists of the local wildflower that grew on the island of Jersey, where she was born in 1853. Jersey is a British territory, off the coast of Normandy, which possesses a French influence in the language and culture. It was also home to other famous society figures. Lucy, Lady Duff-Gordon, famed as a couturier under the name Lucile, and her sister, Elinor Glyn, the original mastermind behind the "It" girl, were just a couple of years younger than Lillie. In the windows of the local newsagent in the island's main town, St. Heliers, she would often admire the glamorous early portrait photographs, or "carte de visite" of society beauty Georgina Ward, Countess of Dudley, and her imagination wandered with thoughts of what it would be like to be so celebrated.

Lillie's mother, Emilie, was a noted London beauty, and her father, William Corbet Le Breton, a womanizing reverend who was given a post on the island. Lillie was their only daughter, and with six brothers, her childhood was rough and tumble as she strived to keep up with the boys. Even at a young age, Lillie's looks provoked jealousy among the local girls, and they were also mystified by the freedom she was given to be a tomboy, as if she was defying her sex. There were rumors she wore boys' clothing on early morning horse rides, that she placed raw mince on her face at night, and rolled naked in the early morning dew to keep her skin pure.[3] Maybe these stories were prompted by the skin treatments she received after a horrific, potentially life-changing accident.

When she was eleven, her father bought her a small spirit stove to play around with, and the flames caught the edge of her long hair, rapidly spread to her face and neck. After hearing her screams, her mother frantically beat them out, and thanks to the medical care she received, her skin healed without scars.[4]

Sarah also suffered the trauma of being burned during her childhood. While living with the Breton nurse, she fell into the lit fireplace. "I was thrown, all smoking, into a large pail of fresh milk" she wrote in her memoirs. Her face was slathered with butter, the dressing was changed every two hours, and under this rigorous protocol, her skin was saved from permanent scarring. The accident had one welcome side-effect. She relished the attention she received from her absent mother.[5]

Her father died suddenly while overseas, and without a loving mother, she fell into fits of uncontrollable rage whenever she was told to do something she didn't want to. Perhaps it was a cry for attention because of the lack of love in her life; she needed to win it in other ways, and it also pushed her drive to succeed. After a stint at boarding school she was sent to an expensive convent near Versailles. The little girl was so transfixed by the sober drama of the nuns that she thought seriously about being one herself. As she embraced religion, she suffered serious bouts of pneumonia, later romanticizing her hovering between life and death.[6]

After leaving the convent in 1859, there was a question of what to do with the fifteen-year-old girl, and her future choices were limited, given she was the illegitimate daughter of a courtesan. She could marry into the bourgeoisie, she could follow her mother into Paris's demimonde by collecting wealthy lovers, or she could be an actress.

With this in mind, her mother's lover Charles, Duc de Morny, half-brother of Napoleon Bonaparte, and close friend to the novelist Alexandre Dumas, took Sarah to the theatre for the first time. In her memoirs she described the power of this performance, that she felt deeply she wanted to be an actress.

"When the curtain slowly rose, I thought I was going to faint. It was as if the curtain of my future life was being raised."[7]

Morny also used his influence to secure her a place at the prestigious Paris Conservatoire, where her silvery voice and pale, thin strangeness made an arresting impression. She adopted a new name, Sarah Bernhardt, in tribute to her Jewish mother, and after graduating, again with the help of Morny and Dumas, she joined the most prestigious acting company in France, the Comédie-Française.

One of her first roles was in Jean Racine's *Iphigénie*, but when her nerves got the better of her, she rushed through her lines and left the audience underwhelmed. In another performance, Molière's *Les Femmes Savantes*, she was savaged by critics, and her mother was even more critical. "See! The whole world calls you stupid, and the whole world knows that you're my child!" It caused Sarah such despair that evening that she "wanted to see what death was like."[8]

Sarah's younger sister Regine often visited her backstage, and one evening, when she accidentally stepped on the train of the star performer, Madame Nathalie, the older actress shoved Regine hard against a marble pillar. Sarah's famous temper got the better of her, and she slapped Nathalie across the face, refusing to apologize for it. She was swiftly fired from the company, and the incident would be the first to earn her notoriety. She signed up with another troupe, but frustrated at not being given decent roles, she quit, and instead toyed with the idea of being a courtesan like her mother.

She ran with the fast society set, pushing herself while struggling with a persistent cough and a flush of fever in her cheeks. She also earned a mention in *The Book of Courtesans*, a leather-bound record kept by Paris's vice squad, as being popular with "old men and especially members of parliament."[9]

Following a trip to Belgium, and an affair with Belgian aristocrat Henri, Prince de Ligne, she gave birth to a son, Maurice in 1864. Despite her pleas, the prince refused to acknowledge his child and rather than hiding in shame at his illegitimacy, it gave her a determination to do all she could to provide for him.

Back in Paris, she was given the opportunity to read for the owner of the Théâtre de l'Odéon Félix Duquesnel. "She wasn't just pretty, she was more dangerous than that," he would say. She was "a marvellously gifted creature of rare intelligence and limitless energy and willpower."[10]

The co-director of the theatre had thought she was too thin, and the voluminous rococo costumes, combined with her frizzy hair, made her look like a broomstick. When she starred in the 1868 revival of *Kean* by Alexandre Dumas, critics finally took notice. What she excelled at was dramatic androgyny, and she was given a chance to prove herself when she played one of her first "in breeches" roles in *Le Passant*, as the young Renaissance troubadour Zanetto. Receiving a standing ovation, and with well-wishers leaving flowers in her dressing room, it made her an overnight star. After performing it at the Tuileries Palace before Napoleon III and his wife, she wound up in bed with the emperor. She also added Charles Haas, one of the most fashionable figures in Paris, to her list of lovers. She held court in the salon of her apartment with a circle of wealthy men, some of whom chipped in to buy her the coffin lined with pink satin that she would become infamous for.[11] In 1870, following the outbreak of the Franco-Prussian War, she also demanded that they supply food, clothing, and medicine to treat wounded soldiers, and with singular determination, transformed the Odéon into a military hospital.[12]

Once the war was over, she took to the stage as the Spanish queen, Doña Marie de Neubourg, in the Odéon production of Victor Hugo's *Ruy Blas* in February 1872. The power of her performance cemented Sarah as the greatest actress in Paris, and when the Comédie-Française begged for her to return, she agreed.

She was mobbed by fans who gathered outside her dressing room, and as her fame increased, so did the criticism. Her thinness and her frizzy hair, both unfashionable at the time, were a punchline: "When she gets in the bath, the level of the water goes down!" and cartoonists depicted her as a broomstick. The size of her body even made it into critiques in the States when the *Boston Post* described her as a "living skeleton."[13]

Rather than dragging her down, she chose to wear tighter gowns to enhance her ethereal features, and to embrace the darkness every time she was described as looking consumptive. Her bisexuality was mythologized, she was at times a genius, a decadent mistress, and a gothic queen. She wore a hat made of a stuffed bat, there were stories that she played croquet with human skulls, and her biggest stunt of all, a perfect marketing trick, was when she hired a photographer to capture her sleeping in her coffin. She played dead, posing with her hands across her chest and with flowers on her body, and then issued these images to the press.

The morbid story had first emerged in 1873, when her beloved younger sister Regine, gripped by the morphine addiction and tuberculosis that would kill her, came to stay with her. Sarah gave her the comfort of the bed while she slept in the coffin. As she would write: "Three days after this new arrangement began, my manicurist came into the room to do my nails and my sister asked her to enter quietly because I was still sleeping. The woman turned her head, assuming that I was asleep in the armchair. Then, seeing me in my coffin, she rushed away, shrieking wildly. From that moment on, all Paris knew that I slept in my coffin."[14]

Like other eccentric "It" girls Josephine Baker and Jayne Mansfield, she was famed for her menagerie of exotic animals. She lived and traveled with her cheetahs, tigers, and lion cubs, a monkey, and an alligator named Ali Gaga. Although she wasn't adept at looking after them; Ali Gaga's diet of milk and champagne would lead to his untimely death.[15] The press recorded her every move, and when they wrote something she didn't like, she sent off a sharp telegram to the editor, threatening to sue if they didn't print it. As she developed a talent for sculpting, she posed in a white silk pant suit to publicize her new profession as an artist, and this led to further ridicule in France.

Just as Sarah was making a name for herself on the stage, fourteen-year-old Lillie was desperate to be a social butterfly and begged her mother to allow her to attend the island's dances and picnics. All eyes turned to her as soon as she entered the room, and she received her first proposal from an army lieutenant stationed on the island, which her parents sensibly turned down.

Lillie came to realize that Jersey was too small for her ambitions, and she was desperate to break free. She knew that marriage was the only practical option for a woman to lead an independent life, and dreaming of a Prince Charming to help her, along came Edward "Ned" Langtry, a twenty-six-year-old Irish landowner whose first wife had died. She was particularly impressed by his luxurious yacht, and she set about pursuing him for a proposal.[16]

She was twenty when they married, but shortly after their wedding, she came down with a near-fatal bout of typhoid fever, and when she eventually pulled through, she was determined not to waste any more precious time on the island. She set her heart on London, and in 1876 he sold his yacht to fund their move to an apartment in fashionable Belgravia. Within the salons and drawing rooms of its white stucco apartments gathered some of the most prestigious names in the city, and they could be spotted going for a turn in nearby Hyde Park and Buckingham Palace Gardens. It was a closed-off world that was almost impossible to break into for someone without a name, but Lillie was driven by a determination to achieve this life of riches and fame, and so she formed a plan.

She began celebrity-spotting—encouraging introverted Ned to go with her for walks in Hyde Park, or to circle art galleries and museums in the hopes she could spark a conversation and gain an "in" with the "it crowd." Seeing Thomas Heron Jones, seventh Viscount Ranelagh, with his two daughters at the Royal Aquarium in Westminster, she struck up a conversation, and Ranelagh, who had a keen eye for art and for beautiful women, invited Lillie and her husband to his popular Sunday afternoon parties where bohemian artists and actresses mixed with high society.

This invitation, Lillie would later say, "completely changed the current of my life," as shortly after, she received another prestigious invitation, to attend

Georgina, Lady Sebright's bohemian Sunday evening parties at her home on Lowndes Square.[17]

Tragedy struck shortly after her arrival in London, when one of Lillie's brothers was killed in a horse-riding accident, and in her grief, she insisted on wearing black for mourning. Her simple black dress was unadorned with jewels, as per the rules for bereavement, and she twisted her hair carelessly in a knot at the nape of her neck; a style that would spark a trend as the "Langtry knot."[18]

Feeling "very un-smart and countrified" among the wealthy guests dripping in bright silks and diamonds, she slinked off to sit in a chair at the edge of the party. The guests, a "who's who" of illustrious Londoners, were intrigued by this beautiful woman in her little black dress, and vying for her attention was John Everett Millais, whose *Ophelia* had made a star of Lizzie Siddal, American artist James McNeill Whistler, and Frank Miles, artist-in-chief to the periodical *Life* whose portraits of society women were reproduced as penny postcards.

She was on such a high by the time she returned home that she could have danced around her room, and there was further excitement the next day when invitations for dinners and soirees piled up in their reception.[19]

It was almost instantaneous the way Lillie captivated society, and despite the little she possessed, and that she was a Breton and therefore a foreigner, she had executed her master plan perfectly. One of the first invitations she and her husband accepted was for a society dinner where one of the guests was Lord Randolph Churchill (father of Winston Churchill). In a letter to his wife Jennie, he described her as "a most beautiful creature, quite unknown, very poor, and they say has but one black dress."[20]

As artists scrambled for her to be their model and muse, she was now the new face of a movement. Millais described her as "quite simply, the most beautiful woman on earth" and when his painting, *A Jersey Lily*, was exhibited at the Royal Academy in 1878, it was roped off to protect it from the swell of the crowds.[21]

Frank Miles depicted the model languorous against a backdrop of lilies, and this painting was snapped up by Queen Victoria's youngest son, Prince Leopold, who was often present when she was posing for it. He hung it over his bed in Buckingham Palace, that is, until his disapproving mother insisted he take it down.[22]

Lillie was awed by the "staggering" transformation in her life as she posed at artist's studios by day, and accepted multiple invitations for soirees. Her nights were filled with a dreamy list of balls, dinners, concerts, and the opera, and often she was buzzing so much that she couldn't sleep when she got home. Instead, she changed into her riding habit, and took her horse for a dawn walk around Hyde Park.

In May 1878 *Vanity Fair* asked: "Why do all our ladies dress in black this season?" The answer, of course, was Lillie, as other women hoped a bit of her magic could rub off on them. Every one of her fashion whims was immediately copied, despite her self-described "indifference at the time to elaborate frocks." One morning, she twisted a piece of black velvet into a turban, stuck a quill through it, and went for a walk in the park. A few days later, the hat appeared in every milliner's window, described as "The Langtry Hat," which complemented the "Langtry hair" and the "Langtry shoes."[23]

Sarah Bernhardt established her celebrity status through the use of photography portraiture. *LA County Museum of Art.*

By the 1860s photography was a burgeoning industry, and portraits of celebrated beauties could be purchased by all classes of society from shops and newsstands. On the cusp of fame as an actress, a teenage Sarah posed for photographer Félix Nadar, and with a heavy cloth draped around her body, the images revealed a calm, regal beauty that showed a hint of the defiance she would adopt in later portraits. There was another, much more risqué, photo from the same time in which she is topless, with a fan over her face to disguise her identity. She may have posed for it because she needed the money, and like Marilyn Monroe when she was a struggling actress and dancer, it was an early example of a starlet using her own attributes to survive in her world.[24]

Lillie was one of the most popular subjects of photographs that were sold on every street corner in London. If Paris Hilton could claim she invented the selfie, then Lillie could take credit for the thriving interest in commercial portrait photography. With Lillie's image so readily available in print shop windows and on newspaper stands, ordinary women wanted to have their portraits taken too, often using a variety of props, costumes, and expressions borrowed from celebrities. Known as "the carte de visite" these were flirtatiously swapped on house calls or pinned to walls and pasted in photo albums to show off their social connections to family and friends.

Photography only encouraged Lillie's reputation and celebrity to explode, and her face was so recognizable that she was mobbed when spotted at the theatre or on the street, where she ran the risk of being pushed by the crowds around her. One young woman in a black dress was relaxing on a bench in Hyde Park when she was mistaken for Lillie. A surge of people from across the park rushed toward her, and the crush was so severe that she was knocked unconscious and had to be taken to hospital.[25]

In her memoirs, she reflected on her experiences with instant fame. "It would be difficult for me to analyse my feelings at this time," she wrote. "To pass in a few weeks from being an absolute 'nobody' . . . to find myself not only invited to, but watched for at all the great balls and parties; to hear the murmur as I entered the room; to be compelled to close the yard gates in order to avoid the curious, waiting crowd outside, before I could mount my horse for my daily canter in the Row; and to see my portrait roped round for protection at the Royal Academy—surely, I thought, London has gone mad, for there can be nothing about me to warrant this extraordinary excitement."[26]

Crowds would gather around Lillie's carriage, and when she went for her daily morning ride on Hyde Park's "the Row," she was always accompanied by admirers. As socialite Margot Asquith remembered, that in these days when "London worshipped beauty like the Greeks," great ladies would stand "on iron chairs in the Park to see Mrs. Langtry walk past."[27]

In the decadence of the late Victorian Era, where sex was hidden behind closed doors, it was common for married couples to have affairs. By the end of 1877, she was the constant companion of the Prince of Wales, the womanizing and decadent eldest son of Queen Victoria, and later Edward VII. She had first met the prince, known as Bertie, when she was seated next to him on his yacht moored off the Isle of Wight. Despite being in the company of her husband, a flirtation began. As his mistress, she was given access to this exclusive life, which followed a set calendar for the season—sailing in Cowes in August, stalking and grouse-shooting in Scotland in the autumn, and weekend house parties over winter.

The Prince of Wales's wife and mother to his six children, the Danish Princess Alexandra, was aware of their affair, and like the whole of society, she was charmed by this sparky, congenial, and intelligent beauty. But if Lillie was to maintain her position, she needed to ensure the prince didn't tire of her. Just as she could be replaced as a painter's muse by the next "It" girl on the scene, she was aware of how savage fame could be.

As they danced the polka on polished wood ballroom floors, the taste for the bird-of-paradise gowns rubbed off on Lillie, and she ordered expensive creations from dressmakers on credit. At a ball at the prince's residence, Marlborough House, she wore a yellow tulle gown covered in gold fishnet, under which were held beautifully preserved butterflies. The next morning the maids swept up the scattered insects from the ballroom floor.[28]

"I was absolutely idle, my only purpose in life being to look nice and make myself agreeable," she said. Over the summer of 1878 she found that admiration could soon turn to ridicule. The downfall seemed to happen within months, and the gossip even reached across the Atlantic. An article in the *New York Times* on July 15, 1878, stated: "London is busy with the frivolity of the season, and more particularly with gossip concerning 'the reigning beauty' . . . every art shop has a study of her. All the photographers fight about her. You hear her name wherever you go in society . . . be she present or absent. You rarely see her husband. She has one . . . The Prince of Wales rides with her often, and his carriage frequently stands at the door."[29]

At a fancy dress ball, when she heard the prince was to dress as Pierrot, she arrived as Pierrette, but it was just too blatant in its acknowledgment of their affair, and she ended up humiliated. At another ball, with Lillie drunk on champagne, she and the prince were laughing and teasing one another, but Lillie took it a step too far, when she dabbed the back of his neck with a spoonful of strawberry ice. He went red with anger, and swiftly left the ballroom, leaving Lillie to face her cancellation from society. She found her invitations withdrawn, and she was left to ride alone in "The Row."

She and Ned were also hit with financial troubles. With his income having dwindled due to the collapse of his family's business, they were in so much debt that bailiffs seized the contents of their home to sell it at auction.

Now no longer in favor with the prince, and with Ned leaving London in a depression, she sought comfort with other men, and she fell pregnant and gave birth to her daughter, Jeanne Marie in 1881, believed to have been conceived during an affair with Prince Louis of Battenberg.

Society may have cast her out, but the artists and writers stood by her, and Oscar Wilde was convinced that she belonged on the stage. As Sarah

Bernhardt had proven, Bohemian women could follow their own creative path as she thrived as a working single mother in Belle Époque Paris.

When the Comédie Française theatre troupe came to Britain over the summer of 1880, its star, Sarah, replaced Lillie as the hot new phenomenon who held London spellbound, and she was given the nickname, the "Divine Sarah." She toured the UK for six weeks, dazzling audiences with her performances of Phèdre and Hernani.

With a desire to control her own career she quit the theatre company and arranged an ambitious fifty-date tour of the United States. In New York she performed for the first time the role she would be most famous for, and the one she would play over 3,000 times—*La Dame aux Camélias*, or *Camille*, written by her old friend Alexandre Dumas. Audiences were moved to tears as Camille dies in her lover's arms, and throughout her career she would ensure there were plenty of death scenes to similarly trigger emotions. Like a method actor of the 1950s, she researched medicine manuals and visited hospitals and morgues to make her death scenes even more authentic, whether she had been poisoned, stabbed to death, or succumbed to tuberculosis.

There was a fanaticism around her, something akin to Beatlemania. Her adoring fans gathered below her hotel window, making shrines to her, having known where she would be from the newspaper reports with the latest information transmitted by the new telegraph cables.

Her fame was one that took advantage of all the latest technologies. Photos of Sarah dressed in the elaborate costumes of one of her characters could be ordered in print shops and sent out in the post, and in New Jersey, she paid a visit to Thomas Edison, who recorded her uttering lines from Phèdre on one of his early phonograph machines.[30]

She earned millions from ticket sales, and her income was further bolstered by being the face of brands including Pears soap and Columbia Bicycles. She returned to Europe in 1881 as an extremely wealthy woman. As she toured Europe, she chose to play the types of figures where she could sink her teeth into the drama and use as vessels to express her own emotions—Empress Theadora, Cleopatra, Princess Fédora Romazoff (setting a fashion trend for the soft felt hat she wore).[31]

As her biographer, Robert Gottlieb, wrote, Sarah was "a child of the Romantic movement, and her theater was the theater of feelings, of rebellion, of the Self." She used her performances to understand the trauma of her childhood, to "safely vent her most powerful feelings. In her alternating suicides and murders she could act out both her often-proclaimed death wish and her rage at her tormentors." He added that these death scenes, by poison, stabbing, tuberculosis, "not only gratified her audiences but were undoubtedly essential to her inner life."[32]

Lillie made her debut in the play *She Stoops to Conquer* at the Haymarket Theatre in February 1882. She may have been shunned by society, but the Prince and Princess of Wales were seated in the royal box to watch her debut, and her name drew in a crowd who queued for hours outside the pit armed with sandwiches and campstools, in preparation for the long wait until the doors opened.[33]

Realizing how valuable she was for publicity, the Haymarket hired Lillie to continue starring in their productions. Lillie left her baby in London while she toured across the UK and Ireland to rapturous crowds, and in October 1882 she embarked on the journey across the Atlantic to perform in the United States. Waiting for her at the harbor in New York was Oscar Wilde with a bunch of lilies in his arms, and a crowd of thousands cheering. As she traveled in her carriage up Fifth Avenue to Central Park, she was "mildly mobbed" by curious onlookers who recognized her from her photographs.

New York's Gilded Age adored the arts and beauty and Lillie was a perfect symbol of bohemian glamor. The fashions she had introduced in London, such as the black velvet "toques," were in Manhattan's shop windows, and in beauty salons women asked for their hair to be done in the famous loose knot.[34]

In 1887 Lillie was in New York at the same time as Sarah Bernhardt, and when they dined together several times a week, she noticed that it was Sarah who took all the attention, as "her magnetism held them in its spell." It was here that the two actresses took part in a joint photography session with New York publicity photographer Napoleon Sarony, resulting in an intimate portrait of the two most famous actresses in the world.

With her status as a global celebrity, Sarah embarked on a world tour, and from 1888 to 1892 she traveled to Egypt, Russia, South America, Australia, New Zealand, and the South Pacific. She used the new modes of travel, such as the steamship, to take her to Australia, and her own private carriage to travel on newly constructed railway lines, as she performed in small-town music halls and even in circus tents.[35]

While Sarah embarked on the equivalent of a rock stadium tour, Lilie also crossed the States in her own luxury railway car, the "Lalee." One of her stops was in the Texas town that the infamous Judge Roy Bean had named Langtry after being wowed by a photograph he'd seen of her. By the time of her visit, in 1903, the judge had already passed away. She embarked from her private train in the blazing sun, her long skirt sweeping across the dry desert covered in sage brush and cactus, and was greeted by a crowd of cowboys who gave her a personal tour of the Jersey Lily saloon.[36]

After divorcing Ned, Lillie had become an American citizen, and she purchased a ranch in Lake Country, California, where she established her own winery. In 1899, at the age of forty-seven, she married a man in his twenties, Hugo de Bathe, who she later found out had a penchant for chorus girls and had only married her for her money.

Sarah also lived by her passions, and she chose to be swept up in a love affair with a Greek aristocrat Jacques Damala, whom she married in 1882. He was a gambler, a drug addict, and a sly womanizer who Bram Stoker would say inspired his Dracula, and he put Sarah through misery. As Robert Gottlieb writes in his biography: "One of the great mysteries is why a flock of great women stars at the very summit of their art—assured in their talent, in firm charge of their careers, worshipped by both sexes—should have allowed themselves to be degraded by unworthy men."[37]

It was a question that could be asked of Lillie and other "It" girls who found themselves taken advantage of by fame-hungry cads. Maybe it was a way for a celebrated woman, so used to being worshipped and obeyed, to be dominated, and to give in to her unflinching need for love.

As she accumulated great wealth, Sarah splashed it on furniture and art, on curiosities picked up on her travels, and on expensive fashions and jewelry, including specially commissioned art nouveau headdresses by Lalique, with floral motifs and lashing of pearls.

In 1894 she commissioned Czech artist Alphonse Mucha to produce an art nouveau poster for the Sardou melodrama *Gismonda* at Paris's Théâtre de la Renaissance, and he would go on to create further artwork and jewelry for her, including a lavish snake bracelet for her role in *Cléopâtre*.

For Sarah's performance of *La Dame aux Camélias* in Paris in 1896, Mucha created a poster in which she was depicted in a white gown against a starry backdrop, and with a camellia in her hair. The swirling, romantic art nouveau illustration made a strong impression on Coco Chanel. The teenager was in Paris to see the performance, and she was so overwhelmed by it that she would choose the camellia as one of the motifs for her future couture house.

In 1899, aged fifty-four, Sarah took on the role of Hamlet in a touring French production. Women had played Hamlet previously, but Sarah was attacked for now trying to steal men's roles. She knew that her gender-blind casting would be controversial and she used it as a savvy means of further boosting her career and defying her age.

Because there was a lack of decent roles for older women, she continued to play masculine parts, including Napoleon II at the age of fifty-five. In 1900 she became one of the first actors to star on film, and in 1912 she played Queen Elizabeth I for Adolph Zukor's Famous Players studio in Hollywood, which helped to break some of the prejudice that the theatre world felt about cinema as a low-class medium.

After Lillie and Hugo de Bathe split, she returned to England to begin a third career in horseracing, and in 1897 her Australian steed, Merman, helped her become the first woman to win the Cesarewitch Handicap at Newmarket racecourse. While celebrating, she heard the news that Ned had died in a Chester asylum, having been found seriously injured and incoherent by police at a railway station. In June 1897, he had given an interview to a press agency where he spoke of his heartbreak over the marriage and the surprise at her pregnancy. "Here, for the present, is the close of my unhappy domestic drama . . . it was a love match; she left me, she is Mrs Langtry; she is my wife."[38] There were jokes and insinuations—that Lillie had arranged his death to get rid of him permanently, and that she'd even been driving the train that struck him.

Lillie spent her final days living in Monaco, where she took pleasure in gardening. When she was in her seventies, she was asked by a reporter as to whether she would have been happier without the fame and beauty. "What woman would not be beautiful if she had the chance?" she said. "Life has taught me that beauty can have its tragic side. It is like great wealth in that respect. It promotes insincerity, and it breeds enemies. A really beautiful woman, like a very rich man, can be the loneliest person in the world. She is lucky if she knows her friends."[39]

In 1906 Sarah injured her knee falling on the deck of a ship and refused to be treated by the doctor. It was then made worse during a performance of *La Tosca*, when she flung herself from a tower, only to find there was no mattress to cushion her fall.[40] After years of pain she chose to have her right leg amputated in 1915. As war raged in Europe, she embarked on a tour of the front to entertain troops, visiting makeshift hospitals in ruined cities while hopping on her one leg, or being carried in a chair.

She continued to act, playing a thirty-year-old male drug addict in *Daniel* at London's the Prince's Theatre in 1921. In her last years, Sarah suffered from kidney disease, and on the evening of March 26, 1923, her doctor made the announcement from the window to the crowds below, "Madame Sarah Bernhardt is dead." She was placed in her coffin, with the Légion d'Honneur that she had been awarded in 1914, resting on her body. There were claims that a million people came out for her funeral, lining the road to watch her procession to Père Lachaise cemetery.

At the time of Sarah's death, Lillie was in the process of publishing her memoirs, which was heavily censored as it featured no mention of her daughter. She died of influenza on February 12, 1929, at the age of seventy-five, and the news brought her back to public consciousness again.

By the 1920s, a time of rapid changes in technology and entertainment, Lillie represented the old vestiges of fame. *The Guardian* naïvely predicted in its obituary of her that the celebrity and worship that Lillie experienced, to have artists, writers, and royals eating out of her hand, was not likely to happen again. "A world with the 'movies' and the wireless to amuse it, a world, moreover, in which the sexes meet on more practical terms than in the past, has more to do than mob a handsome woman for the sake of her looks."[41]

Lillie's name became more obscure, but in the fifties, Sarah Bernhardt was a recognizable shorthand for esteemed acting, even mentioned by Marilyn Monroe in *The Seven Year Itch* ("Every time I show my teeth on television, I'm appearing before more people than Sarah Bernhardt appeared before in her whole career"). And just as he immortalized Marilyn, Andy Warhol created a silkscreen portrait of Sarah as part of his 1980 series, *Ten Portraits of Jews of the Twentieth Century*.

Mark Twain may have said, "There are five kinds of actresses. Bad actresses, fair actresses, good actresses, great actresses, and then there is Sarah Bernhardt." But for Sarah, she believed that for a woman, "there are three subjects and three alone, no matter how many varieties one may mention. They are love, maternity, and sorrow."[42]

Shooting Stars

Gibson Girl to Silent Screen Star

Mabel Normand in 1918. *Picture Lux/The Hollywood Archive/Alamy Stock Photo.*

Very few celebrities had their own adjective to describe the type of behavior they personified, very few had their name in the title of their films, and even fewer earned notoriety from not just one, but two, spectacular murder trials. All these things were true of Mabel Normand.

As arguably cinema's first "It" girl, fifteen years before the expression was conjured up for Clara Bow, Mabel was beloved by her millions of fans around the world who felt like they knew her personally from her high-energy performances in a raft of short films like *Mabel's Busy Day* and *Mabel's Strange Predicament* (both 1914). There was even an expression, "Mabelescent," to describe a certain zingy, free way of being that was her specialty on screen.

Mabel's "It" girl status bridged the eras, first as a Gibson girl model in the burgeoning fashion and advertising photography at the dawn of the twentieth century, and then as one of the original screen idols when cinema was in its infancy. She was the complete embodiment of this innovative new mass entertainment in all her mischievous, coltish glory.

Mabel was small, just five feet tall, but she filled every room with her mane of chestnut hair, pouting lips, and large, expressive, chocolate eyes that revealed a warm but vulnerable heart. Her regular co-star Charlie Chaplin described her as being "pretty and charming," with "full lips that curled delicately at the corners of her mouth, expressing humor and all sorts of indulgence."[1]

Like Clara Bow, Mabel was a manic, clownish presence on the screen, diving into lakes, pratfalling and taking custard pies to the face, and she was billed in interviews as a sweet girl with a sweet tooth, given her penchant for eating ice cream at any time of day. She affectionately called those she liked "Old Peach," she arrived two hours late for press interviews, and she struggled to stay still, or on topic, for more than a few minutes, as if her brain couldn't keep up with the intensity of her life.[2]

Her talents went beyond just being a beautiful face with a knack for comedy. She was one of the first women to write, direct, and star in her own movies, and to head her own studio. Her joyous, silly performances made audiences laugh around the world, but it masked a great deal of pain. "I get terribly blue and sad," she confessed to *Motion Picture Magazine*. "Life is such a rush."[3]

For Mabel, the attention was too much. She had so much money she didn't know what to do with it, and the sheer amount of publicity she received led to long bouts of anxiety, depression, and drug abuse. When her name was linked with an infamous Hollywood murder, and then a shooting, in the 1920s, she was placed as a real-life Roxie Hart.

It was the dream combination—a salacious murder in a glamorous town, and a beautiful, but promiscuous actress with a drug problem. She personified, for some, all that was wrong with Hollywood and the indulgent, wealthy lifestyles it created.

Like many of the founders of Hollywood, she came from very humble origins; born Mabel Ethelreid Normand in 1892 in Staten Island. She was a restless girl, creative, artistic, and always on the move, and at Staten Island's Westerleigh Collegiate Institute she thrived on the stage, even though she didn't complete high school. "I was tremendously ambitious in those days," she told the *LA Examiner* in 1924. "We had very little money and even my occasional trips home were a great expense. I wanted to finish as soon as I could, so I could learn more about the things that particularly interested me. I was crazy about music and drawing. I wanted to be a big musician. And I've never really lost that desire."[4]

She was born at a time of great change in mass media and entertainment. A year after her birth, American inventor Thomas Edison introduced the Kinetoscope peep-box viewer, which revealed a moving image on a short loop of celluloid. In Paris in December 1895 the Lumière brothers unveiled the Cinématographe with the first ever film screening, where they showed ten short films over twenty minutes. It was a phenomenon, and both the Lumière brothers and the Edison Company came up with new ideas to enhance the storytelling techniques. One of the first of these films, 1896's *La Fée aux Choux* (*The Fairy of the Cabbages*), was directed by a pioneering woman, France's Alice Guy-Blaché. That same year Edison released the eighteen-second long *The Kiss*, which showed actors May Irwin and John Rice puckering up together. It was so controversial that there were calls from religious and moral groups for censorship of this new industry.

The first cinemas in the United States were known as nickelodeons—a portmanteau of the five-cent coin, and "odeon," the Greek word for a covered theatre. The first to be opened exclusively for showing films was the Harris brothers' nickelodeon in Pittsburgh, Pennsylvania, and by 1908 around 8,000 had sprung up around the country. Cinema proved to be overwhelmingly popular with the working classes (the upper and middle classes thought it vulgar) and young Mabel was crazy about it, often attending screenings with her mother.

She dropped out of music school at fourteen years old to take up work in the mailroom of the Manhattan pattern company, Butterick.

Told she was far too pretty to be a mailroom girl, she was sent to the art department to model for the company magazine. Every morning, she would take the ferry from Staten Island to Manhattan, and would spend her day working with artists and photographers for a variety of modeling campaigns.

The use of live models for black and white photography and colorful illustrations for advertising and for pin-ups had taken off by the early 1900s. They supported an explosion in print media, particularly with photo-led weeklies like *Life*, and women's magazines such as *Cosmopolitan, Ladies' Home Journal*, and *Harper's Bazaar*.

She was only fourteen or fifteen, but she embodied the beauty ideal, with her fresh, youthful face and her mound of hair that was the "in" look of the era, and as she posed for these images, she enacted different gestures and emotions, which would give her good grounding for the exaggerated movements of silent cinema. She was soon in high demand among New York's top artists, James Montgomery Flagg and Charles Dana Gibson, whose "Gibson girl" had changed the pervading image of womanhood.

He depicted the active, modern, upper-middle-class "New Woman," who was a fresh and natural alternative to the buxomly "gay-nineties," where women were upholstered in heavy, ornate gowns and dripped with jewelry. The "New Woman" was independent, active, and sporty, often taking part in horse-riding and golf, and she was aware of her power as a beautiful woman. She was expected to have a body that was willowy and slender, yet with curves in all the right places. She was, according to writer Nichi Hodgson, "a fully clothed, proto-Page Three girl" (the topless models that appeared on page three of British tabloids from the 1980s to the 2010s).[5]

Yet the "New Woman" was also a reflection of the women's rights movements in her bold desire to educate herself and earn money through independent employment. In 1942, Gibson gave an interview to the *New York Times* where he spoke of the impact of his creation, which he first sketched in the 1890s as an idealized notion of haughty beauty, modeled initially on his wife.

"You must remember that women were just coming into their own when I began to draw. In those days their place was in the home. . . . Women have widened their sphere since then, but they are still women, for which we are truly thankful."[6]

The most notorious of the Gibson girl models was Evelyn Nesbit, who posed for one of his famous illustrations, 1903's *Woman: The Eternal Question*, which was a simple pencil silhouette of her profile, with her long, thick hair cascading down her shoulders.

A 1903 portrait of Evelyn Nesbit. *Harvard Theatre Collection.*

Florence Evelyn Nesbit, originally from a small town near Pittsburgh, was first discovered in 1899 as she gazed at a window display lusting after fabric she couldn't afford. On the other side of the glass was an older woman who happened to be an artist and who was struck by this beautiful ragamuffin with the dark, curled hair.[7] Evelyn's father had died suddenly just four years before, leaving her mother penniless and evicted from her home. Her mother struggled to find work as a dressmaker, so they moved to Philadelphia in the hopes it would offer more opportunities. She secured a job at Wanamaker's department store, and brought her daughter, Evelyn, and son Howard, into employment there too.

After being discovered by the artist, Evelyn agreed to sit for her, and realizing that she would earn so much more money as an artist's model than a shopgirl, she pursued work with other artists in Philadelphia. With her dark hair and pale skin reflective of her Scots-Irish background, cascades of curly hair, an oval face framing large eyes and full lips, she was also considered "exotic." Gibson had declared slenderness the new beauty, and he also celebrated the "melting pot" beauty of American women, which led to a fashion for racial ambiguity, in much the same way as the Kardashians would meld cultures a century later.

Evelyn moved to New York with her mother in late 1900 to capitalize on the interest in her, and after being hired by painter James Carroll Beckwith, he shared his discovery with other artists. There was a duality to the way she was depicted in her portraits, as both innocent and suggestive, as if the teenage girl was being used to fulfill the Lolita fantasies of older men. This contradiction was demonstrated in contrasting works. In a 1901 painting by Beckwith her breasts are exposed as she slips off a robe, and in a 1903 photograph by Rudolf Eickerman, she resembles a flower child with a floral band across her forehead. When the writer Lucy Maud Montgomery saw this image in *The Metropolitan Magazine*, she clipped it out and pinned it to her wall, helping to inspire her lead character in *Anne of Green Gables*.[8]

As Evelyn wrote in her memoirs, "I was smaller, slenderer; a type artists and, as I learned later, older, more experienced men admired. I had discovered in the studios that artists cared little for the big-breasted, heavy-hipped, corseted figure, preferring to paint the freer, more sinuous, uncorseted one with natural, unspoiled lines."[9]

As she worked with Gibson and other illustrators, her face appeared on the covers of *Vanity Fair*, *Harper's Bazaar*, and *Cosmopolitan*, on packs of playing cards, tobacco cards, and to illustrate sheet music. More suggestive pin-up style photography was also used for postcards and calendars, where she dressed up as exotic fantasy figures like Cleopatra and Helen of Troy. In one of her most popular photos, she wears a kimono while reclining on a polar bear rug, playing up to the image of the soft, innocent but sexually compliant young woman.

Evelyn grew tired of the long hours spent posing in studios, and so she pleaded with her mother to let her try out as an actress. She was hired as a Florodora girl at the Casino Theatre on Broadway in July 1901, when she was still just fifteen years old. Combined with her career as a pin-up, Evelyn was pursued, and preyed on, by rich, older men who were attracted to the virginal Lolita fantasy. Married architect Stanford White, who at forty-six years old, was three times her age, ingratiated himself with her mother, and rented them a more luxurious abode as a means of grooming Evelyn. On one of their first chaperoned dates, he took her to his apartment to show her the large red velvet swing suspended from the ceiling, and which he encouraged her to sit on while he pushed it, softly introducing her to one of his kinks.

One evening, when he took her back to his apartment while her mother was out of town, he encouraged her to change into a kimono, and then got her so drunk that she blacked out. She awoke the next day to the realization that he had raped her. Overwhelmed by what had happened to her, and unsure of how to process it, she continued to sleep with him, but also dated others in the hopes they might secure an escape. John Barrymore, yet to become the lauded actor of stage and screen, was captivated after seeing her perform in Broadway's burlesque *The Wild Rose*. He was a handsome twenty-one-year-old, but her mother thought him unsuitable because of his lack of funds, and she put an end to the relationship.

Evelyn was also pursued by a rich railroads boss, Harry Kendall Thaw, who spent his money feeding his cocaine addiction and preying upon young women, with whom he took pleasure in beating. In 1903 Evelyn underwent surgery for appendicitis, which may have been cover for an illegal abortion. To aid her recovery, Thaw persuaded her to come with him on a trip to Europe. She was initially accompanied by her mother, but with tensions between the three, Mrs. Nesbit returned to New York and Evelyn went alone to Paris with Thaw. As he pressed her into marriage, she confessed to him that she wasn't the virgin he thought she was, as she'd been raped. Thaw was obsessed with her virginity, and he imprisoned her in an Austrian castle, where he sexually assaulted and beat her over a two-week period. Evelyn had been thrown into an adult world, her status as a model had left her unprotected from predatory men, and given the attitudes of the time, that a woman who was raped was "damaged," she worried that no respectable man would want her. Back in New York she told friends what Thaw had done to her, and she was warned about his unhinged, morphine-crazed behavior. But Evelyn was desperate to escape poverty and to have some security, and so she gave into Thaw's demands and agreed to marry him in April 1905.

In June 1906, while watching a rooftop theatre show at Madison Square Garden, Thaw took the opportunity to exact his revenge on Stanford White. After spotting him in the audience, Thaw drew his pistol and shot his rival to death, while screaming, "You ruined my wife!"

Arrested for murder and placed on trial, he pleaded temporary insanity, and Evelyn, having been offered financial protection by Thaw's wealthy mother, agreed to testify on his behalf. Given her status as a beautiful "It" girl, the trial was a sensation, with tabloids headlining the latest twists. Yellow journalism was at its height and there were a group of female reporters, nicknamed "sob sisters," who wrote emotively and melodramatically to appeal to women readers.[10] Across two trials in 1907 and 1908, Evelyn's appearance on the witness stand was captivating as she revealed the horrific details of her rape. In the press, she was painted as a former good-time girl who had brought her troubles on herself, and was now a pitiful, wilted hermit who was quite different from her days as a "toasted beauty of society . . . the girl who was tireless in the pursuit of pleasure."[11]

Ultimately Thaw was acquitted but was placed in a mental institution for several years. After the trial, Evelyn gave birth to a son, was eventually granted a divorce, continued to work in vaudeville and in silent cinema, and opened her own Manhattan tearoom, The Evelyn Nesbit Specialty Food Shop in 1921, which may have been a cover for a speakeasy. Given the trauma she had been through at such a young age, she struggled with alcohol and morphine addiction and attempted suicide on New Year's Eve 1925. Her life was once again headline news. In her recovery she continued to tour, performing burlesque in Panama, and then, in the fifties she served as a technical advisor for a film based on her life—*The Girl in the Red Velvet Swing* (1955). Shortly after the film's completion, she collapsed from a stroke, and passed away eleven years later in a Santa Monica nursing home, with her many obituaries headlined with her link to the sensational murder trial.[12]

From Evelyn's experience it was clear that a salacious murder and a beautiful female celebrity was a combination guaranteed to sell newspapers.

At the same time as Evelyn was giving evidence in Thaw's second trial, Mabel Normand was modeling everything from stockings, to combs, gloves, jewelry, lingerie, and sheet music. She struggled with the frustration of her ambitions, that she posed in borrowed gowns that she couldn't afford, and her likely ADHD made it hard for her to concentrate. "I hated to stand still," she admitted. "I hated to be simply a means by which someone else was creating something. I wanted to do it myself, but I couldn't. I had only the longing, without the ability."[13]

Mabel had heard that there was work to be found at the new film studios that had opened around the city, and she was introduced to the director DW Griffith at American Mutoscope and Biograph Company, located on Fourteenth Street. Initially founded by an inventor who had worked under Thomas Edison, it was now one of the leading production companies in the country.

Given her experience as a model for Gibson and Flagg, Griffith thought she would make a pretty addition to the film set, and she agreed to do some work as an extra. It was an exhausting day and by the time she got home to Staten Island it was 2 a.m. and her mother was frantic with worry. Not wanting to put her family through the stress, she decided to stick with modeling for its more reliable hours, choosing not to return to complete her scenes the next day. "I never expected to face a movie camera again. But Fate must have decided otherwise," she said.[14] She tried again, this time at Vitagraph Studios in Flatbush, Brooklyn, where she was taught comedic skills by popular duo John Bunny and Flora Finch. In a series of short films, she created a character, Betty, who liked to play pranks on John Bunny, including in 1911's *Troublesome Secretaries*, and she quickly became a hit with audiences.

Making movies suited Mabel's restlessness. She struggled to stay still while posing for illustrators, but the more energetic she could be for motion pictures, the better, although sometimes this veered into being hyperactive.

Three months later, outside the Forty-Second Street subway, she ran into a colleague of Griffith's at Biograph, Mack Sennett, and he scolded her for not having come back to complete her scenes. Over a malted milkshake, Sennett raved about working with Griffith, and persuaded her to return. Griffith gave Mabel the lead in the 1911 dramatic short film, *Her Awakening*, but it was when performing an impressive dive into water in Mack Sennett's *The Diving Girl* (1911) that she thrived.

At the beginning of 1912, Mack Sennett was heading to California to establish his own studio, Keystone, and he persuaded Mabel, who had become more than a colleague, to join him. New York's film companies were upping sticks to take advantage of the year-round sunshine and the expansive, undeveloped land among the orange groves and cattle ranches.

They arrived in August 1912 and one of Mabel's first starring roles at the new Keystone studios was *The Water Nymph*, in which she again dives into a pool of water. It further cemented her as a daring black-tight-clad "Venus," but she wasn't just a sex object, she was more a tomboy figure with her expressive, hyperactive comedy. She would wink at the camera as if she was letting the audience in on a secret, she would go cross-eyed or pout to indicate shock, and would flutter her hat to communicate excitement or dread.

Mabel was fearless when it came to doing her own dangerous stunts, even shrugging off her injuries and near-misses, which always made great newspaper copy. With her athletic prowess, she swam and rode horses and motorbikes, floated in hot-air balloons, she was dragged through mud by a rope, and jumped from great heights. She also was game for all the now-archetypal moments of silent cinema, including being tied to railway lines by the villain with a big moustache.

By 1913 Mabel was receiving huge amounts of coverage. Her portrait was splashed in *Motion Picture Story Magazine* in June 1913, with her dark curls piled on her head to reveal a bare neckline, and which emphasized her large eyes. Fan letters were pouring into the studio and smitten audiences sent in their tributes to the movie fan magazines, including poetry that eulogized her "winsome smile" and "pretty pout."[15]

Sennett believed the key to making a lot of money was to provide slapstick comedy that would appeal to a mass audience, so he introduced his bumbling "Keystone Cops" and hired an English vaudeville performer, Charlie Chaplin, who specialized in an acrobatic kind of slapstick.

It was in one of Mabel's self-titled short films, *Mabel's Strange Predicament* (1914), that Chaplin introduced his character, the Little Tramp, for the first time. She was the perfect complement to Chaplin's slapstick and as her popularity soared beyond that of cinema's ringleted sweetheart Mary Pickford, her name would guarantee packed audiences. The gossip columnist Gertrude Price, who specialized in writing about the early cinema stars, said: "Mabel belongs to the new generation where the watchword is: do anything, dare anything, and get away with everything!"[16]

With her name recognition she was one of the few actors whose own name appeared in the title, from the Mack Sennett–directed *Mabel's Lovers* in 1912, to a whole series of further movies, some of which were directed by Mabel herself. The fun-loving tomboy got into a series of scrapes in *Mabel's Adventures*, *Mabel's Awful Mistakes*, and in her self-directed *Mabel's Busy Day* she plays a hot dog vendor who is taken advantage of the hungry crowds, including by the Little Tramp. It was a symbolic moment for a star who was under enormous pressure to appeal to her fans and to make them laugh.

When Chaplin left Keystone, Mabel teamed up with Roscoe "Fatty" Arbuckle for a series of "Fatty and Mabel" films that began shooting in January 1915. They were perfect foils to one another—she was petite, he was a hulking, baby-faced presence, and it was this absurdity that made them such a successful pairing.

If the Gibson girl had reflected a new autonomy in women who demanded the right to education and jobs, then Mabel was the epitome of the new woman. She was completely uninhibited—acting the reckless, hard-partying flapper eight years before the term went mainstream. She was the Cinderella for the Jazz Age, the girl from Staten Island who landed the dream life. She wasn't a vamp or a virgin; she was a down-to-earth tomboy who was perfectly attuned to the mood of the country as it declared war on Germany in 1917.

Hollywood's players were accumulating massive wealth in a town that flaunted wealth and luxury in its sprawling Spanish colonial mansions, private country clubs, and decadent nightclubs. Film stars were the new royalty, and as their image was projected around the world and printed in popular fan magazines, and with Mabel as the face of Coca-Cola in 1916, she was a truly global icon. "Many of us became queens overnight," said actress Madge Kennedy. "But Mabel became a goddess."[17]

If life as one of the world's biggest celebrities appeared to be easy living, she felt like she was being worked to the bone by Sennett, and the drinking and the dabbling in the readily available pick-me-ups on set exacerbated her depression.

She was hurt by Mack's frequent womanizing, when she wanted to settle down and have children. He proposed in June 1915, but it didn't offer her the security she needed given his affairs, and by September she had to take time off work due to a concussion caused indirectly by his cheating. There were a number of different accounts as to what had happened. The actress Minta Durfee claimed Mabel had walked in on Mack in bed with another young actress, Mae Busch, and that Mae had hurled a vase at Mabel's head in surprise, believing she was an intruder.

Her mental and physical health took a further beating when she caught tuberculosis, a deadly infection that killed thousands a year, and for which there was no firm cure. To ease her coughing, she took sips of a liquid that she called her "goop" which contained an opioid, and which she mixed with the cocaine prescribed by her doctor.

Despite her ill health, her career was thriving as 400 fan letters arrived for her every day from all over the world, and she laughed in wonder at all the babies who were now being named "Mabel Normand."[18] With support from Mack's new company, Triangle Film Company, in 1916 she founded the Mabel Normand Feature Film Company, and a studio was built for her on Sunset Boulevard. She was now the head of her own studio, and she chose *Mickey* as the first feature, in which she played a coarse mountain girl sent to live with relatives in the east and who must adjust to being a fish out of water. In one memorable scene, she dives nude into a lake—referencing the early screen moments that made her a star. At this point, Mabel looked increasingly tired and ravaged from the medication she had been given for her illnesses. As Minta Durfee said in an interview with archivist Don Schneider: "That little thing would have a hemorrhage of the lungs and then she would take a swig out of a bottle, to stop the bleeding, and the coughing, and do all of her own stunt[s], nobody did any stunts for her."[19]

Mickey's release was put on hold due to Triangle's financial problems, and in the meantime, she was wooed by independent producer Samuel Goldwyn with the offer of a huge contract at $1,000 a week.

When *Mickey* was eventually released in 1918, in part thanks to a big publicity campaign by Mack Sennett, it brought Mabel to new levels of fame. "We make big money," Mabel told reporters, "but it only brings us headaches and heartaches, sapping our strength and powers of resistance."[20]

She was one of the highest-paid women in America, and with more money than she knew what to do with she splashed her cash on New York couture, lavish jewelry, a sixty-foot yacht for taking friends to Catalina Island, and she bought her parents a house on Staten Island. Ever eager to learn, she took piano and French lessons, and bought up a library's worth of books.

Wealthy men like Prince Mohammed Ali Ibrahim of Egypt, who proposed, and the Prince of Wales (later Edward VIII), who merely put in a request for a date, wanted to claim her as a trophy. Still, with her humble beginnings, she was suspicious, she said, of "ritzy people."[21]

The first of the sixteen movies she made under Goldwyn was *Dodging a Million*, released in January 1918, in which she played a shopgirl in a Fifth Avenue store, was a departure from the tomboys and mountain girls. Goldwyn tried to tame her partying lifestyle to bring back some of that old vitality. He also pursued her sexually, and when she fell pregnant, it tragically ended with a stillbirth.[22] Physically and mentally traumatized, Mabel's depression spiraled, and she turned to alcohol to blot out the pain. She was earning a reputation among reporters for being uncooperative and late, and for being unable to sit still for more than a few minutes. Over the years she also had a tendency to fudge her biography—she claimed she'd been raised in a convent, and was an orphan, and at other times, that she was privately educated. As William J. Mann wrote, "Rich or poor, it didn't matter to Mabel. All she had ever cared about was that she never be considered ordinary."[23]

Over lunch one day, *Photoplay*'s Herbert Howe observed her ordering nine martinis and a baked Alaska, but he chose not to print their conversation. He built up a trust with her, and as she let him into her world, she confided her fears, her confusion over her feelings for Mack, and her sense of nihilism that she didn't know how long she had left to live. "What's the use of making plans to go places or marry people?" she had said in 1916, and it felt truer than ever.[24]

Unhappy with Goldwyn, Mack persuaded her to come back to work for him. *Molly O* (1921) was marketed as the reuniting of the team behind *Mickey*, and the Cinderella story of a plucky but poor Irish waif would be a huge hit with the public. She may have had 200 movies under her belt, but after *Suzanna* (1923) she would make only two more. Her career was eclipsed by two major scandals which threatened Hollywood's very foundations.

Mabel wasn't the only star struggling under the limelight, and the pressures and temptations that came with being a star. One of Mabel's close friends, Olive Thomas, suffered a mysterious death in Paris at the age of twenty-five. Dubbed "The Most Beautiful Girl in the World," she had, like Mabel, been a model and then an actress, and as she made her name as the first screen flapper in the 1920 movie *The Flapper*, she was a wild child in real life. The First World War had killed off the Gibson girl, and in its wake was the hedonistic jazz baby who was more permissive than ever before.

In 1916 Olive married Jack Pickford, the playboy brother of Mary who had a reputation as a womanizer and drug abuser. They were the epitome of a toxic relationship, with Jack encouraging Olive's most dangerous impulses, and where their heavy drinking would lead to mishaps.

In September 1920 they embarked on a second honeymoon in Paris, where they fully embraced the city's sparkling nightlife. After an evening at a nightclub, Le Rat Mort, they returned to their hotel in the early hours. In the bathroom, Olive accidentally took a swig from Jack's bottle of bichloride of mercury, which he used topically to treat the syphilis he had contracted after their marriage. The poison destroyed her internal organs and after five days of agony, she died. Mabel was devastated as Olive was her partying companion—they were the Britney and Paris of old Hollywood, both enjoying taking advantage of Mabel's cellar which was stocked with bootleg booze.[25]

Further shock hit the film community a year later, when Roscoe Arbuckle was put on trial for rape and manslaughter, following the death of actress Virginia Rappe at a party at a hotel in San Francisco. She died from internal injuries, allegedly caused by the violence of his sexual assault. He may have been acquitted after three trials, but he was effectively canceled, and doubts about his innocence hung over him until his death in 1933.

With so many scandals in a town that set the cultural agenda, Hollywood and its decadent movie stars were held up by moralists as a place of corruption. There were cries for the film industry to be censored to protect the public from such dubious standards.

An advocate for keeping censorship out of Hollywood was dapper director William Desmond Taylor, considered one of the most intelligent and well-read figures in the industry. Mabel had known him for years, but it was in the early 1920s that their close friendship blossomed over a love of books and high culture, although she would always deny their relationship was more intimate.

On the evening of February 1, 1922, Mabel called at Taylor's home to collect some books he wanted to share with her. She declined his invite for dinner as she had an early call in the morning for the film *Suzanna*, but his butler mixed them Orange Blossoms, a favorite cocktail of prohibition-era jazz babies like Mabel and Zelda Fitzgerald.

As she left by chauffeur-driven car, Mabel blew kisses to Taylor out the rear window, and went to bed early. The next day, Taylor's body was discovered by his butler, having been shot through the heart.[26] As the last known person to visit him, Mabel was implicated, alongside another actress linked with Taylor, Mary Miles Minter. She was now at the center of a media storm, and under siege from the press, she tried to appeal to the goodwill of the public that she was innocent. But her reputation was tarnished by association, and there were calls across America for her films to be banned. Mabel went from idol to pariah, where she was mocked in the press, and held up as a corrupting agent by political and religious organizations. All that she had achieved in her life, as a comedienne, a director, a producer, and a movie star, was eclipsed by Taylor's murder. In a self-penned article in the *Los Angeles Examiner* in 1924, she reflected on the torment.

"Those of you who followed the Taylor case, in all its intensity, undoubtedly realize what I went through," she said. "Detectives and district attorneys swarmed around me and my name was flaunted on the front page of every newspaper in the country for weeks. It was a terrible experience."[27]

She struggled to complete *Suzanna*, appearing thinner and sadder in some of the scenes, but it was a huge hit and Sennett next cast her in *The Extra Girl*. It was the first film to offer a behind-the-scenes look at Hollywood, and it fittingly told of a humble small-town girl who finds that movie stardom is a poisoned chalice. But the common criticism was that she just looked too old and worn out for the part of an ingenue.

If Mabel felt like she could finally move past the murder of her friend, shortly after, she was implicated in another shooting. On New Year's Day, 1924 she and another actress, Edna Purviance, called at the home of millionaire Courtland S. Dines. Mabel's chauffeur, Joe Kelly, took exception to something Dines had said, and he returned with a revolver and shot at him. Dines survived and eventually dropped the charges, but it was revealed Kelly was in fact an ex-convict named Horace Greer, and he was deemed to have acted on impulse due to his love for Mabel.

Again, Mabel's connection to the crime was splashed across newspapers, and she went on a press drive to try to reverse public opinion. "Reportorial friends tell me I have become what they call 'good copy.' Whatever that is, I don't like it. . . . So here's hoping the next time I occupy the front page it will be something nice, something wholesome."[28]

Moral groups made further calls to ban her films, and under pressure, some cities even dropped her from theatres. In Tennessee, the Memphis Board of Motion Pictures Censors agreed to ban her films from being shown, as they would "have a disastrous effect upon the youth of the community."[29] Other states, including Michigan and Ohio, followed. In the *Seattle Star*, one letter-writer agreed with these bans, chastising Mabel as a "common cigaret-smoking, booze-consuming, convention-defying individual, and for the sake of our young girls, whose welfare is worth a thousand Mabel Normands, should be banished from the screen."[30]

Mack Sennett, not loyal enough to take the reputational risk, canceled her next film, and it would mark the end of their working relationship. Mabel was desperate to escape Los Angeles and in August 1925, she rented an apartment in New York while she found work on the stage. Her first play, *The Little Mouse*, was to earn her $1,500 a week, and a percentage of the profits, but it turned out to be a disaster after several rewrites and was destroyed by critics.

She didn't want to be driven off the screen, and rather than retire, she signed with Hal Roach Studios in March 1926 for the film *Raggedy Rose*, which was a Cinderella tale of a waifish girl, whom she seemed too old to play.

In September of that year, she and her longtime friend and fellow actor Lew Cody got married on a whim. It had been a drunken dare, and while they continued to live separately, he gave her protection and love when she needed it most. The tuberculosis was still in her body, and it came back with a vengeance in December 1928. As her health deteriorated over the next year she was placed in a hospice and passed away on February 23, 1930.

When news of her death broke, the newspaper obituaries hailed her as cinema's first star, the tragic figure whose status as a film industry pioneer had been tarnished by scandal.

She had been cinema's unofficial "It" girl, and at the same time as Mabel's career was imploding, another vivacious and comic actress with a mop of cherry red hair was making an impact. Self-aware enough to recognize the similarities, Mabel, in the last years of her life, would even name her chow puppy "It Girl"—in tribute to this hot new star, Clara Bow.[31]

Josephine Baker, Florence Mills, and the Harlem Renaissance

Josephine Baker in her dressing room in Paris. *Pictorial Press Ltd/Alamy Stock Archive Photo.*

Josephine Baker high-kicked onto the stage of the 63rd Street Theatre to rapturous applause. With her arms linked around the waists of the two dancers beside her, the sixteen-year-old was in joyous synchronicity with her chorus line, all in matching white top hats and white and brown polka dot jumpsuits. She'd dreamed of this moment for years, having auditioned several times for *Shuffle Along*, the first Jazz Age Broadway hit that was written, produced, and performed solely by African Americans, and which had transformed Florence Mills into a huge star. After numerous failed auditions, Josephine had been told she was too young, and that she should come back when older, but it had also been disheartening to think that maybe it was because her skin was too dark.

Professional Black dancers on Broadway and in New York's jazz clubs were subjected to the "paper bag test," where their skin was not to be darker than a brown paper bag. Florence Mills said she was "coal black and proud of it," and she refused to use lemon juice or bleach to lighten her complexion. In the years after the First World War there was a call for pride and self-confidence among Black women as they broke free from the constraints of white beauty standards, and Florence Mills and Josephine Baker led the way.

Shuffle Along not only launched Florence and Josephine as Harlem "It" girls who redrew what it meant to be an African American woman. But upon its arrival on Broadway in 1921, it was also credited with kick-starting the Harlem Renaissance, a creative movement of African American literature, music, fashion, and arts in the 1920s.

Florence and Josephine were crossover celebrities at a time when racial segregation was a part of American life, and Black performers were shut out of white society. They brought their syncopated rhythm to Europe, fascinating and thrilling society in Paris and London. At the same they were placed as exotic beings whose appeal to white audiences lay in the "primitiveness" of their dance movements, and both played into these roles as a way of taking ownership. They may have been denied entry in New York's whites-only department stores, but the very thing they were discriminated for also led to them being applauded and celebrated and emulated.

Florence Mills, born in 1896 in Washington, DC, was the daughter of two enslaved people who had moved from Lynchburg, Virginia, to the capital in search of a better life. After her father died from tuberculosis, her mother worked in a brothel laundry to support her three daughters. Living on the breadline in the slum area, Goat Alley, music was a comfort in the face of hardship, and Florence would come alive when she sang and danced, captivating the neighborhood children as she flew like a lightning bug.

Florence began performing in front of audiences from the age of three, earning extra money for the family by entertaining the local bordello workers. Her specialty, for which she won prizes, was the Cake Walk, a performative dance that dated back to the antebellum, when enslaved people would dress up and parody their white owners, and by the 1890s it had become a craze in Black revues and stage shows. She also received invitations to perform for Washington DC's, rarefied circle of diplomats, including from the British ambassador's wife, Lady Pauncefote, who asked for Florence to entertain her guests.[1]

Florence may have found a new world opening up to her, going from the bordello to diplomatic drawing rooms, and even performing on stage with the burlesque star Bonita, but racial segregation was still very much a part of her life. After being invited to perform at a whites-only theatre, she brought along her siblings and a friend to support her, only to find they were forbidden from entering. She threatened to cancel the show, until management relented.

Her performances with Bonita raised questions among the moralistic New York Society for the Prevention of Cruelty to Children, also known as the Gerry Society, a religious group working for the protection of children, and they removed Florence from her home in 1904 and placed her in the care of nuns. She was away from her family for two years, but once she was able to join them in Harlem, her mother altered her age on her birth certificate so she could perform with her two older sisters, Olivia and Maude, as the Mills Sisters.[2]

They traveled the East Coast, performing in Black vaudeville theatres that were part of what was known as the Dudley circuit, and it was clear that Florence was the star of the show. She was small for her age, appearing much younger than her sixteen years, and she was full of energy, practicing her acrobatic moves over and over until she had perfected them.

Her sisters were tiring of touring, feeling they were getting too old for a life on the road, but Florence was determined to keep going. Arriving in Chicago, she moved into a South Side boardinghouse that was popular with jazz club performers. Also staying there was Ada "Bricktop" Smith, who was a regular at the Panama Café, styled like a European society café, or a café-concert, with the singers moving around the floor between the tables in exchange for tips.

She recommended Florence to the owner, and while he thought her too skinny and young-looking, Ada agreed to coach her. They both teamed up with Cora Green to perform as the Panama Trio, and with their energetic moves, sweet singing, and Bricktop's patter, they became so popular that Black businessman Claude A. Barnett hired them to model his Kashmir cosmetics line. In 1917, when the Panama Café was forced to close after a stabbing, Bricktop left for Los Angeles and Florence found her way to the Tennessee Ten.[3]

She was hired to be the prima donna in the troupe of singers, jazz musicians, and dancers, which included the acrobatic performer Ulysses "Slow Kid" Thompson, whom Florence fell hard for. When the United States entered the Great War raging in Europe, Thompson was drafted and sent to France, where he entertained troops in the Army band as a "clown drummer."

After he returned, Florence moved with him to New York to perform with the Tennessee Ten at the Columbia Theatre, New York. The show had a mixed act of vaudeville performers, including Bert Lahr and Jack Haley, who later starred in 1939's *The Wizard of Oz*. Florence wowed the reviewers with her bird-like soprano, and for the agility of her dance moves with her lithe, light frame. She was shy and reserved off the stage, but as soon as she stepped onto it, her large, expressive eyes lit up as she used comedic pantomime expressions to accompany her dance moves. Thompson saw how talented she was and took up his role as both her manager, and by 1921, her new husband.[4]

Florence arrived back in New York City as it flourished with a wave of creativity under the Harlem Renaissance. Jazz had arrived in New York from New Orleans, and together with the writers and intellectuals in the area, it was the soundtrack to a thriving and unique culture. The twenty-five blocks of Victorian brownstones and tenements of upper Manhattan had filled with an influx of migrants escaping from the segregated south as part of the Great Migration. James Weldon Johnson, a leading figure of the Harlem Renaissance, called it "a city within a city, the greatest Negro city in the world."[5]

With the backdrop of a booming stock market, and a sense of freedom and hedonism in the air, jazz and blues pulsated in the clubs and bars, as great musicians Louis Armstrong and Duke Ellington shook off the restrictive legacies of minstrel shows and southern stereotyping. It was in Harlem's nightclubs that the "Roarin' Twenties" dance crazes originated, as the Charleston, the Black Bottom, and later, the Lindy Hop, were mimicked and popularized by white thrill-seekers as the sound and style of this district became big business.

In Harlem's thriving queer culture, Black lesbians and gay men were free to express their true selves. The Blues music of Bessie Smith, Gladys Bentley, and Ma Rainey celebrated the "Bulldaggers," or butch lesbians, as they performed in tuxedos and top hats. The Saturday night beauty contests at the Savoy ballroom, and the Drag Balls which satirized fashion shows, all reflected the embracing of diverse sexuality and self-expression. Ethel Waters remembered the 1920s as "the great time of drags in Harlem with fashion parades for the male queers dressed in women's clothes."[6]

In their downtime, Florence and "Slow Kid" immersed themselves in Harlem's nightspots and speakeasies, where they mixed with other performers like Bojangles, who taught her tap dancing, and the comedy duo Flournoy Miller and Aubrey Lyles, who were the creators and stars of *Shuffle Along*.

Miller and Lyles had first conceived the idea of creating an all-Black Broadway show after meeting the songwriting team Noble Sissle and Eubie Blake at an NAACP (The National Association for the Advancement of Colored People) event in 1920. Loosely based on Miller's script for *The Mayor of Dixie*, Miller and Lyles played two grocery owners who compete in a small-town mayoral contest. As well as being the first all-Black show on Broadway for over ten years, its narrative broke from the minstrel stereotypes, and unapologetically featured a typically taboo romance between two Black characters.

They secured the 63rd Street Theatre, an obscure theater on the very edge of Broadway, where the first rows of seats had to be removed to make way for an orchestra. Opening on May 23, 1921, just a week before the Tulsa race riots broke out in Oklahoma, destroying one of the most successful autonomous Black enclaves in the country, *Shuffle Along*'s success defied the hatred. Running for 500 performances, it was the second longest Broadway run for 1921, and was the hit of that sweltering summer, "selling out mostly to white people."[7]

Lester Walton, the drama critic for the African American newspaper the *New York Age*, and manager of Harlem's Lafayette Theatre, likened it to a steamroller crushing "many of the barriers that have stood in the path of the colored show's progress.

"There are but few dull moments in *Shuffle Along*," he added. "There is always something to hold one's interest be it dialogue or song. As for the comedy work of Miller and Lyles, they have written so many bright lines and humorous situations for themselves you are likely to temporarily forget all about the Ku Klux Klan."[8]

Florence joined the show in August 1921 to replace Gertrude Saunders, and at first her castmates were unsure what to make of this small, unassuming figure who arrived backstage, according to Bee Freeman, "wearing a black rusty looking dress. It seemed like she had no glamour at all."[9] To celebrate her debut night, "Slow Kid" brought an entourage to watch and cheer as she performed her first number, "I'm Craving for That Kind of Love." As she moved forward onto the stage, getting closer to the footlights as she belted out "Kiss Me," the audience screamed in appreciation, and she received seventeen encores; and not just from her husband and his friends. She was able to handle both the love ballads and the jazzier tempos, and as Noble Sissle tried to define her appeal, he described her as "Dresden China, and she turns into a stick of dynamite."[10]

This was a star-making turn as she stole the show with her sweet but powerful voice, and the cute-as-a-button face that belied her energetic, tomboyish moves, such as the "buck and wing" tap dancing. "I never dance like a girl. I prefer to dance like a man," she said in 1925.[11]

In an interview with the *Pittsburgh Courier* in February 1925, she credited *Shuffle Along* with kick-starting her career. "No one of the family was in the profession before; just my two sisters. We were in vaudeville, the Mills Sisters. I was the youngest. Now they've dropped out. I don't like to think of that part of my life; it was too horrible. I like to think I started with 'Shuffle Along.' It's hard getting to the top, and when you're there it's hard starving."[12]

With *Shuffle Along* a huge hit on Broadway, Harlem's entertainment was now the fashionable experience for white Manhattanites. Thousands flocked to Harlem to listen to jazz and to the erotic cabarets that offered the "real" experience of dancing the Charleston at the Cotton Club, which opened in 1923, and which excluded Black guests. Langston Hughes was scathing that "strangers were given the best ringside tables to sit and stare at the Negro customers—like amusing animals in a zoo."[13]

It angered him, the way that Black culture was so often met with contempt yet became a fashion trend among the very population who derided them. In the secret exclusive clubs of Harlem, away from white eyes, novel dance styles were created and consumed for an exclusively Black audience, as musical innovations thrived. In May 1926 Hughes wrote in *The Nation*: "We younger Negro artists who create now intend to express our individual dark-skinned selves without fear or shame. If white people are pleased we are glad. If they are not, it doesn't matter."[14]

Because a lot of money came from white audiences, there were clubs that played up to their expectations, toying with the notion of the antebellum south that many of its founding residents had escaped from. One of these establishments was the Plantation Club, owned by producer Lew Leslie, which re-created the antebellum south. The ceiling was decorated with a giant slice of watermelon, with its seeds as electric lights, a painted backdrop featured a steamboat on the Suwannee River, and a hut where a "mammie" cooked waffles and flipped flapjacks.

Florence Mills performing in the Plantation Revue. *Jerome Robbins Dance Division, The New York Public Library.*

Leslie described Florence as the "world's greatest colored entertainer"[15] and he booked her to appear with her husband in "Plantation Revue," an after-show performance on the roof of the Winter Garden Theatre. Florence's name blazed across the marquee as she performed on stage with her backing chorus dancers the "Chocolate Drops" and played up to the exotic stereotypes of jungle rhythms and Polynesian grass skirts. "It's not really South sea," Florence explained. "It's jungle; or, what I imagine the jungle might be like. I have never visited a jungle. It's an emotional dance. I like it."[16]

If *Shuffle Along* had been a huge success, then Plantation Revue was even more so, transforming her into the top Black female entertainer in the city.

Charles B. Cochran arrived in New York in late 1922 to search for Black performers he could bring back to London for a novel show. Having seen

Florence in *Shuffle Along*, he considered her to be the shining star, so appealing because of her combined magnetism and lack of affectation, and opted to adapt Plantation Revue for a show called *Dover Street to Dixie*, with white performers in the first half, and Black performers in the second. Dixieland jazz had become all the rage in London in the early twenties, but as well as being considered an American curiosity, it was also met with deep suspicion. The *Daily Mail*, which referred to it as "jazzmania," insinuated that it was tawdry, in the same way it would later decry rock 'n' roll as "voodoo."

Florence Mills was nervous in the days leading up to the start of her show in London—she was used to American audiences but was worried about how she would be received in a foreign country, where the culture was completely different. Aware that the English wouldn't understand the meaning of some of her songs, she changed the lyrics, because "they didn't know what momma in 'You've Got to Kiss Momma Every Night' meant. So I changed it to 'sweetie,' and then they knew."[17]

Back in New York, she turned down an offer from the great impresario Florenz Ziegfeld to be the first Black woman to star in his Follies, instead choosing to be part of an all-Black cast in Lew Leslie's *Dixie to Broadway* to "give my people the opportunity of demonstrating that their talents are equal to the most exacting demands of this popular form of entertainment."[18]

New York critics hailed her, but they struggled to define her magic, as if they couldn't get to grips with the culture it celebrated—at times described as grotesque, at others, a form of undefinable beauty. The *Evening World* described her as a "slender streak of genius, about five feet tall, born a shade or two South of the color line." The *Telegram and Mail* called her a "sensational little personality, slim, jaunty, strung on fine and tremulous wires," while Heywood Broun in the *World* said she was "like that of no one else. She does not precisely sing but she makes strange high noises. . . . Sometimes the intent is the creation of the grotesque and then it fades into lines of amazing beauty. Now I have seen grace."[19]

A clear sign of her celebrity was a profile in *Vanity Fair* in February 1925. In the photo, taken by Edward Steichen, she played up to her tomboy persona in her Dick Whittington stage costume, complete with a knapsack on a stick slung on her shoulder. "Florence Mills Leads a Harlemquinade on Broadway," said the caption, and underneath, "The exotic rhythm and accelerated pace, which have created a furore for the Negro Revue, have reached a climax in Dixie to Broadway."[20]

While Florence had returned to Harlem after her successful tour in Europe, there was another alumnus of *Shuffle Along* who was about to find extraordinary fame and celebrity on the other side of the Atlantic. On stage at the Théâtre des Champs-Élysées, with only a handful of feathers to cover her naked body, and at the Folies Bergère in 1926, wearing a rope of pearls and her famous "banana skirt," Josephine Baker had become a phenomenon in Paris. Her presence was everywhere in the city; postcards were on display in newspaper stands, Parisiennes sported their own version of her glossy Eton crop, and she was fetishized by those who had the fortune to meet her. When Ernest Hemingway took to the dance floor with her in a club in Montparnasse, he boasted that "the place was set on fire by the most sensational woman anybody ever saw. Or ever will. Tall, coffee skin, ebony eyes, legs of paradise, a smile to end all smiles."[21]

Josephine's story began in the ghetto of St. Louis, and while her sheer energy and charisma had led her to the clubs of Paris, she never forgot the hardships she experienced. "A black childhood is always a little sad," she told Marcel Sauvage, the co-writer of her 1927 biography, but she was hazy about some of the early details of her life. "I don't lie," she said. "I improve on life."[22]

She was born in 1906 as Freda Josephine McDonald in St. Louis, to Carrie McDonald, a single mother and dance hall performer and adopted daughter of two former enslaved people from Little Rock, Arkansas. Given that she was born in a white hospital, she was convinced her absent father was white. At other times she professed he was a "good-looking boy with olive skin" or a Spanish dancer, which was all part of her desire to blur the lines of truth.[23]

Her mother struggled in abject poverty, and Josephine was forced to work as a domestic help at the age of eight. What gave her hope was a love of dancing, performing in her makeshift theatre in the cellar of her home and on the streets because, she said simply, "I was born in a cold city."[24] By thirteen she had left school to work as a waitress, and she also had a shockingly young and short-lived marriage to a railway porter.

In 1920 the fourteen-year-old, now divorced, met Clara Smith, a boisterous singer whose stage outfit included a bright red wig and glamorous feather boa, when she was performing on stage in St. Louis. Clara was part of a new wave of lesbian singers who were out and proud, and she offered Josephine singing lessons at a price—if the young hopeful went to bed with her.[25] It was just one example of the exploitation of poor young girls that was normalized and uncontested. Observing her talents for comedic dancing, Clara asked Josephine to join her vaudeville group, the Dixie Steppers, and so, by fourteen she was traveling from town to town, until she ended up in New York City. Josephine had married for a second time, to William Howard Baker, in 1921, and while she had left him when she went on the road, she kept his surname as her stage name.

Clara introduced Josephine to the queer culture of Harlem, and she was inspired by some of the touches Smith brought to the stage, such as toying with a long silk handkerchief. Everyone was talking about the smash success of *Shuffle Along*, and Josephine was desperate to be part of the show. She failed her first audition, but was given backstage work as a dresser, before finally crossing onto the stage as a chorus girl on the touring leg in Boston, and then on Broadway.

When she joined the chorus line of the 1924 Broadway musical *The Chocolate Dandies*, a new production by Sissle and Blake, she was given her own solo dance number. As she recounted in 1929: "I was no longer a chorus girl . . . I was a feature player in my own right; I had grown used to seeing my name in lights—but there always remained some of the thrill which I experienced the first time. I was billed as a comedienne—that was my forte. It was glorious to make people laugh—to take them out of themselves, to make them feel happy. I don't believe there is any greater compensation than knowing that you are doing something to make the world happier!"[26]

As well as the high energy of her dance moves, honed by her study of classical ballet techniques, she used facial expressions to generate laughs. She believed it was these comedic touches that helped to bring the audience onto her side. On May 28, 1922, the *Brooklyn Eagle* quoted Josephine's philosophy of performance. She believed that if people danced successfully with their faces and hands they wouldn't have to worry about their feet, because it was personality that counted.[27]

Next she was snapped up by the venue that had made Florence a star, the Plantation Club on Broadway, this time as the top-billed, highest-paid chorus girl of Tan Town Topics. Florence Mills had excelled at singing and acrobatic, boyish moves, but Josephine was a dancer who mixed the sensuality she had learned from Clara Smith with the comedic touches that always generated a laugh. She relished seeing her name as the highlight of the night, of being the star in every room in Harlem when she burst in wearing satin and faux pearls. But all that glory was undermined when she wasn't allowed into the white-only theatres of midtown or to shop at the department stores of Fifth Avenue. She was unfettered in her own district, but in the rest of white Manhattan she was limited in her choices, purely because of the color of her skin.

One evening she was visited in her Plantation Club dressing room by Caroline Dudley Reagan, a theatre impresario who persuaded the nineteen-year-old to come to Paris to perform in a show called "La Revue Nègre." It was being developed by Rolf de Maré for a run at the Théâtre des Champs-Elysées, with a vision of transporting his Parisian audiences straight to Harlem with jazz and modernist dance. He had initially hoped for Florence Mills as the lead Black dancer, but her costs were prohibitive, and so he turned to Josephine as the latest star of Plantation Revue.[28]

According to Caroline Dudley Reagan, in Paris Josephine would be able to find the pure, unfettered freedom, and stardom, that she craved. It was in the cobbled streets of Montmartre and the boulevards of Montparnasse that jazz and ragtime throbbed through the smoky, cavernous nightclubs. It was here that African American musicians had set up home after fighting in France during the war because of its liberalism. Florence Mills's friend and bandmate from the Panama Trio, Ada "Bricktop" Smith, had moved to Montmartre in 1924, where she would set up her own nightclub, Chez Bricktop, which attracted Hollywood stars, socialites, and international playboys.

Shortly after her arrival in Paris in September 1925, Josephine was dismayed to discover that the classy show she had been promised now required her to be completely nude. It was insulting as it tied her to the fantasies of the exotic woman in "primitive" art, such as the paintings by Paul Gauguin of Polynesian woman. But she had little choice without a means of getting home, and a week later she made her first appearance on the Théâtre des Champs-Elysées. The packed audience included notable figures like Gertrude Stein and Maurice Chevalier, expat Americans, reporters and critics, all holding their breath to see what they could expect from Josephine, who had been depicted so seductively in illustrations for the show by Paul Colin.

As part of the final act, she came on stage in front of a jungle backdrop, wearing the scantest feather loincloth, and balanced upside down on the shoulders of her male dance partner with her legs in splits. The audience burst into applause and laughter as she performed her signature comedic facial expressions, alongside high kicks and splits, the cross eyes as she ferociously danced the Charleston—bringing it to Paris's stage for the first time. André Levinson, the ballet critic, described her as "the black Venus that haunted Baudelaire" and that her performance showed "a wild splendor and magnificent animality."[29]

As she later described, she was "driven by dark forces I didn't recognize, I improvised, crazed by the music, the overheated theatre filled to bursting point, the scorching eye of the spotlights," and by the end of performance, the audience was intoxicated.[30]

On the back of glowing publicity, there was an intense scramble to get hold of tickets, and she was so popular that she knocked Anna Pavlova out of her upcoming spot. Josephine was the star attraction, the exotic beauty who was as streamlined as the new Art Deco movement that had only just been given its official title that very year, and which melded African arts with its worship of geometry and sleek, gleaming surfaces. With her short, lacquered hair, and her strong, toned body, she was considered the perfect figurehead for the *années folles* as the *garçonne*, the French version of the flapper.

For Josephine, her idolatry was not just about being a celebrity, it was also an acknowledgment of her as a person on an equal level with every other performer. This had been impressed upon her right from the opening night, when she was invited to sit with the white performers and crew at the opening night after-party.

Josephine found the Montmartre and Pigalle areas to be much like Harlem, alive with the roar of traffic, the bustle of people brushing past one another. She could now afford to stay in a luxury suite in the Hôtel Fournet, and to buy hats and dresses and furs at the department store Galeries Lafayette without the restrictions that were placed on her in the States. Like Sarah Bernhardt, who had died just a few years before, she collected pets, adding to her collection rabbits, snakes, and parakeets, as well as a cheetah, Chiquita, whom she led around with a diamond collar and leash.

She was invited to the salon of Paul Poiret, the eminent Paris couturier, and he draped silvery fabric on her body to create a gown that made her feel "like a sea goddess emerging from the foam." Josephine also sketched her dream dress, a pink fringed flapper dress, and he promised that he would create it for her and launch it as the "Josephine Baker" dress for his next collection.[31]

In 1926 she was poached by the Folies Bergère, the oldest music hall in Paris, to headline in a luxuriously extravagant show that would be the pinnacle of her career. Once again, Josephine was cast in the exotic role, and she would do a jungle dance wearing a pearl bra top and the now infamous skirt of jewel-encrusted bananas. Sliding down a pole disguised as a tree, she then performed the Charleston at rapid speed, doing the splits, then arching her back as she crawled on all fours.

As Judith Mackrell writes in *Flappers*: "The glitter of the performance came, principally, from its confident spirit of mockery: Josephine was playing with this jungle imagery, rather than letting it play her."[32]

Josephine was thrilled to see her name in lights, the thousands of fan letters that filled her dressing room, the huge posters plastered outside the theatres with her name and body in brilliant color, and the postcards for sale that were splashed with her glorious image. She was still only twenty-one years old, but she was the girl of the year, the symbol of the Charleston and of American freedom as she drove around Paris in a coffee-colored Voisin motorcar with snakeskin upholstering. There were even Josephine Baker dolls for sale which promoted her skin color and her hair style, and which reflected the advertising campaigns aimed at white women to copy her style.

She was hired to be the face of Bakerfix, a glossy hair pomade that was developed to emulate her look, and Nancy Cunard, the heiress with a fixation for African American culture, donned a black skullcap to achieve the effect of Josephine's glossy Eton crop.

Even though she was setting new beauty standards, Josephine had been ingrained with feelings of shame around her skin, at times trying to lighten it with lemon juice, or a burning goat's milk and bleach formula. In Harlem, where the flourishing beauty business offered hair pressing for Black hair and skin whitening products, shop windows began displaying the Josephine Baker dolls, evident of a new sense of Black pride. African American girls looked up to her as a symbol of beauty and hope, at a time when there was an increasingly fervent Ku Klux Klan who regulated segregation.

Despite her worship in France, she was also mocked. Sem, the famous cartoonist who had captured Coco Chanel as the purveyor of feminine fantasy, depicted her with a monkey tale poking out of her evening gown. It was a hurtful reminder of how women of color were treated, and she needed to push her career beyond being the novelty Charleston dancer who specialized in the Banana Dance.

In 1926, on the other side of the English Channel, Florence Mills was the "It" girl of the London stage, having returned to the city to headline Lew Leslie's Blackbirds at the Palace Theatre after a run in Paris at the ultra-fashionable café-concert Les Ambassadeurs. The show incorporated song and dance numbers with comedic interludes, and it sparked a mania among London's glitterati. A regular in the audience was Edward, Prince of Wales, who proudly told the press that he saw the sold-out show eleven times. In its review, London's *The Times* praised Florence for her "personality, humour, agility, and a voice worthy of better uses." The reviewer had prepared for an "orgy of jazz" and given the high energy of dancing, that "life in Dixieland must be terribly exhausting."[33]

Florence was a representative of the emancipated Black woman, with her Eton crop and flapper gowns, and she was splashed as a celebrity in Britain's newspapers, sharing her own recipe for a New Orleans Christmas Loaf in one paper, and in another, inspiring a new shade of stocking. She took the opportunity to visit Black communities in the city, to put on a special performance for a children's hospital, and to act as an outspoken critic of racial inequality.[34]

If audiences thought they could enjoy a frivolous Harlem show, her feature song, "I'm a Little Blackbird Looking for a Bluebird," delivered a call for race equality. By performing for London's high society, she brought her message directly into the heart of Mayfair, although she was still treated as an exotic fascination. Socialite Brenda Dean Paul was particularly entranced. "I feel so utterly at home with these enchanting people that every other white person in the room seemed positively genteel and almost indecently defined," she said.[35]

Through 1926 she performed with the Blackbirds over 300 times in London, and it took a huge toll on her health. She fell ill with tuberculosis and was forced to return to New York to recover. In October 1927 she was hospitalized for a serious ailment, believed to be appendicitis. But she was too weak, and on November 1, when her sudden death at the age of thirty-one was announced, the public was stunned.

As reported in the *New York Age*, crowds filed past her body in an open casket at the undertakers, and an estimated 150,000 mourners lined Harlem's streets to pay tribute to the "dainty little comedienne, singer and dancer . . . whose talent, grace and winsome sweetness had won for her a place on the very topmost rung of the Ladder of Fame."[36]

If white audiences were shocked by her death, then Florence's death really hit hard in Harlem. Fats Waller recorded "Bye Bye Florence" in November 1927 and Duke Ellington dedicated his 1928 composition "Black Beauty" to her. Constant Lambert, an English composer who had watched her perform in *Dover Street to Dixie* in 1923 and in *Blackbirds* in 1926, wrote a piano tribute, *Elegiac Blues*, inspired by the opening fanfare of the latter show.

By the time of Florence's death, Josephine Baker had become the most celebrated nightclub performer in the world.

In December 1926 she opened her own Montmartre nightspot, Chez Joséphine, situated on Rue Fontaine. The party didn't get going until the wee hours, and then she would make her arrival, sailing past guests that included the Aga Khan and Colette, and into her dressing room covered in photographs of herself, where her maids helped her get ready for her show-stopping performance.[37]

As she embarked on an ambitious world tour to Europe and South America in 1928, she showcased a new look. She said goodbye to the Jazz Baby, in favor of sleek glamor that fitted the mood of the thirties, where sweet escapism and ultra femininity was an antidote to the hardships of the Great Depression. As Janet Flanner wrote in the *New Yorker*, "Her caramel-colored body which overnight became a legend in Europe is still magnificent, but it has become thinned, trained, almost civilized."[38]

Josephine would find that outside Paris, Europe wasn't the safe haven she had hoped for. She had been looking forward to touring Austria and Germany, where the Weimar Republic of the twenties had offered a similarly free, expressive, and debauched culture. However, racial prejudice was tightening its grip during the economic crisis. She was driven out of Berlin after only three weeks of a six-month tour, and once Adolf Hitler's Nazi Party seized control, propaganda minister Joseph Goebbels placed her as a representative of degenerate art.

Following the outbreak of the Second World War, she never forgot her own experience with the Third Reich and was determined to do all she could to prevent their victory. Because of her celebrity, she was able to hide in plain sight, and so she became a secret agent for the French counterintelligence agency, the Deuxième Bureau. Initially they were concerned about her Mata Hari status as a beautiful and seductive dancer, that if discovered, she would be shot, but in 1937 Josephine had given up her US citizenship and declared she had "finished with the exotic."[39]

She and her handler Captain Jacques Abtey embarked on a wartime affair and they fled Paris just before German forces swept into the city in June 1940. She leased a chateau in the Dordogne, where she hid resistance members and planned out counterintelligence moves. There were trips to Spain and Portugal where she buried intelligence dossiers under stage costumes in her trunk and in North Africa she entertained US troops.

In 1957, Baker was awarded the Legion of Honour for military service during the war, and her postwar life was similarly dedicated to a cause. She was determined to put an end to racism and went undercover in the American South in 1948 as part of an exposé for a French newspaper.

She refused to perform in segregated clubs, and publicly shamed those who did so. In Manhattan's Stork Club in 1951, Baker walked out in disgust, but newspaper columnist Walter Winchell was present to witness it, and rather than supporting her, he accused her of having "Communist sympathies," and her work visa was revoked.[40]

In February 1952 she returned to St. Louis to deliver a speech against segregation of schools, where she said, "I ran away from home. I ran away from St. Louis. And then I ran away from the United States of America, because of that terror of discrimination, that horrible beast which paralyzes one's very soul and body."[41]

Josephine had struggled with fertility issues during her latter two marriages, and in the 1950s she adopted children from around the world as she toured, naming the band of thirteen her "Rainbow Tribe."

When she died in 1975 of a cerebral hemorrhage, she was given full French military honors at her funeral. Josephine pushed her way out of poverty and segregation to become one of the most celebrated icons of the twenties, and one of the most famous women in the world. She was the rare "It" girl who crossed the race divide, and then used her fame to fight racism and bigotry through political activism.

From Flapper to "It" Girl

The Madcap Spirit of the Jazz Age

Clara Bow in 1927, wearing her favorite bathing suit, socks, and heels combination. *Alamy.*

"**I** smile, but my eyes never smile," Clara Bow once told reporters. She was asked if she was like the flappers she played on screen, and she sighed, "I wish I were. She's much happier than I am."[1]

The jazz-loving flapper was the stock character that Clara specialized in; the flirtatious good-time party girl who cavorted and kissed across the screen in short skirts and with a cocktail in hand. She hadn't been the first—that honor had been given to Olive Thomas, the tragic star of 1920's *The Flapper*. And there were others who were equally popular. Colleen Moore's *Flaming Youth* (1923) summarized the postwar generation in one pithy title, and Joan Crawford was the champion Charleston dancer who would be described as the face of a movement by F. Scott Fitzgerald. But it was Clara whose flame blazed the brightest.

Clara's disillusionment with life was rooted in the trauma of an awful childhood in extreme poverty and was further exacerbated once she achieved incredible fame. She may have earned the riches and renown from the public that she had craved, but behind the scenes she was dismissed as cheap and tacky, and her complicated love life was dragged out in the burgeoning celebrity gossip columns. She was too honest, too vulnerable, and it allowed her to be abused by the very media that had built her up.

In an industry where actors were often required to change their name, she was born simply Clara Bow, on July 29, 1905, in Prospect Heights, Brooklyn, to Robert and Sarah Bow, second generation English and Scots-Irish immigrants. Her mother had already lost two children in infancy, but against the odds both Sarah and her daughter Clara survived. Later, she would say: "When I have told you about my short life, maybe you will understand why, in spite of its incongruity, I am a madcap, the spirit of the jazz age, the premier flapper, as they call me. No one wanted me to be born in the first place."[2]

The Brooklyn tenements of her early childhood were hellish slums without safety or sanitation codes, and where tuberculosis, influenza, and cholera spread freely among the human sardine-can apartments. She was hungry and cold for much of her childhood, and it was a struggle to survive day by day, week by week.

Her father was only reliable when it came to his drunkenness and violence. Her mother suffered personality-changing seizures following two head injuries—once when she fell out a window at sixteen, and then when she fell down a tenement staircase when Clara was just six, thought to have been a suicide attempt. As a child Clara was lonely, sensitive, and, as she recollected, the "worst-looking kid on the street." Shunned by the girls because of her scraggly looks and "carrot-top" hair, she ran with the neighborhood boys, who taught her how to perfect that right hook.[3]

She only had one real friend, a younger boy, Johnny, who lived in the same building. When a fire in his room exploded, his clothes caught alight and as he called out to her for help, she sprang into action and rolled him in a carpet to extinguish the flames. But his burns were so bad that he died in her arms.[4]

In later therapy sessions, she would find that the reason for many of her psychological problems in adulthood could be linked back to childhood trauma. Her mother frequently brought different "uncles" back to the apartment to earn some money to put food on the table. During these sessions, Clara was locked in a cupboard, but it didn't filter out the noise of her mother having sex with them. Just a few years later, after her mother was placed in a sanatorium, and Clara lived with her father, he expected his daughter to do everything a wife should do, from cooking and cleaning, to going to bed with him. Her biographer David Stenn made the claim that she was raped by her father, but she chose to remain loyal to him throughout her adult life because she had been so deprived of love.[5]

She found escape from this horrendous childhood by going to the movie theatre. There were, by 1920, over twenty thousand cinemas in the United States, as well as countless nickelodeons which had offered cheap populist entertainment in the early days of its invention.[6]

As the flicker of the silver screen transported her to new worlds, she was able to temporarily blot out the misery in her life.[7] Clara was of the first generation to grow up with films and she couldn't get enough of the gossip and the glamor. She would pore over the pictures of the stars in the twenty-cent fan magazines like *Motion Picture* and *Photoplay*, imagining that one day she could appear in them too. There were dozens of these publications, all featuring similar content, such as stills from the latest releases and studio portraits of the stars, alongside insight into their luxury lifestyles. Much of what was printed was dreamed up by the press agents to create an interesting backstory, or to soften some of the harsher realities.

In the January 1921 edition of *Motion Picture* she spotted an announcement for a "Fame and Fortune" contest by Brewster Publications, which called for applicants to send in their details alongside two pictures. With minimal prospects beyond her teenage job on a Coney Island hot dog stand, this promise for "the key to success" offered an escape route to fame and adoration, and she begged her father to lend her money to get the photos taken. To her surprise he agreed to pay for a session with a cheap Coney Island photographer, but she was dismayed at how awful she looked. Still, she was invited to the Brewster Publications offices to take part in a screen test. As she walked into the reception area, the other hopefuls sniggered at the sight of her in her best outfit, a plaid dress and red tam o'shanter, and she took a seat, already feeling deflated about her prospects. She didn't think much of her looks, so was taken aback when one of the men in the office pointed her out as "an interesting face—that kid with the red tam and the gorgeous eyes."[8] Clara was the last to be called, but she spent those hours observing every mistake the other girls made. She noticed they were all doing bad impersonations of the stars they'd seen on the screen, rather than creating a natural and original interpretation of the scenes they were expected to act. Clara realized in that moment that to be truly special, she had to be original, and so when it was time for her screen test, she threw her energy into romping in front of the camera.

A few days later she found out she was the winner, and her photograph, this time taken by a professional studio, was splashed in the January 1922 issue of *Motion Picture Classic*, announcing it as a "A Dream Come True." As the magazine stated:

"She is very young, only sixteen. But she is full of confidence, determination and ambition. She is endowed with a mentality far beyond her years. She has a genuine spark of the divine fire. . . . She screens perfectly."[9]

Going to the movies was one of the most popular leisure activities, particularly for the working classes, and by the middle of the twenties, 50 million people in the United States, around half the population at the time, attended each week. The film industry may have shone like a glamorous mecca to girls like Clara, but to moralists, it was a place of debauchery and sin. With all that money flowing through the community, it was a hotbed of decadence, and this reputation had only grown with every scandal, from Olive Thomas's death to Fatty Arbuckle's rape trial and Mabel Normand's involvement in the unsolved murder of William Desmond Taylor.

These scandals provoked outrage among powerful church groups, and to try to keep them placated, the studios chose to self-regulate by enlisting former Postmaster General William Hays to create a moral code for which films should operate. As president of the Motion Picture Producers and Distributors of America (MPPDA) he sought to smooth over scandals. One of his first measures was to introduce a morals clause in every actor's contract, and if breached, they would face suspension. In 1934 he would introduce the Hays Code, which enforced strict censorship rules on filmmakers. The movies that came before 1934 were later referred to as "pre-code," and often featured nudity, sexual innuendo, infidelity, drug use, and nefarious characters who didn't suffer repercussions.

When Clara's mother found out her daughter was planning to be a sinful actress, she ranted that Clara would go straight to hell. One night Clara woke up to find Sarah hovering over her, butcher knife in hand, preparing to slit her daughter's throat. Clara was frozen in fear, but before her mother could bring the knife down on her, she was gripped by a seizure and collapsed on the ground.[10]

Realizing she was now too dangerous to be with her daughter, Clara's father Robert committed Sarah to an asylum. The memories of her mother trying to murder her would haunt Clara for the rest of her life, keeping her restless at night as she struggled with insomnia.

Clara's road to fame wasn't as simple as winning a competition. The girls at school had ridiculed her for it and she struggled to get her foot in the door of New York's movie studios. "There was always something. I was too young, or too little, or too fat. Usually I was too fat," she remembered.[11] Clara's curvy body didn't follow the fashion for lean, streamlined figures, and she also had a very young face which didn't offer the sophistication that was usually required for a star.

Finally, she landed a small role in *Beyond the Rainbow*, and she was giddy with excitement at the opportunity to earn fifty dollars for one week's work. It opened in February 1922, and as she sat in the theatre with a friend to celebrate her debut, her high quickly turned to a low when she realized all her scenes had been cut.

Her fortunes changed when director Elmer Clifton, looking for a fresh-faced, and cheap, talent for his whaling drama *Down to the Sea in Ships*, spotted her contest photos. He invited her to audition and was impressed by the sixteen-year-old's spark and vivacity, and that her young face was perfect for the role of a tomboy stowaway. Filming took place on location in the coastal village of New Bedford, Massachusetts, and it earned her favorable notices. She was honored as one of the thirteen WAMPAS Baby Stars of 1924—a promotional campaign by the Western Association of Motion Picture Advertisers to recognize the up-and-coming actresses who had star quality.[12]

She was frolicking on a table while filming a scene for *Enemies of Women* in January 1923 when her father came on set to tell her that her mother had died. From joy to sorrow, from dancing on tables to breaking down in tears at the loss of her mother, this would be a familiar pattern in Clara's life.[13]

Her acting career was flourishing, and she was given another tomboy part in *Grit*, penned by F. Scott Fitzgerald, where she played a streetwise urchin. When Jack Bachman from Hollywood's Preferred Pictures visited the set, he was impressed enough by Clara to invite her to California for a three-month trial at his studio. She was terrified of the idea, having never traveled beyond New England, but with her father's encouragement she took the train west in July 1923, accompanied by a studio chaperone.

Her first film was a period operetta, *Maytime*, which was followed by the leading role in First National Pictures' *Black Oxen*, based on the bestselling novel by Gertrude Atherton. Director Frank Lloyd had tested fifty actresses for the role of precocious flapper Janet Oglethorpe, but it wasn't until Clara walked into his office that he found his ideal: "Independent, intelligent, keenly sensitive and delightfully inquisitive and aggressive. To try to make a flapper out of some established actress would be folly. Flappers aren't made; they're born."[14]

When *Black Oxen* was released in January 1924, Bow was singled out for her "adorably played" performance of, in *Variety*'s words, "the horrid little flapper." Its release came only six weeks after Colleen Moore's performance in *Flaming Youth*, which would define this hedonistic generation who were burning out to forget the trauma of war.

"The flapper was already well established, but no one had portrayed her," Colleen Moore later remembered. "I knew she was an established type because these were the girls my brother used to bring home from college, that's how I knew about them . . . I never even had a cocktail until I was probably about thirty. A flapper I wasn't, but I was the right age and looked the part and I had the bangs and I was it."[15]

The word "flapper" had initially been used to describe a young fledgling bird at the turn of the century, and by 1918 it had morphed into a fashionable and frivolous young woman whose permissive behavior shocked the "old fogies." She was, according to F. Scott Fitzgerald in *Flappers and Philosophers*, "a flirting, kissing . . . sort of mental baby vamp." Clara and Colleen blazed on screen as careless, expressive, exciting representations of a rebellious phenomenon. Fitzgerald, who considered the flapper a fleeting beauty whose sparkle faded the older she got, would later call Clara "the girl of the year," and the "quintessence of what the term 'flapper' signifies. . . . There were hundreds of them—her prototypes . . . patterning themselves after her."[16] After *The Perfect Flapper* (1924) Colleen declared she'd had enough of playing the trope because "people are tired of soda-pop love affairs," which had been popularized after the war,[17] but Clara Bow was fizzing with ambition to fill her spot.

The Plastic Age was Bow's fifteenth film of 1925, and it was the one that made her a star. The *New York Times* in their July 1926 review singled her out as the reason to see it, with her "eyes that would drag any youngster away from his books, and she knows how to use eyes, shoulders and all the rest of her tiny self in the most effective manner. She radiates an elfin sensuousness."[18]

While her curvy body may not have fitted the mold of the boyish flapper, Clara's image, with her short, tousled hair, her heavy kohl-rimmed eyes, the beauty spot and cupid-bow lips, would become the beauty ideal, sparking a wave of copycats. She changed her hair color to caramel or cherry-cola on a whim, and it was said that sales of henna tripled when it was discovered Clara used it to dye her naturally lighter hair.

Off-screen, she was a vision in red, often spotted driving about town in her red roadster, with her dyed-red chow dog beside her, and her hair a blazing ball of fire. She may have won over audiences as the hottest new thing, but the Hollywood in-crowd shunned her. With her penchant for adding a belt to every dress to enhance her waist, her insistence on wearing ankle socks with her heels, and the cheap jewelry, they thought she was tacky and embarrassing. Mary Pickford and Marion Davies, who ruled the colony, refused to invite her to their glittering parties because they thought she was vulgar. Yet she was her own worst enemy when it came to making social blunders. Invited for dinner at a Beverly Hills hotel by her frequent director Frank Tuttle, she turned up wearing a belted bathing suit and heels, violating both the hotel's rules and social codes.

When Preferred Pictures filed for bankruptcy, the studio's major talents, including Clara, went to Paramount Pictures. After the studio cast her in 1926's *Mantrap*, playing a manicurist who just can't help flirting, it firmly established her as one of the brightest stars who exemplified a generation of freedom-loving women. She followed it with the First World War aviation drama *Wings* (1927), and she may have been the only female in the cast, just the "whipped cream on top of the pie," as she described her role,[19] but she helped make it a sensation, breaking box-office records as women flocked to see a film designed to appeal to men. It also had the distinction of being the first film to win an Academy Award for Best Picture at the inaugural ceremony in 1929.

In September 1926, Clara was called to her boss B. P. Schulberg's office in the middle of shooting *Wings*, where she was introduced to the English writer Elinor Glyn. She was informed that from now on she would be known as the "It" girl. It was a common publicity gimmick in Hollywood's star system to bestow an actress with a nickname. Barbara La Marr was known as the "Girl Who Is Too Beautiful," Mae Murray was "The Girl with the Bee-Stung Lips," and now Clara was the "It" girl who would star in 1927's *It*, based on Glyn's story. Audiences came out in record-breaking numbers to see her, and as a trendsetter she also helped to popularize the "little black dress." Her shopgirl character, Betty Lou, doesn't have an evening dress to wear to a date, so instead, adapts her simple black work dress, transforming it into a chic cocktail gown. It was a moment that all young working women could identify with, and Clara was their girl; she acted how they wished they could behave in real life.

Mary Pickford may have been "America's Sweetheart" playing chaste little girls with corkscrew curls, but Clara's characters were in control of their sexuality. Coming from a humble background, she was entirely relatable to the audience of young women who worked as shop assistants and secretaries. She was the jazz baby of the Jazz Age, dancing to the gramophone in her living room or on the table of a café, completely free in how she moved and lived.

Clara was the biggest star in Hollywood, and her life would never be the same. "Once Elinor Glyn called her the 'It Girl,' it changed Clara completely," said her friend Charles "Buddy" Rogers, who starred opposite her in *Wings*. "She had always put on this act because she was so shy and insecure. Now Clara believed she was the 'It Girl.' She tried to be vivacious, she tried to be fascinating, she tried to be clever, and she just worked her body and mind and soul to death."[20]

After a succession of hits, she had become a commodity, and new movies were churned out to cater to audience expectations. She often worked from six in the morning to midnight, six days a week, and when she got home she struggled to switch off, regularly staying up all night drinking and gambling. Yet despite the bone-aching exhaustion, she pushed herself to be the sparkling flapper on screen.

She was typically cast as manicurists, shopgirls, or spunky tomboys, who had names like "Kittens" or "Rosie O'Reilly" or "Hula." Like her characters, Bow developed a reputation as a man-eater, and there were plenty of rumors about her insatiable sexual appetite. Her first great love was Mexican actor Gilbert Roland, whom she met on the set of *The Plastic Age*, when they were both twenty. They bonded over their insecurities—he struggled with English, and she felt like an outcast in the industry she was dedicated to. Her racist father, whom she still doted on and whom she had allowed to move into her Bel Air home, was disgusted that she was dating a Mexican, and warned her away. She also struggled to stay faithful due to her deep desire to be loved. She had a long affair with *Mantrap* director Victor Fleming, who wanted to marry her, and at the same time bedded Gary Cooper, who she first co-starred with in 1927's *Children of Divorce*. She was so smitten with him that she pushed for Cooper to be cast in *Wings*, ultimately helping to launch his career.

Clara was a huge American football fan, and she was particularly attracted to the boys of the USC football team, known as the Trojans. Hollywood possessed the sexual double standards of the time, that a man who pursued women was a stud, but a woman was a slut, and tales of Clara's promiscuous behavior became legend. In Kenneth Anger's notorious 1959 gossip tome *Hollywood Babylon*, he recounted as fact the stories that she bedded the entire team at an orgy at her house. The truth was far more boring—because of their training, after a couple of hours of mostly sober socializing, the players returned to their dorms to get a good night's sleep. But still, the idea of Clara being a vulgar floozy stuck, and she found herself at the center of much gossip and inuendo.

Gossip columnist Adela Rogers St. Johns became a confidante of Clara's, and during their time together, often spent at USC games, Adela discovered that the real Clara, beyond all the high jinks, was full of anxieties. "There seems to be no pattern, no purpose to her life," she wrote. "She swings from one emotion to another, but she gains nothing, stores up nothing against the future. She lives entirely in the present, not even for today, but just for the moment. And you go on loving her, feeling sorry for her, and praying that she won't get into any real trouble."[21]

Their intimate conversations were turned into a frank three-part autobiography of Clara's life. *My Life Story* was more revealing of a Hollywood star than anything that had come before, given that their backstories were often invented by a studio publicist. Yet it further isolated Clara from her peers, as they were horrified that she would be so open about her experiences of poverty and familial mental illness. In a revealing interview with *Photoplay* in October 1929 she conveyed her desire to find a man to fulfill her loneliness. "I'm unhappy, desolate. My mind goes on even when my body sleeps. I've always given. I've had no childhood. My mother's illness. Her horrible death. The demands that have always, always been made upon me. But I could be happy, I believe, if I could find the right man." On her bedside were bottles of sedatives to try to quiet her restless brain and help her sleep, and she played over in her mind how she was treated by the "frightful snobs." "I'm a curiosity in Hollywood. I'm a big freak because I'm myself!"[22]

She was growing tired of the madcap roles where she cavorted on screen in lingerie and felt she should advance her career by doing more dramatic parts. But she couldn't escape these formulaic roles that built on the "It" girl phenomenon. *Red Hair* and *Three Week-Ends*, both based on Elinor Glyn's stories, were a continuation of the flirty, free-spirited young woman.

For *Red Hair*, Schulberg came up with a gimmick for Clara, where the opening sequence used the new and very expensive two-strip Technicolor, to give audiences the chance to see Clara, and her famous hair, in glorious color. She was most afraid of another novelty—the talking picture. With the rush to get on the talkie bandwagon following the release of *The Jazz Singer* in 1927, Paramount pushed Clara into doing a voice test in December 1928. She was terrified of the microphone, and she was worried about the reaction to her thick Brooklyn accent, aware that other careers had imploded due to disappointing speaking voices. *The Wild Party* went into production on January 2, 1929, and she struggled all the way through, at times looking like she was visibly recoiling from the sound equipment. Yet she had a sympathetic female director, Dorothy Arzner, who created a fishpole mic that would follow Clara as she made her signature ad-libs around the set, and the film proved to be a huge hit.

At this point she was receiving 45,000 fan letters in a month, more than double any star in movie history, yet her salary, and contract, didn't reflect her popularity. Attached to her contract was a good-behavior bonus of $10,000 for each film, which would be placed in a trust fund for several years, provided she didn't create a moral scandal.

When Clara had an affair with a married man from Texas, William Earl Pearson, whose wife threatened to go public, the studio bought her silence with the money from Clara's trust fund. Yet Clara, not known for her discretion, accidentally revealed the truth about her affair to a reporter, and soon it was headline news.

Clara was notoriously bad at her finances, and with a penchant for gambling, she was in debt to Paramount, which had bailed her out of debt on numerous occasions. One of the people closest to Clara was her hairdresser, Daisy DeVoe, who, it was later revealed, used a spectacular bleach and henna technique to make the star's hair shimmer on screen. Clara trusted Daisy completely with her secrets, and so she hired her as a personal secretary to manage her finances. Daisy opened bank accounts which only she and Clara had access to and would pay her own expenses from it; a move that would come back to haunt Daisy when she was accused of fleecing her boss.

Her spectacular fallout with Daisy would lead to the most sensational trial since Roscoe Arbuckle's. Clara had met the man who would become her husband, the western actor Rex Bell, and he and Daisy were both possessive and overprotective of Clara. Rex believed Daisy was taking money from Clara's account, and when confronted with it, Daisy threatened to release all the information she had on Clara from their intimate chats. Clara went to the police, and Daisy was arrested, where she was found to have taken jewelry and $20,000 in cash and personal papers, which she claimed she was keeping safe.

The January 1931 trial was billed as the blonde versus the redhead, and was a perfect example of how two women could be paired against each other in the media. Daisy was articulate on the stand, whereas Clara was nervous and hoarse from bronchitis, and many of the personal letters and telegrams that Daisy had taken were read aloud in court, and then printed in the papers and fan magazines. "Of course, Clara always had a lot of boy friends but I think she cared most for [Pearson]," she testified.[23] She also revealed the star's poker addiction, the alcohol-fueled parties and the bills for rum that Daisy had to pay for, and that she bleached the star's hair to make it red, with bleach considered an arbiter of brash character. "Don't forget this either—Daisy's hair is bleached," Clara retaliated on the stand.[24]

Following the stock market crash of 1929, extravagant lifestyles were unforgivable, and her spending orgies, her gambling, and her affairs did not stand her in good favor with the public. By the end of the trial, when Daisy was found guilty, Clara was well and truly exhausted by the fame merry-go-round, and what she desired more than anything, and hoped for, was to marry Rex, which she did in 1931, and to start a family of her own.

The final push to send Clara over the edge was when a magazine called *Coast Reporter* reported a salacious exposé on her, which detailed incest, drug addiction, lesbianism, and bestiality, with a grotesque story that she performed intimate acts with her Great Dane. It was libelous and ridiculous, but no one stood up for her to say it wasn't true. The paper was even sold outside Paramount's main gate, and when she saw a copy of it, she vomited in her dressing room. She begged Paramount to give her some time to recover, as she was "on the verge of a nervous breakdown."[25]

It wasn't until she collapsed with shattered nerves and was taken to a sanatorium that the studio released her from her contract. She had been the biggest movie star the world had ever seen, but she was unprotected and condemned, and at the age of twenty-six was washed-up. Clara moved to a vast ranch on the California-Nevada border with Rex, and the dusty landscape proved to be a peaceful sanctuary away from the gossip and the headlines.

Still, her time in Hollywood wasn't quite over. Paramount may have been happy to see the back of her, but other studios expressed interest. She negotiated a two-picture deal at Fox and *Call Her Savage* marked a spectacular comeback in June 1932, where she was now one of Hollywood's highest-paid stars. It was followed a year later by *Hoopla*, but by this time she'd had enough and opted out, refusing any new offers.

In September 1937 she opened her own "It Café" on Hollywood and Vine while recovering from a miscarriage, but when she found out she was pregnant again, she was given doctor's orders to put her feet up and the café closed shortly after. She and Rex retreated to their Nevada ranch, where they raised their two sons, Tony and George.

Yet this domestic bliss proved elusive, as she found herself plagued by anxiety-induced headaches, backaches, and cramps, leaving her confined to bed. After the Second World War, Rex spent much time in Las Vegas to stand as a candidate for the Republican party, leaving Clara even more isolated. She refused to socialize and was afraid to leave the house. When her sons found her unconscious in bed one morning after taking too many pills, Rex decided that for the good of the children they should separate. As he worked on his political career, Clara retreated further from the world and was diagnosed with schizophrenia.

Without the fame, she was lost—her identity had become so entwined with being a jazzy "It" girl she was frightened to only be herself. Retiring from the screen had taken away her own agency. She hadn't found the idyllic life she had desired, and instead was haunted by her childhood trauma and the mental health issues that manifested in poor judgment.

On September 28, 1965, Clara's obituary appeared as a small column on the front page of the *New York Times*, among the latest Cold War headlines. The piece noted that she had been suffering with ill health for years and that she'd been under treatment in a rest home for insomnia. Clara, the article said, "best personified the giddier aspects of an unreal era," and that "It" still signified her "toss of a boyish bob, her brazen sauciness and the energy of her Charleston high kick."

In the decades after she left Hollywood, Clara had become a forgotten relic, unappreciated and unacknowledged for her vast contribution to culture. As she hid away from the world, she watched and admired Marilyn Monroe, feeling protective of the woman she saw as her successor. Marilyn paid her own tribute to Clara when she posed in a series of Richard Avedon photographs that referenced past icons. The baton of "It" girl had passed to Marilyn, whose life followed a similar trajectory. They both had a mother with a mental illness, their traumatic childhoods were marked by abuse, they were commodities who were exploited and underpaid, and they were both considered vulnerable, sexy babes who died too young.

8

Brenda Frazier and the Café Society Debutantes

New York's "Top-Notch Debutante"

Brenda Frazier Leads Season's Glamour Girls

By JOAN DURHAM,
AP Feature Service Writer.

New York—They've picked the No. 1 glamour girl of New York's debutante season already.

Of course raven-haired Brenda Diana Duff Frazier won't have her debut for two full months yet, but she gets around—every night—and neither the columnist nor the stag lines await debuts to award popularity prizes.

Well, she does have everything—or nearly everything. Looks, brains, poise, money. At 17, her lustrous hair, which she won't brush up from its long flowing bob, her ivory skin, aristocratically arched eyebrows and carelessly graceful walk would make a professional model envious.

That's the way the columnists see her—at night clubs and theaters. I went calling on Brenda at her home to see what sort of a girl a top notch New York debutante really is.

She is amazingly human and friendly.

Brenda and her mother, Mrs. Frederic N. Watriss, live in a luxurious but home-like double-suite in Carlton House, at the Ritz-Carlton hotel.

Calling on them is pleasant and stimulating, although Mrs. Watriss isn't fond of letting Brenda be ex-

CAMILLA COMMENTS

High-necked, dark fall dresses plead for some gay flash to brighten them, and a jeweled clip, pin or necklace is just the answer. A Moline jewelry store is showing extravagant-looking copies of Tiffany numbers in gold plate and rhinestones, accurate copies of platinum and diamond baubles whose price tags bear four figures.

One of the handsomest clips is of lustrous gold barred in rhinestones, and the clip part has an engaging safety feature. Instead of simply clasping it to a fold of the material, you also pin in the ends of the hinged part, holding the ornament securely. That way, it can also be worn as a lapel gadget.

A handsome necklace boasts a simple but heavy gold flower with a center of rhinestones on a double gold cable, the whole thing so plain yet rich-looking that it would give an air to the simplest black or deep brown dress.

A new type of cleansing cream is being featured at the cosmetic counter of a Moline department store this week. One of the latest products of a very well known beauty house, it is intended to solve the problems of the woman with a dry skin, for it is a cleansing cream built on a lubricating base so that it leaves the skin soft and smooth, retaining the natural oils.

Is it a sweater that looks like a

Brenda Frazier dunks a doughnut at the opening of a New York night spot.

Brenda Frazier hit the headlines, and sparked debate, in 1938, for dunking a doughnut into coffee during her coming out season. *Author's collection.*

As the flapper faded from the screen, and the original "It" girl, Clara Bow, was all but forgotten, the replacement expression for the thirties was *glamor*. Derived from the Scottish word "gramarye," meaning magic or enchantment, it was applied to Hollywood movie stars in George Hurrell portraits and society debutantes with similar impunity.

With the Wall Street Crash of October 1929 triggering the devastating Great Depression, glamor was a means of escapism. It took attention away from the breadlines and the grim headlines about savings being wiped out and rising unemployment. Millions may have been out of work, but at least the stars on screen offered a glimpse into a luxury world as they slinked around streamlined art deco apartments in white satin gowns, and as they blew out cigarette smoke, they were as cool and remote as the ice in their cocktails.

Hollywood PR departments worked their magic to build up the auras of Greta Garbo and Marlene Dietrich by placing features on their style and makeup secrets in fan magazines, and by using advertising to create an aspirational lifestyle. Film magazines taught readers how to get the look of their favorite stars, and in turn there were affordable products that women could buy to emulate them; lipsticks, shampoo, hair curlers, soap that promised the same glowing complexion as Carole Lombard.

They could buy dress patterns to copy the gowns and suits worn by Joan Crawford, beloved for her roles as shopgirls and hoofers who used their beauty and brains to enter rarified Park Avenue drawing rooms. They could style their hair in the pageboy do of Greta Garbo or bleach it into a platinum halo like Jean Harlow. These images of impeccable glamor lit a spark of joy within the factory worker and shopgirl who could imagine they too possessed that indefinable factor of the screen goddess. Joan Crawford and Carole Lombard may have lived the café society life on screen, but it was the debutantes of New York who were living it for real. Following the lives of wealthy, reckless heiresses was an escape from the real-life struggles of the Depression era, in the same way that watching the Kardashians' extravagant lifestyle was soothing to their fans during the 2008 financial crash and the cost-of-living crisis.

In November 1938 debutante Brenda Frazier was splashed on the cover of *Life* magazine as an example of the new café society. In place of the flapper, the New York debutantes were the new "It" girls. They were rich, beautiful and possessed that essential feminine quality, "grace," and with their moneyed background, there was no need for them to work. In the midst of the depression, they were the bright society jewels who carried on as if nothing was wrong as they danced and drank all night.

Café society in New York was centered around El Morocco and the Stork Club, where photographers would capture Hollywood stars mixing with royalty, and rich society girls like Brenda whose exploits were always fascinating to the press. She had thick, shoulder-length raven hair with a widow's peak, her powdery-white and luminous skin was framed by dark arched eyebrows, and her lips and nails were vixen red. She was described as having a Hedy Lamarr intensity, and a quality that Florenz Ziegfeld said was "Glorified."[1] She could be found most nights sipping champagne and cocktails in Manhattan nightclubs, a cigarette in one hand as she soaked up the attention in the room.

It was Brenda who inspired Walter Winchell's phrase, "celebutante" in his April 7, 1939, "On Broadway" column; an expression which would later define good-time heiresses like Paris and Nicky Hilton. In the late thirties Brenda dominated the media headlines as the "debutante glamour girl." In just a six-month period, a clipping service found there had been 5,000 mentions of her. Just as letters to Clara Bow marked "The It Girl, Hollywood" arrived for her in the tens of thousands, fan mail was addressed only to Brenda Frazier, New York. She had become so recognizable that she was mobbed by crowds of people who all demanded her autograph. At the Easter parade in 1939 she had to be rescued by the police when she was engulfed by a 200-strong crowd.[2]

"I'm not a celebrity," she insisted to one reporter. "I don't deserve all of this. I haven't done anything at all. I'm just a debutante."[3] With $4 million in a trust, which she said she couldn't access, she came to epitomize the "Poor Little Rich Girl." Her relationship with fame was intense and devastating. She had a life-long struggle with eating disorders, and it was said she attempted suicide at least thirty-one times. She later wrote that she had been doomed by an unfortunate childhood and an adult life "plagued by fears and inner emptiness."[4]

Brenda's grandfather was from a prosperous Boston family and made his fortune in the wheat market. Her father, Frank Duff Frazier, didn't possess the same business acumen and instead was an alcoholic and womanizer who was drawn to "tarts."[5]

When he married the brazen Brenda Williams-Taylor, the Canadian daughter of a British peer, their marriage was immediately fraught with public fights and open affairs. To safeguard his fortune, Franklin set up a restricted trust fund for their daughter, Brenda Diana Duff Frazier, who was born in June 1921 in Quebec. By the time she was three years old, her parents were acrimoniously separated and couldn't even decide what to call her—she was Brenda in her mother's house, and Diana to her father. "When I clung to my mother, I felt guilty toward my father. I had two parents, in two different homes, yet psychologically I was an orphan."[6]

When nine-year-old Brenda was made to testify during their divorce proceedings in court, this lonely girl with the huge trust fund and morally bankrupt parents triggered much interest in the media. During the protracted custody battle which went on for over seven years, her father died of throat cancer.

Her mother raised Brenda like a pushy stage mother, training her to become a debutante. She insisted she curtsy in front of guests and messed with her daughter's sense of self-worth by telling the twelve-year-old that she should go on a diet. It would have a devastating impact on her disordered eating as she obsessively counted calories and vomited meals for the rest of her life.

Rather than anger at her mother, Brenda later wrote in *Life*, "I feel only pity and sorrow. She was such a charming woman, so intelligent, so witty."[7] As she blossomed into a beautiful teenager, Brenda's debut in society was utmost on her mother's mind. She wanted to shake off their nouveau riche stigma to achieve celebrity status and respect, but in her attempts, her daughter became notorious as a publicity seeker.

At a time when women weren't encouraged to work, marriage was the respectable choice, and the debutante ball was the means of achieving an advantageous match. The coming-out ball was supposed to be a joyous time when a young woman could enjoy the freedom of being a young, single woman before her inevitable marriage.[8]

Yet Brenda peaked too soon as she was forced to grow up too quickly. At the age of twelve she was spending her evenings smoking cigarettes, while draped in furs and long chiffon gowns. At thirteen, Brenda was regularly waltzing all night at the St. Regis hotel and there was no parental supervision to prevent her drinking heavily or having sexual relationships.[9] "My mother always seemed to be visiting friends Christmastime," she remembered, "often in places as far away as Europe, and I was left to open my presents alone, except for the company of a maid or the butler." Instead, she held her own Christmas parties, with fifty guests of her choice, as she was left to her own devices for the season.[10] Her mother was in such a hurry for her daughter to come out in society that she took her to London to present her at court for the debutante season, where she was primped to look much older than her fourteen years.

They returned to New York to prepare Brenda for her American debut, even though it was still a few years away. She may have been educated at the prestigious Miss Porter's School in Connecticut, but the Old Money establishment looked down on she and her mother's antics in the newspapers. Many families, like the Vanderbilts and the Astors wouldn't let their children associate with Brenda. "I had a little talent for music and my teachers said that I had a great deal of talent for art," but, she said, "it was possibly dangerous" as it could be detrimental to finding a match for a rich man who felt threatened by her intelligence.

She was given a boost when the mystery society columnist Cholly Knickerbocker (writing under a pseudonym) encountered Brenda and her mother lunching at the Ritz and wrote in June 1936: "It may seem a bit early, but I—here and now—predict Brenda Frazier will be one of the belles—if not the Belle—of her season."[11]

By 1938 Brenda was enrolled at a Munich finishing school and she was enjoying the normality of her life, of studying French and German, and going to classical music concerts and opera. She would much rather have stayed in Munich, but her mother pushed her to come back for her debut.

She returned to New York for the 1938 season, which kicked off in the fall, and the seventeen-year-old was an instant hit. She was named "No. 1 Glamour Girl" and the "glamour girl of the season," making the cover of *Life* magazine in November, with a photo taken from the night of the prestigious Velvet Ball, wearing a pale pink strapless gown. *Life* praised her as the "outstanding debutante" for her "long hair, her vivacity, and splendid figure she is superbly photogenic, and publicity is the lifeblood of new society." They noted that she "never wears a hat" and her tortoise-shell rimmed glasses "vanish at the approach of a photographer."[12]

The season was a whirl of parties. The dance floors of ballrooms were a cloud of chiffon and white satin, the hum of chatter and giggles and the clack of high heels on polished floors as they danced the waltz and the rumba to live bands. These balls often went on until the early hours, when guests would be fed reviving scrambled eggs before heading home, just as the city's morning deliveries were being made. On just a few hours' sleep, Brenda spoke with the press from across the country who had gathered to meet the most in-demand debutante. "I love being a deb," she said. "I'm going to a tea dance this afternoon. Golly, my feet hurt. Out to dinner tonight and then dancing later."[13]

She later confessed that she had been miserable most of the time, and that her mouth was set with a "painted-on smile" and her head "as straight as if it were in a vise, fearful to move it lest I disarrange my hair."[14] Still, she was being interviewed by dozens of nationwide journalists who reported with great enthusiasm on this filthy rich, raven-haired beauty. As an Associated Press piece detailed, after a leisurely morning, her days began at noon, and involved meeting her contemporaries at 21, the Coq Rouge, Trouville's or the Stork Club, "lunching, committeeing or both."[15]

She generated thousands of mentions in the papers, and in December 1938, Cholly Knickerbocker looked back with glee at their 1936 prediction. "Brenda has become a newspaper and magazine 'personality' in the public's eyes," they wrote. "And she belongs to the public created for her just as much as if she were a 'movie star' or an operatic diva."[16]

Yet the more publicity Brenda received, the less likely it was that she'd have any part in the more established, and insular, debutante presentations such as the Junior Assemblies. Her mother spoke of her disapproval of the publicity because she realized it was backfiring on her desire to be taken seriously. "I dislike it intensely. Why, my daughter can't even go to supper without being photographed and somebody asked me the other day how much her publicity had cost? Of course, people who haven't a beautiful daughter don't realize how difficult it is for a mother to curb publicity."[17]

Society reporters blamed Brenda's rejections on a particular incident when she was photographed at the opening of a new restaurant, the Iridium room, at the St. Regis hotel, dressed in pearls and a black gown, as she daintily dunked a doughnut into her coffee. It was a move that was criticized as inelegant and common, but she was supported by etiquette experts, including Emily Post, who pronounced this doughnut-dunking correct for informal occasions.[18] The image was splashed across newspapers and it even won first prize for Associated Press photographer Anthony Camerano at the 1939 New York Press Photographers' Association awards.[19] While the moment was treated as a novelty, Claudette Colbert had done the same thing with a doughnut when she played an heiress in Frank Capra's *It Happened One Night* (1934).

Failing to have her debut approved by the exclusive organizations, her mother decided she would throw the flashiest ball in New York for her daughter herself. Brenda made her official debut into society on December 27, 1938, at their ball at the Ritz-Carlton hotel, with 2,000 invited guests, and many more gatecrashers. Her mother chose a late start time so as not to compete with other balls that were happening that same day, and she booked extra rooms at the hotel for those who needed to get away from the party or couldn't make it home.[20]

Frazier brushed her hair, applied more red lipstick, smoothed down her white satin ball gown, and waited to make her entrance into the ballroom of the hotel. Having come down with a winter cold, she had spent the hours before trying to recover with a combination of milk and Coca-Cola.

It was just before midnight that she swept into the ballroom with a bouquet of orchids and with her mother, who was dripping in jewels, beside her. The room was already buzzing with guests including Elsa Maxwell, Cornelius and Grace Vanderbilt, *Vogue* publisher Condé Nast, Douglas Fairbanks Jr., and heiress Doris Duke. With the presence of the old society families and the major figures in publishing, it was a sign that she had officially been accepted. One thousand quarts of champagne were consumed by the guests and party crashers, and despite feeling awful, she took to the ballroom floor to dance the rumba with a line of suitors. The party went on until 6:30 a.m., and by this time, tired and with swollen feet, Douglas Fairbanks Jr. draped a tablecloth around her bare shoulders. "Doug said I was shivering; that the hall must have grown cold. But the hall was not cold at all. I was shivering from exhaustion," she later remembered.[21]

The next morning, as papers reported on her debut, the *San Francisco Chronicle* headlined what everyone else was thinking: "Brenda is finally out, now we can all relax."[22] The reports may have praised her radiant debut, with *Time* hailing it as a "champagne christening," but she later wrote in *Life* that she hated every minute of it.

"I fell into bed afterward, the ordeal over, in such a state of collapse that I still cannot remember what happened all the next day. I rose again, of course, put on my fixed smile and started my long year of lunching with friends at the Stork Club, going to other debutantes' parties, serving on endless charity committees."[23] She described the charity committees as the worst part, with millionaires praising themselves for hosting a ball that raised just $1,500 for a cause.

Her fame now extended from high society into the living rooms of America. She was even approached by Hollywood for a screen test, but it was considered so unimpressive it wasn't taken further. She failed to live up to the hype, and so had to settle for her sponsorship deals as the face of soap and perfume. She even appeared in an advert for a Studebaker automobile, proclaiming it thrilling to drive even though she had never learned; there had been no need to, given her family had their own chauffeur.

She may have been the toast of New York, with Joan Crawford clamoring to be photographed with her at the Stork Club, but she said she was also resented. "No previous debutante had ever received such publicity, and some of the arbiters of society strenuously objected."[24]

She was also aware that if she didn't marry well, the whole year would be wasted. She was pursued by eccentric Hollywood producer Howard Hughes, and dated the *New Yorker*'s Peter Arno, who was twenty-one years older.

In 1941 she married former-football-star-turned-banker John Simms "Shipwreck" Kelly in 1941, but she missed the café society when she was stuck out on a farmhouse on Long Island. They had a daughter, Victoria, in 1945, but they divorced ten years later. She had a short-lived second marriage to an aviator, Robert Chatfield-Taylor, a "gentleman in every sense of the word," who stood by her during her increasingly fraught mental health crises. After two marriages, she conceded she had never experienced true love.[25]

She hadn't been given the chance to form her own identity, rather it had been set for her, and it led to misery. Being a debutante was not a gilded lily. Woolworth heiress Barbara Hutton and Doris Duke, whose family fortune was in tobacco, were also pushed by ambitious parents. Barbara, who even had a television movie, *Poor Little Rich Girl*, made about her life, came out to society at her star-studded debutante ball in 1930, at the height of the Depression. She lived it up lavishly, and had spent almost all her billion-dollar inheritance by the time of her death.[26]

Celebrity had not been good for Brenda. Having suffered from anorexia and bulimia, she was painfully thin, her bedside table was scattered with prescriptions and she tried so many times to kill herself her arms were crisscrossed with razor-blade scars. In her self-penned article in *Life* in 1963 she revealed she had attempted suicide in a Boston hotel suite two years before.

She had swallowed all the sleeping pills in her possession and laid back in her bed, waiting to slip away. She later said she was just one pill short of ending it all, and she reflected on the reasons why she had been so desperate to die.

"If I had been thinking more coherently, I might have mustered one small last laugh. I had been the most publicized debutante in history; the newspapers never called me just Brenda Frazier but 'glamor girl Brenda Frazier.' I was supposed to be the envy of all American women. But here I was, just two decades later, at the age of 39, at the end of my line."[27]

By the mid-sixties she had faded from her "It" girl days, and in a portrait by Diane Arbus in 1966 she was painted as a tragic Miss Havisham figure in heavy white rice powder and red lipstick, a ghost clutching onto her past beauty.

She died from bone cancer in May 1982 at the age of sixty, but there was little celebrating of her life. Brenda hustled to achieve her fame, putting her on a par with Paris Hilton and Kim Kardashian, but rather than making her happy it had led her down a path of misery, as if she was always trying to grasp the high that she had first experienced in her early moments of celebrity.

"It's an intoxicating thing, especially when you are young and naïve, to open the morning newspapers and find your name there," Brenda reflected. "I hated the job of being a debutante but enjoyed the rewards."[28]

9

The Wartime Pin-Up Girl

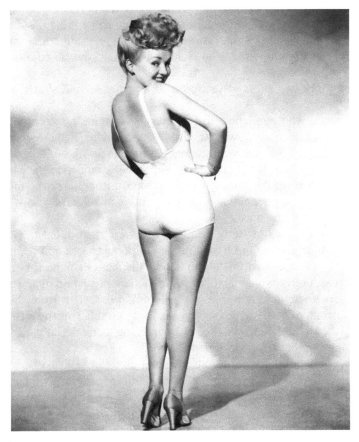

With this 1943 photo, Betty Grable became the most popular pin-up in the world. *Frank Powolny/20th Century Fox/Kobal/Shutterstock.*

When Betty Grable walked into Frank Powolny's studio on the Twentieth Century Fox lot in summer 1943, she assumed she would be posing for the usual publicity photos to promote the film she was working on—a "gay nineties" musical, *Sweet Rosie O'Grady*. Her hair was done in the period style, with curls piled up on her head, but rather than the ruffles and sequins of her musical hall costumes, she chose to wear a white, one-piece bathing suit, teamed with a leg-extending pair of heels.

As she tried out a variety of different poses, Frank, an Austrian native who had been the Fox still photographer since 1923, snapped away. He was an old hat at capturing the biggest stars, and his work was frequently shown in newspapers, magazines, and theatre lobbies around the world.[1] But it was one pose, with her hands on her hips, as she peers coyly over her shoulder, with an inviting wink at the viewer, that would make history.

As Powolny recounted to the *Los Angeles Times* in 1982, "I asked Betty if she'd like to have a back shot, just to be different," he said. "She said, 'Yes,' and began to clown around. 'You want it like this?' she asked, posing. And I said, 'Yeah.'

"I made only two shots of that pose. It was the second shot that became famous."[2]

There was a wholesomeness to the image despite its provocativeness, but still Betty tried to play down the risqué aspect when later recounting the story. She claimed that she was pregnant at the time with her eldest daughter Victoria (born in March 1944) and was hiding her stomach to the camera, but whatever the reason, the image was distributed to publicize the movie, and it quickly became a phenomenon among American soldiers who were being shipped out to fight overseas.

Five million copies of Betty's saucy pose were distributed to GIs during the Second World War, and it also helped to popularize a new vernacular— the "pin-up"—first coined in 1941 to denote the mass demand for one image, typically a seductive woman, which could then be posted up on a wall. These images were cheap and portable, and offered an escapism from the tedium, and the horrors, of being in active service. Betty Grable was the all-American girl who they could fantasize about in freezing barracks and foxholes, or when flying bombers over occupied Europe.

This type of publicity photo, also known as a "cheesecake" shot, was a staple for Hollywood starlets to get their name out there, as they posed in swimsuits or shorts with a bright and wholesome lipsticked smile on their face.

Grable's image was also a real-life incarnation of the Petty girl—the feminine fantasy illustrations by George Petty that appeared on the pages of *Esquire* from its founding in 1933. The magazine had been devised for increasingly fashion-conscious men, but rather than the sartorial spreads, the most popular content were the illustrations of glamorous, scantily clad women. Like the Gibson girl who preceded her, the Petty girl with her long legs and tiny waist was an idealized version of femininity. She was a good girl acting naughty, always smiling at being caught in a cheeky pose, and with a one-liner caption underneath.

Similarly, Peruvian-American illustrator Alberto Vargas created a wartime phenomenon for his sexually provocative images of women with exaggerated curves. Vargas had honed his skills as the artist in residence for showman Florenz Ziegfeld in the 1910s, and as a commemoration of Olive Thomas, following her tragic death in 1920, he painted from memory a sensual image of the silent star with one hand clasping her nude breast, the other holding a rose to her face, which Ziegfeld kept on the wall of his office. In Hollywood, his illustrations further took on elements of modern glamor, styled with the hair and costumes that mimicked the current trends of the stars.

In October 1940, Vargas's first illustration appeared in *Esquire*, depicting a woman reclining panther-like on a bed while talking on the phone, with her sheer negligee clinging to every curve. She was clearly rich, a femme fatale, and a departure from the wholesomeness of the sporty Petty girls, who were less exaggerated in their voluptuousness. Vargas also used an airbrushed technique to achieve peach-skinned, glossy, perfection. It was printed side-on over two pages, as if its purpose was to be ripped from the magazine and pinned to a wall.

With millions mobilized during the war, the Petty and Vargas girls were in such demand that *Esquire* distributed nine million copies of the magazine to send to American troops free of charge. They fed into a desire for female iconography among sex-starved men and were a connection to the home front, a representation of the girl waiting back in America for them. Reproduced on the sides of jeeps and on the nose of bombers, they were a symbol of womanly power, as if they were the goddess Athena guiding their way into battle.

The Gibson girl fed the imaginations of young men at the turn of the century, and now the voluptuous Petty and Vargas girls represented American notions of freedom. Just as the Nazis believed women should be devoted to traditional roles and conservative dress, rather than the trappings of makeup and modern dress, the Vargas girl was an American knickerbocker glory, with all the frills to make her as sensual as possible. The most famous Petty girl was the one painted onto the nose of the bomber the *Memphis Belle*—a blonde coquette in a red swimsuit, flashing her legs and her derriere as she talks on the phone.

As a more sensual version of Rosie the Riveter, the illustrations depicted women actively involved in the war, not just playing dress-up, and patriotic in their embracing of the mission. It was a new type of populist sexuality, a war goddess who was inspiring to the women taking on new roles in society. As Maria Elena Buzek writes in her essay, *War Goddess*: "Vargas conjured up lemon meringue blondes with bodies just as steely and dangerous as anything rolling off the assembly line in Dearborn and Detroit."[3]

It wasn't just men who adored them; at a time when women were entering the workforce in droves, donning work overalls and uniforms, these pin-ups acted as flirty, feminine inspiration to break through all that khaki and navy serge. Wartime demands meant that women were now doing jobs that they had previously been told were beyond their capabilities. While actresses, singers, and female celebrities typically transcended notions of the virtuous woman who was modest and chaste, real women were also being fed the line through advertising campaigns, films, and magazine editorials that their patriotic duty was to be as inviting as possible, with red lipstick, a winsome smile and a ready availability to please. They took on the real-life representation of the Varga girl by being strong and capable, but also sexually open and appealing, and began posing for their own pin-ups to send to their boyfriends or husbands. Actresses like Betty Grable, Veronica Lake, Rita Hayworth, and Carole Landis brought the dream girls to life. The fantasy pin-up always captured women in a moment when they were cheerful, compliant, and sexual, but they never revealed her realness, and her fallibility. Betty Grable had a bawdy sense of humor, often making wisecracks and burp jokes which defied the angelic appearance, and she avoided premieres and public events because of her social anxiety. Yet she always made time for the soldiers who adored her and was one of the regulars at the Hollywood Canteen—a venue established by Bette Davis in 1942 as a place where servicemen on leave could meet and dance with the stars.

As *Modern Screen* wrote in 1945: "if you think Betty Grable is simply a decked out blonde baby doll who can sing and dance and act a little—a walking Petty girl pin-up with nothing but luscious looks on the ball—then you've got another think coming. Because there's plenty more to Betty than just lovely legs. Yes, indeed!"[4]

Despite Betty's stratospheric rise to top box office star, she wasn't an overnight sensation, having grafted in movies and on stage since the early 1930s. Born in 1916 in St. Louis, Missouri, her mother, Lillian, was desperate to turn her angelic little girl into a star. She was encouraged to perform whenever she could—tap dancing in hotel lobbies while on vacation and appearing in vaudeville shows with comedic hoofers like Jack Haley and Bert Wheeler.[5]

When word spread that a movie talent agent was visiting St. Louis, Lillian ensured Betty was given an introduction, and when they suggested that she bring her daughter to Hollywood, she drove the family cross-country to Los Angeles in the summer of 1929. Betty was only thirteen, but she pretended she was fifteen to meet the age criteria to be a chorus girl at Fox Studios. She was sacked when the truth was revealed, but she was signed up as an all-smiling and dancing Goldwyn Girl at producer Samuel Goldwyn's studio, appearing in *Whoopee!* (1930), *Palmy Days* (1931), and *The Greeks Had a Word for Them* (1932).

She further made an impact at RKO when she was given her own number in the Ginger Rogers and Fred Astaire musical *The Gay Divorcee* (1934). With her newly bleached blonde hair and plucked eyebrows she looked every inch the perky starlet, and back home the *St. Louis Star and Times* reported "Betty Grable's Star Beginning to Twinkle."[6]

In summer 1935 Betty and her mother were on a day trip to Catalina Island when they met Jackie Coogan, the former child actor, on board the ship. When their engagement hit the headlines, Grable was catapulted to fame. She and Coogan married in November 1937, and they acted out the Hollywood dream, enjoying ice cream sodas at C.C. Brown's on Hollywood Boulevard, or going to champagne parties at Carole Lombard's house in Malibu.

Jackie Coogan was locked in a court battle after he discovered that the millions he had earned as a child actor, and that he was supposed to receive at twenty-one, had been squandered. It put stress on their marriage, and after their divorce in July 1939, Betty was seen out on the town with womanizing band leader Artie Shaw. Her photo was splashed across fan magazines, but she was dropped by her studio once again, and instead accepted the lead in *Du Barry Was a Lady* on Broadway in November 1939. Glowing reviews transformed her into the toast of Broadway as she dined at the Stork Club every night with showbiz favorites like her castmate Ethel Merman.[7]

She was settling into a long run for *Du Barry* when Darryl Zanuck at Twentieth Century Fox asked her to replace the ill Alice Faye in the musical *Down Argentine Way* (1940). Basking in her stage success, and with her ten years' experience in front of the camera, she thrived on screen.

With war in Europe having broken out in 1939, she did an early piece of wartime propaganda, starring in the hit *A Yank in the RAF* (1941) as Tyrone Power's love interest, a nightclub singer and member of the Women's Auxiliary Air Force. In the musical *Moon Over Miami* (1941) she and Carole Landis were perky sisters waitressing in a hamburger drive-in, who go to Miami to search for rich husbands to help save their restaurant. It was in Technicolor that she really blossomed, and her blonde hair, now worn in the longer pompadour style of the forties, shimmered under the Klieg lights, and her cheeks flushed with effervescence. With her bubbly energy, Betty was the girl next door, appealing equally to men and to women, and *Footlight Serenade* and

Springtime in the Rockies (both 1942) enhancing her status as a star. But no movie could touch the phenomenon of her pin-up. Once it was circulated in 1943, it catapulted her to the number-one favorite female star, ahead of Rita Hayworth, whose 1941 *Life* photograph by Bob Landry had been the most popular image up to that point.

Before her pin-up, Betty was already celebrated for her legs, and in February 1943 had imprinted one limb in cement outside Grauman's Chinese Theatre on Hollywood Boulevard. *Life* magazine in June 1943 hailed them as a "Hollywood landmark," and over a five-page spread where her head was lobbed off to focus in on her body, she posed in swimsuits, pulled on a pair of stockings, and climbed into a jeep in tiny shorts. "They seem to get me around the lot all right," she joked. "They are fine for pushing the foot pedals in my car."[8] To further promote her as "the girl with the million-dollar legs," Twentieth Century Fox engaged Lloyd's of London to take part in a publicity stunt to insure her legs for $1 million.

She was now Hollywood's biggest female draw at the box office, and with her July 1943 marriage to bandleader Harry James she became even more popular among the bobbysoxers who idolized her husband. In just one month 90,000 fan letters poured into the studio. Her films were lightweight froth, but they were bringing in the audiences, and even though Darryl Zanuck thought she should challenge herself with more dramatic roles, she wanted to stay within her comfort zones. The film *Pin Up Girl*, released in spring 1944, was conceived to capitalize on the popularity of the image. "I'm no Bette Davis. I just want to make pictures people will like," she pleaded.[9]

She was enormously popular, one of the most famous women in the world, and the highest paid in America, but was Betty Grable a true "It" girl? She didn't seek fame by spending her evenings in nightclubs, and she tried to avoid Hollywood premieres, as she felt too self-conscious under the glare of camera flashes. While she appeared in the gossip columns for her marriage to Jackie Coogan and Harry James, and her romances with George Raft and Artie Shaw, she didn't court it. But along with other pin-ups of the war years, she set the female standard of beauty, and popularized a new form of mass media.

Rita Hayworth, when she was still an unknown dancer named Margarita Cansino, was pushed into spending her evenings in nightclubs by her first husband, an older businessman, Edward Judson. He knew that having her photo splashed in papers as the latest girl about town was a way to boost her career. Her striking looks were noticed by film studios in the late 1930s, but given how shy she was, she felt uncomfortable about all this publicity. "I had to be sold to the public just like a breakfast cereal or a real estate development or something new in ladies' wear," she said.[10]

To further sell her as a star, her Spanish heritage was erased as she was transformed into the all-American Rita Hayworth by dyeing her hair red and using electrolysis to raise her hairline. Her *Life* magazine pin-up, in which she knelt on a bed in a negligee with an inviting smile, was almost as popular as Grable's, and with her lead role in *Gilda* in 1946, she became Hollywood's most desirable star. This femme fatale was completely unlike her true self, and she famously lamented that her marriages failed because men "went to bed with Gilda and woke up with me."[11]

Rita became a huge celebrity, but there was a constant cycle of hot young starlets who had their moment of fame on the back of an impressive movie debut and through well-placed gossip pieces in the fan magazines. With the fickle nature of Hollywood, the girl who was the cat's pajamas one minute could burn out and disappear just as quickly.

"Picking the newcomer who is going to click is in an industry in itself, for the movies are forever on the prowl for someone different," wrote the *Chicago Tribune* in February 1941. "The choice involves agents, casting directors, test directors, producers—and chance. Fortunes are gambled on young women . . . and sometimes the winnings are handsome. So it may be that Veronica Lake will be the find of 1941."[12]

Veronica Lake made a spectacular debut in *I Wanted Wings* in 1941, as a nightclub singer with a blonde sweep of hair which instantly earned her the nickname "the girl with the peek-a-boo hair," "the Peeping Pompadour," and "the Strip-Tease Hair-Do."

In advertising for *I Wanted Wings*, a piece of American Air Force propaganda, she was billed as "The blonde bomber," with her face and breasts featuring more prominently than the two male leads, Ray Milland and William Holden. She wasn't just a pin-up for men, as her hair became one of the most requested styles in hairdressing salons, and an article in *Life* magazine in November 1941 provided the intricacies of how she looked after her hair, from shampooing it twice a day to rinsing it with vinegar.[13] Her signature also became a popular punchline for comedians at the time. "I opened up my mop closet the other day and I thought Veronica Lake fell out," joked Groucho Marx.

As the *Chicago Tribune* added in their article on how to make a star: "In the cinema Cinderella game you first find the girl. She must be striking, rather than beautiful; if she's both beautiful and striking, so much the better. It wouldn't hurt any if she could act. And she must have another name."[14]

Veronica Lake did have another name. She was born in 1922 as Constance "Connie" Ockelman in Brooklyn, and her early life was marked with tragedy when her father was killed in a workplace accident. After moving to Florida with her mother and new stepfather, the teenage Connie exhibited behavioral problems, and received a diagnosis of schizophrenia. She refused to accept this, and instead embraced the attention her blonde looks and full bust received, entering and winning local beauty pageants.

The family moved to Los Angeles in 1938 on the vague promise that Connie might make it as a movie star, and like many hopefuls in Hollywood, she found work as an extra. She was spotted on the MGM lot by director Fred Wilcox, and struck by her stunning, glacial beauty, he ordered a screen test.

Producer Arthur Hornblow Jr. was mesmerized by the way her blonde hair curled over the eye, and he cast her in *I Wanted Wings*. He thought the name Connie Ockelman sounded too clunky, whereas Veronica was much more sophisticated, and if you added Lake, well it was like sinking into her blue eyes. She was signed to Paramount Pictures and shot to instant stardom in classic forties film noirs like *This Gun for Hire* (1942) and *The Glass Key* (1942).

She was just five feet tall, doll-like and delicate-featured, but with the blonde sweep, and the clinging, sultry gowns that accentuated her curves, she dominated every scene. The adulation didn't last long, as rumors began to appear that she was temperamental and unreliable on set. Veronica was a heavy drinker, and while men could get away with turning up hungover, for women, it was unacceptable.

There were also stories that she had come between Hornblow and his wife Myrna Loy, when in reality, Veronica claimed the producer had tried it on with her, but she rejected him. She was in love with her husband, the art director John S. Detlie, and achingly lonely during the location shooting for *I Wanted Wings*, she impulsively drove all night to Gallup, New Mexico, where he was working on a film. In Arizona she was caught in a storm and her car veered off the road, skidded and overturned. She escaped with bruises and a cut leg, but she was also left with a bad reputation for abandoning the set.[15]

On her next film, *Sullivan's Travels* (1941), she was reportedly so difficult that her co-star, Joel McCrea, refused to ever work with her again. Pregnant during the making of the film, she questioned whether she really wanted the fame that came with being a movie star, and she recoiled against the sexual harassment and verbal abuse she experienced on set.

Her mental health problems were further triggered during her second pregnancy. She went into premature labor after tripping over a lighting cable during the making of *The Hour Before the Dawn* in late 1943, and her baby son died just a few days later. She and Detlie divorced, and she married for a second time, to director André de Toth. He was abusive and controlling, and she turned to drink to further cope with the pressures of marriage and fame. Her starry ascent as one of the hottest pin-ups of the Second World War was lightning quick, but it never sat easily with her, and just as soon as she found fame, she rebelled against the constraints of Hollywood. As Veronica said to Dick Cavett in a 1971 television interview, "rather than a sex symbol, I was a sex zombie."

By the late forties, with fickle audiences turning away from her, she was dropped by Paramount. "No asking why I was no longer in favor with Hollywood," she wrote in her memoirs. "Just a long spiral down into a bottomless well, the only buoy a bottle—of Scotch." At the same time, she conceded "I had to get out. I was never psychologically meant to be a picture star."[16]

In 1952, after her finances were wiped out by careless spending, she divorced Toth and moved to New York to find work in television and on stage. By the end of the decade, she had married and divorced for a third time, and was living in a series of cheap hotels to make ends meet.

In March 1962 a reporter discovered the forty-three-year-old employed as a down-on-her-luck cocktail waitress at a shabby women's hotel in New York, and she once again made international news. "GI's pin-up girl Veronica Lake found working in a New York bar," blasted one headline for a syndicated *United Press International* article in March 1962. She was described as a "little overweight and her features have begun to change," and she was nursing a damaged ankle after an ex-boyfriend supposedly "fell on it." The flirtatious locks of blonde hair were also noted as being "nothing more than a fading memory."

In 1971, the Veronica Lake sitting in the chair opposite television host Dick Cavett to promote her memoir was a world apart from the glamor girl of the 1940s. She now wore her hair short, and with her absurdist sense of humor, she was unvarnished and real. She also appeared to be suffering from the alcoholism that would kill her only a short time later.

Veronica sounded optimistic in the last pages of her autobiography. She had traveled to England to perform in local theatres, and she believed more offers were coming her way. "I seem to be coming around full circle to the point where Veronica Lake is almost in vogue again," she wrote. Yet she also hinted at the destructive nature of her lifestyle as a heavy-drinking, junk-food eating ex-star in Miami. In 1973, she passed away as a result of hepatitis and kidney disease. She was just fifty years old.

Veronica wasn't yielding or perky enough to remain in favor through the postwar period, when women were shuttled back into a restrictive feminine box. Being a Hollywood wartime pin-up came with a lot of pressure to live up to the image, and once the conflict was over, it was hard to find a place in this new, more conservative, society. To support men in reacclimatizing from the war, women were pushed out of the workplace and back into the home.

In 1947 Betty Grable was still the highest paid woman in the United States with an annual salary of $325,000, but by the end of the decade her popularity was waning.

Now that she was approaching her mid-thirties, Twentieth Century Fox boss Darryl Zanuck had plenty of bright new things waiting in the wings to take over from his aging star. She was desperate to play Lorelei in the upcoming movie *Gentlemen Prefer Blondes*, and even though she had earned $100 million for the studio, the part went to the new favorite, Marilyn Monroe.

She was teamed with Marilyn and Lauren Bacall in 1953's *How to Marry a Millionaire*, and while her contract gave her top billing, when she was dropped by the studio shortly after filming was complete, Marilyn's name replaced hers as first in the credits and in the promotion.

Despite this, Betty refused to fall for any manufactured rivalry; instead, she agreed to star in *How to Be Very, Very Popular* (1955) on the proviso Marilyn would be cast too. Instead, she got Sheree North, who was being groomed by Fox as a Marilyn successor. The film failed to sizzle, and it would be Betty's last major movie. She took her own show to Las Vegas, where she performed with husband Harry James, and indulged in drinking sessions while playing the slots in the strip casinos.

By the late sixties she and James were divorced, and she began dating a much younger man, Bob Remick, who was just a few months older than Betty's eldest daughter. Betty was wowing audiences with her performance in the stage revival of *Born Yesterday* when she was diagnosed with lung cancer, and she died a short time later, in July 1973, at the age of fifty-six.

After her death, Neil Sedaka wrote a song with Howard Greenfield in tribute, in which he reflected on his childhood memories of Saturday afternoons spent at the picture house, when he would be transfixed by Betty Grable, his movie queen, up on the silver screen. Her legacy as a pin-up girl would be enduring.

The ubiquity of the pin-up during the war, and the need to soothe the damaged male psyche, would, by 1953, peak with the launch of Hugh Hefner's *Playboy* magazine. Aimed at an exclusively male readership with a mammary fixation, it would define the overarching notions of femininity in the 1950s—that of the busty, and dumb, blonde, whose raison d'etre was to be appealing to men. If Betty Grable was reduced to her legs and Veronica Lake to her hair, then the ultimate star of the fifties, Marilyn Monroe, was fetishized, celebrated, and mocked for every part of her body.

Marilyn Monroe, Jayne Mansfield, and the Death of the Pin-up Blonde

Marilyn Monroe surrounded by photographers while filming the skirt-blowing scene in *The Seven Year Itch* (1955). *HA/THA/Shutterstock.*

In the 1950s, the worship of blonde femininity was at its peak, as if it tapped into the very ideal of what it meant to be a woman. Rather than the plucky pin-up who took part in war work, the new "It" girl was completely non-threatening in her sexuality, as soft and sweet and desirable as a strawberry and vanilla ice-cream cone. With its connotations of youthfulness, blonde was the high-maintenance, sunshine-bright hair color that could transform the girl-next-door into a star.

"If I have only one life, let me live it as a blonde," proclaimed a pretty woman in an advertisement for Clairol in the 1950s. Together with the phenomena of Marilyn Monroe, and the message that gentlemen really did prefer blondes, it encouraged three out of every ten American women to bleach their hair.[1]

At the same time as Betty Grable's pin-up was the visual delight of the American war machine, and the aspirational symbol of patriotism, a young woman named Norma Jeane was spotted by a photographer at the aircraft factory where she worked on the assembly line. David Conover had been tasked with taking photos of attractive workers, and when he developed the photos of Norma Jeane with her natural chestnut hair and scarlet smile, he was struck by the power she had in front of the camera. He came back to take more photos of her, and as she posed for him, her power in front of the camera was clear. She would work hard to construct a dazzling identity, with a new name, a new hair color, and a new aura designed to transform her into an enchanting vortex.

Everything about Marilyn Monroe was a creation, from her name to the wispy voice, the painted pout, and bleached blonde hair, and as Sarah Churchwell wrote in her extensive biography of the star, "To be artificially put together by modistes, couturiers, cosmeticians and coiffeurs, leads to a profound loss of one's identity."[2]

Coming full circle from his era-defining photograph of Grable, in 1962, Frank Powolny took the last known still photographs of Marilyn Monroe on the set of *Something's Got to Give*, just a week before her death in 1962. In the lead-up to her final days, she felt a terrible loneliness and a fear of losing her looks, which she believed were key to her power. Without them, what was she?

Marilyn's confused early life was shaped by images of starlets who came before her. Her mother, Gladys Baker (née Monroe) and her best friend, Grace McKee, were two young flappers living and working in Hollywood as a film cutter and supervisor. Grace adored the movies and worshipped the stars on screen like Mary Pickford, and she even persuaded Gladys to emulate Clara Bow by dyeing her hair cherry red.[3]

During a short-lived marriage to Martin Edward Mortensen, Gladys fell pregnant with another man, and she gave birth to her daughter, Norma Jeane

Mortenson, on June 1, 1926, with the father's surname incorrectly spelled on the birth certificate at the Los Angeles General Hospital.

Gripped by depression, Gladys was unable to look after her daughter, instead leaving her with ultra-religious foster carers, the Bolenders. Their strict child-rearing stifled the imagination of the sensitive Norma Jeane, and as she was taught that vanity was a sin, the young girl later confessed her fantasy of stripping off naked at church as a manifestation of the desire for people to notice her.

For a short time, when she was seven, Norma Jeane was returned to her mother's care, but when Gladys suffered a complete mental breakdown, she was passed around different homes, until her mother's best friend Grace took her in for a short time. The little girl would often be left to fend for herself during the day, and the movie theatres on Hollywood Boulevard allowed her to escape to a carefree world of love and adventure. She dreamed that Clark Gable was her real father, and that one day she would be as beautiful as Jean Harlow. Grace worshipped the platinum blonde star, and she promised Norma Jeane she would be just like her one day; she felt real conviction that this young girl would grow up to be a movie star.[4]

While being passed from home to home, Norma Jeane was abused on multiple occasions. She revealed her childhood trauma to Ben Hecht, the screenwriter who had been hired to write her biography in the fifties, and she altered some details for anonymity. Like Clara Bow, she was brutally honest about her childhood, and she was one of the first celebrities to talk so openly about sexual abuse. But the hazy details made it easy for journalists to dismiss her story and call her a fantasist who was eliciting sympathy to further her career.[5]

Some biographers have analyzed her adult behavior as reflective of this childhood abuse, where she perpetually suffered from low self-esteem, feelings of shame, insomnia, and depression, and abused substances to cope.

When Grace got married in September 1935 she dropped her charge at the Los Angeles Orphanage. Norma Jeane couldn't understand why she was being placed there if her mother was still alive—after all, orphans didn't have any parents. She burned with shame over her abandonment, the terror of sleeping in a dorm with many other children, the chores she had to do. She was so frightened that she hardly spoke, and for her well-being it was decided she should stay with Grace's aunt, Ana Lower, who lived in West Los Angeles.

She thrived during this period of her life, helped by the kindness of "Aunt" Ana. At the age of twelve she transformed from a skinny young girl into one who was suddenly aware of the enormous change in the way people treated her. Now she was *seen*. She enjoyed the attention, relished the lingering glances and the whistles, and began wearing tight sweaters and lipstick. The two and a half mile walk to school was "sheer pleasure" as every "fellow honked his horn. And workers driving to work were waving. . . . The world became friendly. It opened up to me."[6]

When she was fifteen, as a means of giving her somewhere permanent to stay, Norma Jeane was encouraged to marry her nineteen-year-old neighbor Jim Dougherty, a merchant marine. He worried she was too young, but her overwhelming beauty canceled out those concerns. When Jim was sent to fight in the Pacific in spring 1944, Norma Jeane went to live with his mother, and she found work at the Radio Plane aircraft plant. It was here, working on the assembly line, that she was launched as a model.

Once she had built up her portfolio, she took it to the Blue Book Modeling Agency, where the founder, Emmeline Snively, was impressed with Norma Jeane's fresh-faced "girl-next-door type."[7] She persuaded the young model to lighten her natural chestnut hair, as blondes were guaranteed to get more assignments, and Norma Jeane proved to be a tireless worker. It led to a screen test at Twentieth Century Fox, and the studio, always with an eye for the next Betty Grable, offered her a movie contract. Casting agent Ben Lyon felt her name didn't do her justice. He immediately saw her as a "Marilyn," and when he asked her what surname she would like, she insisted on her mother's maiden name, Monroe. With her career looking more promising she didn't need a husband holding her back, so she wrote to Jim, asking for a divorce.

She was given bit parts in *Dangerous Years* (1947) and *Scudda Hoo! Scudda Hay!* (1948). But with so much competition from other starlets, she was dropped by the studio. She was aware that the currency in Hollywood was sex, and she was invited to parties hosted by studio execs, where she worked the room in tight dresses, hoping an introduction might lead to work. Orson Welles recalled being at a party where she was surrounded by a group of men, one of whom grabbed and ripped her top. She laughed it off, but she was humiliated and angry.[8]

At one party she met the powerful studio executive Joseph Schenck, who was fascinated by her innocent humor, her shyness despite the way she dressed, and the way she performed as a character—with the heavy-lidded gaze, the open-mouth smile. He asked Columbia Pictures boss Harry Cohen to try her out, and she signed to a six-month contract in March 1948. *Ladies of the Chorus* was Marilyn's biggest break so far, but she was dropped once again, with reports it was because she turned down Cohen's suggestive offer of a private trip on his yacht.[9]

With little success in sustaining a film career, she was short of cash, and on May 27, 1949, she agreed to pose nude for a photographer, Tom Kelley, for $50. She stretched out nude on a swath of red velvet, which she said was "a little drafty," and after the shoot was done, she pushed it out of her mind.

She had spent years grafting and trying to get that big break, with bit parts, modeling gigs, visits to Schwab's drugstore for a discovery like Lana Turner, and she underwent a surgical tweak to enhance her chin with cartilage, in the hopes it might boost her fortunes. She was picked up again by Twentieth Century Fox in May 1950, and was given a small, star-making role in *All About Eve* as Miss Casswell, the dim but fame-hungry blonde starlet who many thought was Marilyn incarnate.

By 1952 a nude calendar with an image titled "Golden Dreams" was appearing on the walls of garages around the country, and there were whispers that she was a blonde Hollywood starlet. On March 13, 1952, the story broke with the headline "Marilyn Monroe Admits She's Nude Blonde of Calendar." Nudity at that time was aligned with pornography, and the scandal could easily have destroyed her career. Fox held urgent meetings to discuss what to do, and they strongly advised Marilyn to deny it. Marilyn refused to be shamed, because "I've not done anything wrong" and explained that she had been "a week behind on my rent" at the time.[10]

This honest admission earned her sympathy, and when a reporter asked her what she had on, she quipped "The radio"—it was the example of the literal humor she was so adept at.

In the process of launching a new men's magazine, Hugh Hefner purchased the negatives for $500 and published them in the first issue of *Playboy* in December 1953. Marilyn never made more than the $50 she had initially been paid and had no rights as to how they would be used. The editorial, like much of the lascivious content at the time, placed her as beyond-human. It said, "There is nothing else quite like Marilyn on this good earth—be it animal, vegetable or mineral. She is natural sex personified. It is there in every look and movement. That's what makes her the most natural choice in the world for our very first Playboy Sweetheart."[11]

In April 1952 she was splashed on the cover of *Life* as "The Talk of Hollywood," illustrated with an image that incorporated all the elements we recognize as Marilyn—the halo of sculpted blonde hair, the beauty mark, the lazy, half-open eyes, the wet red lips parted into a half-smile, and a white off-the-shoulder dress. Inside, the article reprinted the image of the calendar alongside a photo of Marilyn reclining on an armchair in check pants, a sweater, and bare feet. It hailed her as the latest sensation that Hollywood was buzzing about: "the genuine article is here at last: a sturdy blonde named Marilyn Monroe."

While the assumption was made that she was ditzy, the article noted that she may be "naïve and guileless. But she is smart enough to have known how to make a success in the cutthroat world of glamour. She does it by being as wholly natural as the world will allow." She sprinkled her conversation with references to Thomas Wolfe and Robert Browning, and she revealed a disconcerting candor that was endearingly suggestive. "One day this fellow says, 'Marilyn, what do you wear to bed?' So I said I only wear Chanel No. 5 and he groans, 'Oh no, I can't use that.'"[12]

Another profile in *Time* in 1952 compared her to Clara Bow and Jean Harlow for her sex appeal. She would surpass their fame, yet she also possessed a timeless quality that resonated across the eras.

For the December 22, 1958, edition of *Life* magazine, Richard Avedon took photos of Marilyn dressed as the sex symbols that came before her—Lillian Russell, Theda Bara, Clara Bow, Jean Harlow, Marlene Dietrich—and she looks uncannily like them in each depiction. Decades after her death, other "It" girls like Paris Hilton, Lindsay Lohan, Kate Moss, and Madonna in her "Material Girl" music video, would emulate and imitate some of her famous images. Marilyn, therefore, became the magnetic force of all "It" girls who shared that same hunger for fame and the vulnerability, and with her death keeping her in eternal icon status before she inevitably faded into the irrelevance of an aging star.

In the thriller *Niagara*, released in February 1953, her body was once again beyond human; it would be equated with the power of the American landmark it took its name from. For the first time she was in Technicolor, and it brought her to life as she shimmers in a hot pink dress, and in the most famous scene, the camera tracks her from behind as she totters in heels and a tight skirt. Never mind that her character is trying to escape her murderous husband; it was all about the walk. It was a still from this film that would further place her as an eternal icon, and the subject of one of the most famous pieces of modern art, when Andy Warhol reproduced it in his silk-screen print "Shot Marilyns," as a commemoration of her death and as a statement on her commodification.

In *Niagara* the Marilyn image was fully formed, and in *Gentlemen Prefer Blondes*, she would create the personality; the dizzy blonde who is not as stupid as she appears. Her character, Lorelei, is a gold digger who is honest about it, using her kittenish dumb blonde persona to lure in men who want to care for her. "I can be smart when it's important, but most men don't like it," she admits.

In her next movie, *How to Marry a Millionaire* (also 1953), she played another gold digger, but this time her character, Pola, bumbles around without her glasses until she chooses love and acceptance over money.

One of her costumes from *Gentlemen*, a skintight gold lamé, was too risqué for the finished movie. Instead, she was sewn into it for the 1953 Photoplay Awards, and with her drunken wriggling, she shocked Joan Crawford into accusing her of being vulgar and an attention-seeker. Crawford said it was "Like a burlesque show" and "Those of us in the industry just shuddered. Apparently Miss Monroe is making the mistake of believing her publicity."[13] Marilyn often cast a particular pose in each of her movies, which would then become a pin-up freeze-frame. In *Gentlemen Prefer Blondes* she holds her arms above her head while wrapped in hot pink for the "Diamonds are a Girl's Best Friend" number, and in *The Seven Year Itch* her white dress billows around her legs as air blows through a subway grate. For *How to Marry a Millionaire*, she poses in a red bathing suit and heels, one leg extended as she sits on a stool, like a Petty girl on the nose of a bomber. As Sarah Churchwell writes, "for many observers, Marilyn would always be defined as 'cheesecake,' as sex on display, and as sex for sale."[14]

Marilyn's relationship with baseball star Joe DiMaggio further placed her in the grasp of the media as their relationship was gold—the most celebrated sportsman in America and the glamor queen of Hollywood.

On their honeymoon in Hawaii, she was mobbed by fans at the airport who tugged at her clothes and her hair, and in Tokyo, the crowds went so crazy that they flung themselves at the lobby door of her hotel, cracking the glass.[15] While DiMaggio was training Japanese baseball players, Marilyn, who was now the top pin-up girl, or "oomph girl," was invited to do a USO tour of American army bases in Korea.

In February 1954, dressed in just a tight beaded dress that defied the freezing temperature, she took to the stage in front of 70,000 troops, and she loved every minute of performing to the whoops and cheers of her enraptured audience. Afterward, she proclaimed to her husband, "You never heard such cheering!" "Yes I have," he replied. "Don't let it go to your head. Just miss the ball once. You'll see they can boo as loud as they can cheer."[16]

Sick of being given scripts that she felt weren't good enough, she only agreed to do *There's No Business Like Show Business* (1954) if she was given *The Seven Year Itch*, directed by Billy Wilder and based on the Broadway hit by George Axelrod.

Her character wasn't given a name, she was just "The Girl"; a nameless fantasy figure who keeps her underwear in the icebox to stay cool. Filming of the famous subway-grate scene took place on location in New York on September 8, 1954, and the publicity dominated headlines, with crowds gathering on Lexington Avenue in the early hours to watch as huge fans blew air to lift her skirt up around her legs. DiMaggio was watching from the sidelines, horrified at how much his exhibitionist wife was showing to the cheering crowds.

There were stories that a huge fight broke out in their hotel, and that Marilyn was seen with bruises the next day. This image of Marilyn, in the white halterneck dress, an expression of ecstasy on her face as she pushes down her skirt, and "feeling blonde all over," would be the prevailing image of Marilyn, but it was also the end of her marriage—her sensational stardom was a threat to the masculinity of the time.[17]

She felt the weight of her image upon her. According to observers, Marilyn would be lost in her own reflection, as if she was trying to figure out her own beauty. Truman Capote went into the ladies' bathroom of a Chinese restaurant, wondering what was keeping her. He found her gazing into the mirror, "Looking at Her," as Marilyn said.[18] She was trying her best to live up to and perfect the image she created, yet she also wanted to be taken seriously, and to challenge herself in her work.

In December 1954 she fled Hollywood for Manhattan, where she hoped to begin the process of trying to find herself. With her close friend, photographer Milton Greene, she set up Marilyn Monroe Productions with a plan to make her own movies, and she enrolled at the Actors Studio to learn the Method technique, considered the truest form of acting. She was regularly spotted walking the streets in her casual New York wardrobe of camel coats, beatnik black turtleneck sweaters, and black silk dresses, as if she was tapping into a more insular, reflective, and serious side of her.[19]

Her absence was felt in Hollywood, as studios scrambled to discover the next Marilyn, and Jayne Mansfield, Sheree North, Diana Dors, and Mamie Van Doren were all hailed as her replacement. The fifties were obsessed with breasts as a cushioning comfort after the war, and where they reinforced the image of the helpless woman burdened by the statistics of her body.

They may have had the blonde hair, the cleavage, the wispy voice, but none of the imitators could capture her essence despite their relentless pursuit of publicity. Jayne Mansfield, however, was a turbo-charged Marilyn with her white-blonde hair, the exaggerated cleavage, the soft voice, and an absolute love of pink.

The fame-hungry starlet worked hard to get her name out there. Always the most beautiful girl in the room, Jayne had dreamed of being a movie star since she was six years old, and she did all she could to make it happen. "She took any kind of job—addressing envelopes, selling candy—to pay for her singing and dancing lessons," wrote the *Los Angeles Times* in 1956.[20] Born Vera Jayne Palmer in April 1933 in Bryn Mawr, Pennsylvania, when she was three years old her lawyer father died suddenly of a heart attack while driving with Jayne and her mother. Her mother remarried and moved to Texas, and Jayne would always by haunted by his death, as if on a quest to find him in other men.[21]

Jayne excelled at school in Texas, and while she thrived in class and learned viola and violin, she developed early, and like Marilyn, she loved the attention from boys, wearing the tight sweaters made famous by Lana Turner to accentuate her shape. "It is the most wonderful feeling in the whole world, you know, knowing you are loved and wanted," she said.[22]

Jayne was sixteen when she met Paul Mansfield at a party, and they married in May 1950. Six months later the seventeen-year-old gave birth to a daughter, Jayne Marie. Paul was drafted into the army for the Korean War and she reluctantly came with him to train in Georgia, yet she bartered an agreement that she could then go to Hollywood for six months to try to make it.[23]

Arriving in Los Angeles in early 1954, she headed to Paramount Studios to announce her intention to be a star, and this gumption impressed enough to land her an audition. Her monologue from *Joan of Arc*, however, didn't impress—it was her body, rather than her mind, that she needed to reveal. She was also advised to lose weight and to dye her brown hair platinum blonde.[24] She signed up to the Blue Book Modeling Agency, the same one as Marilyn, but she was just too much for some clients. General Electric had to cut her out of their video because her breasts were too big, and they worried it would be a shock to their customers.

In December 1954 she was signed with press agent and publicist Jim Byron, who arranged for her to deliver bottles of Scotch to his press contacts while dressed in a sexy Santa outfit. Her presence made such an impression on the journalists that she featured in the papers the next day.

She also secured an invite for a press trip to promote Jane Russell's movie *Underwater* in January 1955. At a pool event she flaunted herself in a tight red lamé swimsuit, before diving into the water. The impact caused the strap to break, and she modestly tried to cover herself while the photographers snapped away. Jane Russell asked cynically: "Who's the blonde tomato?"[25]

Like Kitty Fisher centuries before, Jayne was practiced in the art of wardrobe malfunctions for publicity, and her dresses burst open and bikini top fell off as if she was in a *Carry On* movie. "I didn't come to Hollywood to be the girl next door," she would later inform her studio. "I came to be a movie star."[26]

After being named *Playboy*'s Playmate of the Month in February 1955, Warner Brothers put in a preemptive offer and signed her to their studio. However, she was dropped just five months later, and reluctantly agreed to audition for the part of Rita Marlowe in the Broadway play *Will Success Spoil Rock Hunter?*[27]

Following the success of *The Seven Year Itch*, its screenwriter George Axelrod penned the play as a satire of Marilyn and when it opened on Broadway in October 1955, Jayne earned plaudits as the vacuous star Rita Marlowe who longs to be taken seriously. She had been handpicked by Axelrod, after he'd viewed hundreds of starlets at a casting. "When an agent brought in Jayne Mansfield, who had done only some cheesecake photos and a couple of movie playgirl parts, the question was answered. Jayne emerged full-blossom in the play. She was not the girl to make boys write clean words on clean fences."[28]

The role made Jayne the toast of Broadway, and she was snapped up by Twentieth Century Fox as their Marilyn replacement. They cast her in *The Girl Can't Help It* (1956), which was a huge hit among teens as the first rock 'n' roll picture that captured the youth subculture, with guest performances by Little Richard and Gene Vincent. She won a Theatre World Award for "Promising Personality" in 1956 and a Golden Globe Award for "New Star of the Year, Actress" in 1957. As much as her career was on the rise, she was determined to milk it for all she could by using her body to create a spectacle. At the premiere of Warner Bros.' *The Spirit of St. Louis* in April 1957, Jayne squeezed into the same gold dress that Marilyn infamously wore at the 1953 Photoplay Awards.[29] She also made sure she was the center of attention in 1957 at a party in Romanoff's, Beverly Hills in honor of Sophia Loren. Seated together, Sophia gives her a distasteful look as her breasts spill out of her dress, and the photo went the fifties equivalent of viral.[30]

Jayne Mansfield taking advantage of the publicity opportunities at a Hollywood dinner for Sophia Loren in 1957. *HA/THA/Shutterstock.*

It was the type of tactic that served starlets on the red carpet in the 1990s—Elizabeth Hurley made a career from a safety-pinned Versace—but in the good and bad girl dichotomy of the era, it was too much. After starring in the 1957 film adaptation of *Rock Hunter*, the *New York Times* described her cruelly—the "frankly grotesque figure and her leadpipe travesty of Marilyn Monroe."[31]

Marilyn was discovered and then made the most of her opportunities, whereas Jayne's career was very much by design. She would do anything for a bit of attention—going shopping in a leopard bikini or walking down Hollywood Boulevard with two ocelots on a leash. "She was a kooky, wild, fun-loving, and totally uninhibited girl," said her former press agent and biographer, Raymond Strait.[32]

Playboy featured Mansfield every February from 1955 to 1958, and this was used by her estranged husband Paul to portray her as an unfit mother as he sought custody of their daughter. A few years later, Jayne became the first mainstream Hollywood actress to appear nude in a film in *Promises! Promises!* (1963) despite being strongly advised against it as a bad career move. *Playboy* took still photos from the set, and these were splashed in the magazine in June 1963, with this sell-out issue quickly becoming a collectors' item. The nudity was condemned by moral groups, and it hurt her image further at a time when her career was in a slump. Still, for a few years in the late fifties, Jayne was thrilled at her new celebrity. As she told Lydia Lane, "When I left Hollywood I was so broke I couldn't treat my daughter to 10 rides on the merry-go-round, and now I have a pink mink stole, a black mink coat and I own my own home."[33] Jayne played up to the expected femininity of the era with her adoration of pink. Lynn Peril in her book *Pink Think: Becoming a Woman in Many Uneasy Lessons* describes how "Pink Think" was a concept for the consumerist and conservative fifties, when women were expected to be meek, gentle, and unquestioning of their place in the world.[34] Jayne believed that a woman should be "as soft as a kitten," with a "voice as soft as a purr," because "it's a certain feminine quality that attracts men."[35]

Pink was the color of this ideal womanhood, particularly when coupled with high-maintenance blonde hair. As part of her calculation to make herself a star, Jayne used this sweet but sickly hue as a tool to place her as the tantalizing "It" girl of flirty, ditzy femininity. "Men want women to be pink, helpless and do a lot of deep breathing," she said. "If a girl has curviness, exciting lips and a certain breathlessness, it helps. And it won't do a bit of harm if she has a kittenish, soft cuddly quality."[36]

Pink, she said, "made me happy," and she drove a pink Jaguar and lived in a home on Sunset Boulevard which she named the "Pink Palace," featuring a pink bathroom and bedroom, and a heart-shaped swimming pool.[37] She would later reflect that it had all been part of a cynical ploy for publicity. "Now I had something to intrigue the photographers. Come up for a drink and paint me pink. I'd invite anyone who had a camera. I'd add I would be happy to pose for any layouts they'd like. I was desperate. I was running out of time."[38]

While Jayne was overexposed, Marilyn embraced art and literature, aligning herself more with the intellectual beatnik movement. She wasn't the bimbo people liked to place her as, and what the imitators couldn't get right was the vulnerability. They could smolder and pout, but they didn't break hearts and illicit sympathy in the same way. "These girls who try to be me—I guess the studios put them up to it, or they get the ideas themselves," she later said.[39]

After a year in Manhattan, Marilyn signed a new contract with Fox, and her first movie as part of this deal, *Bus Stop* (1956), would be produced by her own company. Her character, Cherie, is beaten down by the world, yet she is a smarter survivor than the men, despite the initial impressions and judgments around her appearance. As well as proving her talents, it would be the perfection of the Marilyn character, where her ditsy exhibitionism, the pout, and the halo of hair were a thin mask for her fragility.

This was true of her next film, *The Prince and the Showgirl* (1957), right down to the scene-stealing antics during a press conference when the strap of her dress snapped accidentally-on-purpose, to the patronizing annoyance of co-star Laurence Olivier. It mimicked a scene in the script, when Elsie, an American showgirl in Edwardian England, suffers a wardrobe malfunction in front of Laurence Olivier's Grand Duke. It was also mirrored during a reception where Marilyn was presented to Queen Elizabeth II, whose eyes lingered just for a second on the cleavage spilling out of her dress. Jayne was perceived as desperate for these tactics, but there was something so knowingly innocent about Marilyn, that she could almost get away with it.

Marilyn arrived in England with new husband Arthur Miller to begin filming at Pinewood Studios, but her unreliable behavior on set was now legendary. Miller was shocked by her unprofessionalism, and for the first time understood how damaged she was. One day he left his notebook lying open, and when she read his words—that she wasn't the angel he initially thought, and she was a "troublesome bitch"—she was devastated.

Having had such a fractured childhood, Marilyn desired a family of her own. She and Miller tried to have a baby, but she suffered two miscarriages and an ectopic pregnancy, and with each loss she fell into despair and depression. She was advised to stay away from champagne and pills, but with her state of mind, she increasingly relied on them to get her through the day.[40]

Her next movie, *Some Like it Hot* (1959), was one of the biggest hits of the year. *Variety* said she "has never looked better," while her skills as a comedienne, "with that combination of sex appeal and timing that just can't be beat."[41] But from then on, her life toppled from the high of her popularity in the mid-fifties, to new lows.

Let's Make Love (1960) was not only considered to be a down point in her career, but there was a damaging affair with her co-star Yves Montand. She was bombarded with criticism about her weight, her age, and how long she had left to be a sex symbol. This was particularly upsetting considering she had recently suffered another miscarriage.

Hedda Hopper wrote a nasty open letter to Marilyn in *Motion Picture* magazine in July 1960, advising her patronizingly and cruelly, "Have you a complex about losing babies? You lost two unborn children, one in 1958 and the other in 1959. Is it true that, in sorrow, you even put vodka into your bouillon? . . . Marilyn, don't drink . . . it won't bring back the baby." She also chastised her for having retained her pregnancy weight. "Being overly sensitive about your weight and doing nothing about it makes no sense. You're a star and must know you can't have your cake and eat it too."[42]

Thinking he could help her recover, Miller wrote *The Misfits* (1961) for her, creating the damaged character of Roslyn as a reflection of who he perceived to be the true Marilyn, although here she was more a healer for the three male characters, rather than finding her own identity. During the making of the movie she became more dependent on alcohol and prescription drugs, and she blamed Arthur for the failure of the film and the role she hated. Her marriage fell apart, and they divorced in January 1961. She spoke of how Arthur saw the demon in her, which fed her insecurities and told her she wasn't good enough or smart enough. As her marriage to Miller broke down, she upped her pill intake, which she washed down with champagne.[43]

With her body weak with anxiety, she longed for the comfort of hazy sleep, the "womby-tomby" feeling, as she called it. In February 1961 she asked her doctor to help her find some respite, but when she was taken to the New York Hospital, she was committed to a psychiatric ward, with no access to a phone, completely stripped of power and of identity, and intrusively examined by interns and doctors who all wanted to snatch a look at the famous body. Eventually she was able to make a call to DiMaggio who immediately flew from Florida and demanded her release.[44]

Her mental state was the topic of conversation in the gossip columns, with amateur diagnoses as to what was troubling her—she was thrice-divorced, she was aging, she was childless. Once out of hospital, she set out on a mission to reevaluate her life. With all the comments on her weight, she went on a high-protein diet, and after shedding the pounds, she emerged as a svelte, chic Marilyn for the sixties, and with newly platinum blonde hair, the lightest it had ever been, which she referred to as "pillow slip white."[45]

Now that she was single once more, she was drawn into the hard-drinking, hard-partying Rat Pack circle, where she dated Frank Sinatra, and was introduced to President John F. Kennedy. She fretted about no longer being young and beautiful, but, with the president and his brother Robert F. Kennedy rumored as her lovers, it was a temporary reprieve.

With a refreshed sense of pleasure in her own appearance, Fox offered her *Something's Got to Give*, which had originally been intended for Jayne Mansfield. But with the latter star's popularity fading, it was passed to the original blonde. The script needed work, but in wardrobe tests she was a sleek, glowing Marilyn who looked better than ever.

With her frequent absences from set due to illness, the studio was losing patience with her. The final insult was her abandoning the shoot by flying to New York to perform at Madison Square Garden for President Kennedy's birthday celebrations on May 19, 1962. Everything about it helped shape the Marilyn myth—the shimmering sexuality, the breathy voice, the hint at nakedness, the blonde halo of hair, the lateness. The "It" girl had become an American icon.

For her performance, she asked French costume designer Jean Louis to create a dress "only Marilyn Monroe could wear."[46] Flesh-colored soufflé was studded with crystals to create the illusion of nudity. It further supported rumors she was having an affair with the president.

After calling in sick one too many times, Fox sacked her and filed a $750,000 lawsuit against her. To publicize Marilyn's comeback, she had taken part in a nude swimming scene, and the images were released to the press. But she was devastated at *Photoplay*'s display of the photos, released just before her death, with the question, "Daring? Is publicity—bold and blatant publicity—all that's left of Marilyn's career?" The article asked, "At 36—without a husband, a job or faith in herself—what will happen to Marilyn next?"[47]

All her problems were piling up—the humiliation of being fired, the loneliness, the desire for love and happiness which always eluded her, the worries about getting older and the loss of her looks. Marilyn turned to pills and alcohol to numb the pain and to help her sleep, and increasingly relied on her psychiatrist, Ralph Greenson, for extensive therapy sessions. Despite the feelings of hopelessness, she spent the summer of 1962 proving she could fight her way back. She arranged publicity shoots with top magazines, including interviews with *Life* and *Redbook*, and she also sat with the hot young photographer, Bert Stern, for *Vogue*, who took photos in a suite at the Hotel Bel-Air as he plied her with champagne. She ended up naked under white sheets, deliriously drunk, as she fully inhabited "Her."[48]

In the sixties, the voluptuous body was out, and it was now, thanks to the new British model Jean Shrimpton, chic to be thin. Marilyn began dressing more colorfully, in Pucci orange tops and psychedelic swirls, but having been criticized for her weight gain, she was now chastised for being too thin, and for the natural laughter lines around her eyes, as if it was a sin to show signs of mortality; for being less than an alabaster goddess.

With all the press that she was generating, Fox realized they had just thrown away one of their most valuable assets and they asked her to return to complete the movie. She agreed on the condition that she was given a new script, a new director, and that there would be new scenes that would allow her to use her skills at physical comedy.

But all that potential was lost when she was found dead in the bedroom of the bungalow she had only recently purchased, on August 4, 1962. Even after death she was scrutinized. The coroner's assistant who removed her body from the bed, commented, "She didn't look good, not like Marilyn Monroe. She looked just like a poor little girl that had died."[49]

The conspiracies around her death have helped to elevate her status beyond that of an "It" girl who became the most famous woman in the world. There were rumors that the Kennedys had been involved to hide their affairs with her, that Frank Sinatra and Peter Lawford had helped to cover it up, and each story placed her as a victim who could be manipulated, just as her life was twisted to suit the narrative. It was ruled as a suicide, but maybe it was just a tragic accident of losing count of the pills she had taken.

Marilyn Monroe died before the start of the feminist and civil rights movements, and her death, like President Kennedy's a year later, marked the end of an American way of life. The public had been intrigued by her fragility, as if she needed to be protected. But with her desire to be taken seriously, she had asked for too much. She was supposed to be a pretty, silly object, and the media turned against her, punishing her for getting older, for failing to keep a marriage and have children, and for being too emotional.

Marilyn's death placed her in a permanent icon status as her image was splashed on posters and calendars, on mugs and bags, and most famously in Andy Warhol's screenprints, where she becomes a repetition; a mass-market commodity. The photo that was used, a still from *Niagara*, placed her in that permanent state of ecstasy, with her lips parted, and the hooded, sleepy eyes that promised pleasure.

Like the wartime pin-ups and the nude photos that turned *Playboy* into a brand, Marilyn was a fantasy of idealized femininity, but she was also empowering to women who adored her image and wished to mimic it themselves.

Jayne was devastated about Marilyn's death, and it also made her aware of her own mortality as a star. She was about to turn thirty and despite all the publicity she had received—the 2,500 newspaper photographs and over 122,000 lines of newspaper copy—she had been dropped by Fox, and she had become a joke for her constant need to do "whoopsie" moments. She had met former Mr. Universe Mickey Hargitay in New York when he was a dancer for Mae West's revue show, and the two pinnacles of sculpted beauty were instantly attracted. They got married, had babies, and performed in a hit Las Vegas burlesque show together. They would continue this double-act into the sixties, with the two dressed in matching leopard Tarzan and Jane outfits as he performed acrobatics, and in one stint, lifted her over his head.

While taking advantage of Rome's La Dolce Vita with a role in the 1964 Italian movie *Panic Button*, she had an affair with an Italian producer, and it led to her and Mickey's Mexican divorce. She then discovered she was pregnant, and knowing that being an unwed mother would create further scandal, she claimed they were technically still married, and had their daughter, Mariska Hargitay, in January 1964.

She continued to capitalize on her impersonation of Marilyn. She and Mickey appeared together in a stage production of *Bus Stop* at the Yonkers Playhouse, and then toured with a production of *Gentlemen Prefer Blondes*.[50] Jayne fell for the director of these plays, Matt Cimber, and they married and had a son together, Tony. After they split, she entered into an intimate relationship with her lawyer, Sam Brody, which was abusive, controlling, and destructive. Jayne by this point had fallen into a cycle of pills, alcohol, and LSD experimentation, where she would become aggressive, throwing her diamonds about "like popcorn"[51] and then would accuse everyone in her household of stealing them. Jayne's Hollywood film career was over, her nightclubs were failing to attract audiences, and the blonde bombshell role she had cultivated was passé now that the youthful Mod fashions of The Beatles and Mary Quant were sweeping the world.

In October 1966 at the San Francisco Film Festival, she met Anton LaVey, a leading satanist, and when he and Sam Brody got into an argument, LaVey put a curse on him. He warned Jayne to distance herself from Sam, because after a series of car crashes, he predicted that the final crash would also kill anyone with him.[52]

Jayne Mansfield died in the early hours of the morning of June 29, 1967, when the car she was traveling in to take her from a supper club in Biloxi, Mississippi, to a television interview in New Orleans, slammed into the rear of a truck. She was in the front seat with Sam Brody, and in the backseat were her five children and four chihuahuas. Jayne, Sam, and the chauffeur were killed instantly as the top of the car was sliced off, but the sleeping children all escaped with cuts and bruises. Jayne hit the headlines around the world for the final time, and in one of the many reports of her death, she was described simply as "a smart girl in the tradition of Hollywood dumb blondes and sex symbols."[53]

11

The American Revolutionaries

Edie Sedgwick and Jean Seberg

Jean Seberg in 1957. Her cropped hair and bohemian attitude made her an international star. *Everett/Shutterstock.*

Think of Paris in the 1960s and one image may come to mind. Her blonde hair is dangerously cropped, she wears a striped top or a *Herald Tribune* T-shirt, and she smokes cigarettes as she speaks melancholically of her desire to be free. But she's so much more than her Parisian gamine haircut; she's a revolutionary. She's an American who reads Voltaire, she is a committed champion of social justice, and her fight for the civil rights movement will eventually lead to her destruction.

Now think of New York City in 1965 and imagine a limousine pulling up outside a nightclub. Out totters a woman in sky-high heels, her arms covered in bracelets and her short silvery mop revealing large earrings cascading from her lobes. She's the most famous girl in New York, and inside is Mick Jagger, who is waiting to meet her. As she enters the club with her entourage from Andy Warhol's Factory, crowds surge and almost swallow her, as camera flashes pop to capture that fleeting moment when her star is the brightest in the sky.

Jean Seberg and Edie Sedgwick, both famous for their cropped blonde and silvery hair, were two American icons of sixties' youth culture. Both became the poster girls for the sexual revolution, for their flouting of the conventions of the fifties in favor of a bohemian, sexually free, European way of living. Theirs was a starriness far removed from the Hollywood glamor of a generation before; of Jayne Mansfield's kittenish voice and her love of pink, of the voluptuous bodies that were symbols of soft, helpless, and compliant womanhood. This new movement was edgier, free and uninhibited, and it fetishized youth.

Both Edie and Jean's families were soaked in American tradition, with their bloodlines reaching back to the founding of the United States. Edie rejected her refined Santa Barbara upbringing in favor of squatting in New York with bohemian artists and musicians, while Jean Seberg left the puritanism of the Midwest to become a darling of the French New Wave in Paris.

With her inimitable fashion sense, Edie was Andy Warhol's superstar, a *Vogue* magazine "Youthquaker," the girl everybody wanted a piece of. But the party lifestyle led to serious drug addiction and tragedy. Jean used her fame to support political causes, but she was destroyed by her government working in collusion with the media.

Jean Seberg's origins were far removed from the glitz of Hollywood or the Left Bank bohemianism of Paris. She was a corn-fed Midwesterner, born into an ordinary middle-class family in Marshalltown, Iowa, in 1938. Her father, Edward Seberg, was a pharmacist, while her mother, whose family could be traced back to the Mayflower, worked part-time as a substitute teacher while she raised Jean and her three siblings. With their Swedish and German ancestry, their life revolved around the Lutheran church, and the sermons about the importance of charity would have a lasting effect on the sensitive girl. At the age of fourteen she applied for membership of the Iowan branch of the NAACP, a move that worried her father in case the conservative townsfolk thought she was a communist.[1]

From the age of five she wanted to be an actress, and often, as she walked along the banks of the river as a teenager, she thought of the Betty Grable movies she'd seen and dreamed of her own stardom. She composed poetry inspired by the nature that surrounded her, and in one, compared herself to "a sunflower rising from the sod."[2] Hollywood felt about as far removed from Marshalltown as you could get, but in 1956, when she was seventeen, the opportunity came tantalizingly close.

The Austrian-American director Otto Preminger, known for his boundary-pushing films including *Carmen Jones* (1954) and *The Man with the Golden Arm* (1955), launched an international talent search to find an unknown actress to play the lead in *Saint Joan*, his adaptation of the George Bernard Shaw play of the life of Joan of Arc. Eighteen thousand hopefuls applied, and Jean, without much more acting experience than school plays and New England summer stock, was overwhelmed to discover she was on the shortlist. She traveled to New York to take part in the final auditions and Preminger put her through an intense, grueling test—an ominous sign of things to come. Jean had the spirit of Joan of Arc in her desire to stand up for those without a voice, and as her eyes burned with intense feeling, she won the role.

Her discovery was the equivalent of *Star Search* or *American Idol*, and her victory was announced on *The Ed Sullivan Show* on October 21, 1956. Appearing alongside the director, wide-eyed and oatmeal-scrubbed with her hair neatly pinned up, she was more like a Hitchcock heroine in training than the countercultural icon she would become. Marshalltown's residents were so proud of their local success story that they celebrated her newfound stardom with a homecoming parade.

As the *New York Times* reported: "Introduced to the press yesterday, Miss Seberg proved to be a personification of the Cinderella story. A slim, five-foot four-inch, green eyed miss, whose brown hair has been closely cropped for her screen test, she had acted professionally in only five productions last summer."[3]

She flew to London in October 1956 to begin production, but for a teen-age girl with no experience of how movies were made, it was daunting to be surrounded by an older male cast and crew. Rather than explaining the processes of filmmaking, Preminger berated and bullied her into giving the performance he wanted. The tension became more and more extreme until she was seriously injured while filming the crucial burning-at-the-stake scene. Tied by chains above a burning pyre while a baying crowd of extras looked on, something went wrong with the pyrotechnics as the flames seared her eyebrows, her stomach, and hands. She managed to break free and the crew eventually came to her rescue, but it would leave her with permanent physical scars.

Jean had been embarrassed by the huge amount of press attention after winning the part, and after such a buildup, she was devastated by audience walk-outs and savage reviews when *Saint Joan* was released in June 1957. Viewers found it boring, and critics like those at the *New York Times* described her performance, for all its sincerity, as "callow and unconvincing in a long, difficult and complex part."[4]

The immediate reaction in film circles was to attribute the failure of *Saint Joan* to Jean by writing her off as a hopeless amateur.

She would later say, "I have two memories of Saint Joan. The first was being burned at the stake in the picture. The second was being burned at the stake by the critics."[5]

As part of her contract with Preminger, and before the devastating reviews of *Saint Joan*, she was cast in *Bonjour Tristesse*, an adaptation of Françoise Sagan's cult novel set in Paris and St. Tropez. She arrived in Paris for her costume fittings with Hubert de Givenchy, and while the androgyny of her crew-cut hair had been confusing in America, among the fashionistas of Paris it was gamine chic. The designer persuaded her to crop it rather than grow it out and this hairstyle would come to represent a new bohemian, countercultural femininity.

Given a month to relax in the south of France before filming began, Jean soaked up the easy Mediterranean atmosphere in St. Tropez pavement cafés drinking Pastis and reading classic literature. The respite wouldn't last long as Preminger continued to berate her on set, wrongly thinking this was the way to get the best performance out of her. She was young, inexperienced, and terrified of the older director and she was burdened with anxiety around how disappointing she must be. There were rumors that having divorced his wife, he had his eye on Jean as a "beauty and the beast" love affair, and this further made her feel exposed and ashamed.

"That was a bad time for me. *Confidential* magazine came out with a piece about me and Preminger entitled 'Svengali and the Druggist's Daughter.' It was horrible. My father saw one of the first copies in his own drugstore," she said in 1963. "He was so disturbed, he ran around the whole town buying up all the copies and then burning them. It was a bad, sad time."[6]

The film proved to be another disappointment and the negative reviews threatened to end her career. Rather than return to Hollywood, she embraced friendships with Paris bohemians Françoise Sagan and Juliette Gréco who glowed with youth and symbolized all that was modern and free about the city.

She further escaped from the difficulties of fame with François Moreuil, a French lawyer and cousin of director William Wyler. They were married in September 1958 at the same Marshalltown Lutheran church she had taught Sunday school, and the wedding was billed as the city's social event of the year.

They settled in Paris, and even though she felt like a twenty-year-old has-been, she decided that even if no American producer would touch her "with a 10-foot pole,"[7] she'd try again in France. "I had learned discipline from Preminger. Now I learned mime from Etienne Decroux, who taught Marcel Marceau. I took French lessons, acting lessons, voice lessons. I cultivated the society in Paris of directors, writers, actors. I absorbed from everyone."[8]

She felt alive and appreciated in Paris. She wasn't just some talentless starlet who got lucky. She soaked up literature and art, reading Tolstoy, Pushkin, Flaubert,[9] and the hot new directors of New Wave (or *Nouvelle-Vague*) cinema now admired and wanted her. The French critics, with an eye for the avant-garde, had been drawn to her freshness and unrefined performance in *Bonjour Tristesse* (1958) as the immoral, hedonistic young woman who plots the demise of her father's new lover, played by Deborah Kerr. As François Truffaut, one of the leading figures of the emerging *Nouvelle-Vague* filmmaking revolution, wrote in *Cahiers du Cinéma* in February 1958, "you can't look at anything else. . . . The shape of her silhouette, her walk; everything is perfect: This kind of sex appeal hasn't been seen on the screen."

Jean Seberg's image would be forever connected with her role in Jean-Luc Godard's debut, *Breathless* (1960) as Jean-Paul Belmondo's American girlfriend, Patricia. *Breathless* was shot around Paris on a handheld camera and a shoestring budget, and Godard's guerilla style, with the nonlinear narrative and jump-cut editing, would shift the rules of filmmaking. It was raw and unpolished, and Jean, with her short blonde hair, the cool wardrobe, and the unfiltered realness, appealed to a new generation looking to see beneath the gloss.

Patricia is an American in Paris who is supposed to be studying at the Sorbonne, but dreams of owning a Dior dress and finds herself equally drawn to and afraid of Belmondo's criminal. She is completely disaffected in her statement that "I don't know if I'm unhappy because I'm not free, or if I'm not free because I'm unhappy."

Her ambivalently immoral character may have struggled with that dilemma, but for young Americans she was the epitome of European freedom and of the navel-gazing Existentialist movement that defined Parisian chic. She was the female equivalent of James Dean in *Rebel Without a Cause*, and this role, and its angst, would define her as she returned to Paris time and again to run away from her own troubles. "Life took me there and I just kind of stayed," she said in 1968. "After St. Joan, the New Wave boys defended me. They found out I needed money and work."[10]

American tourists poured into Paris, hoping to catch sight of Jean, or beatniks like her, in the pavement cafés and bookstores of the Left Bank. After the success of *Breathless*, the French-American production *In the French Style* (1963) took advantage of her status as an Existentialist sweetheart grappling with her identity.

By this time her marriage was disintegrating, and she sought divorce on grounds of cruelty. She found comfort with Romain Gary, a French diplomat and writer who was twenty-six years her senior and married to author Lesley Blanch. She latched onto him as a protective figure at a time when she was struggling with fame, and she gave birth to their son, Alex, in July 1962, having kept her pregnancy a secret from almost everyone.

With her vulnerability in *Breathless* seared in his mind, Director Robert Rossen knew that he wanted her to be the beautiful, disturbed asylum inmate in *Lilith* (1964) opposite Warren Beatty. Rossen described her as "a fine instinctive actress of depth and power" who "looks like one of those girls who goes house-to-house selling Girl Scout cookies."[11] In the early sixties, as women were breaking from the shackles of domesticity, and with the introduction of the contraceptive pill welcoming a more permissive era, films like *Lilith* reflected societal concerns over young women. These were cautionary tales warning that they were being driven to nymphomania and psychosis due to the pressures of the sexual revolution and the call for feminism. And the real-life "It" girls like Jean and Edie Sedgwick would be used by the media to hammer home this point.

Edie always knew she was special. She may have been the seventh of eight children, born in 1943 to Alice Delano de Forest, daughter of a Southern Pacific Railroad executive, and Francis Minturn Sedgwick, of the prominent Massachusetts Sedgwick family, but she was sure she was the favorite. Her class-conscious parents, WASPs who followed all the rules and etiquette of their class, had the aura of Greek gods in their tennis whites, but they were also as cold as the bronze statues her artist father spent his days creating.

One of her ancestors, Theodore Sedgwick, was a speaker of the House of Representatives under Thomas Jefferson and signed the Declaration of Independence. Another, her father's aunt whom she was named after, was a noted beauty who sat for John Singer Sargent. Being a muse was in her blood.

Her parents moved from Cold Spring Harbor, New York, to Santa Barbara before she was born, and owned a succession of vast ranches around California, one of which struck oil. Edie adored horses, and she loved the freedom of riding alone on the ranch as a respite from the stifling rules at home. Her father, known as "Fuzzy" or the "Duke," was cruel and domineering and held exacting standards of beauty. He was also a philanderer who didn't hide his love affairs and was abusive to his children.

Edie's prevalent memories were of her father's sexual advances from the age of seven, and later, that one of her brothers suggested they sleep together. "The fact that I find it hard to believe doesn't mean some of it couldn't have been true," wrote her sister, Alice Sedgwick Wohl, in her 2023 biography of Edie.[12]

One afternoon, Edie walked in on her father having sex with a woman who wasn't her mother, and she fell into hysterics at the confusion of what she was seeing. She tried to explain to her mother, but she wasn't believed; instead, her father told her she had imagined it, and even called a doctor who gave her tranquilizers. She was forced to question her own mind under a haze of drugs, and this angst would have a long-lasting effect on her sense of reality.

Edie's brother Jonathan recounted how their mother coped with their father's affairs by going on special diets and declaring she suffered food allergies. Her father was a binge eater, consuming vast amounts of food that he burned off with exercise, and Edie began copying this behavior, veering between anorexia and bulimia, which she called "pigging" and which resulted in her being taken out of school to stay at the ranch, alone with her parents.[13] Even though she said her father kept her housebound like a princess in a gothic novel, Alice said she "grew up with a total lack of boundaries, a total lack of a sense of scale about her."[14]

In 1958 Edie arrived at St. Timothy's boarding school in Maryland, and with her aura of glamor and charm, she immediately shone as the new girl everyone wanted to be friends with. But her golden status quickly shifted as she began to get into trouble for contravening uniform regulations, wearing sneakers instead of saddle shoes, and flying into anger during arguments. What her classmates didn't know was that she was in the grips of anorexia and in 1962 she was admitted to Silver Hill psychiatric hospital in Connecticut to treat her disorders.[15]

This was the same hospital her adored older brother Minty had been admitted for alcoholism at fifteen, and when he killed himself in 1964, it would have a profound effect on her. She seemed to be doing well at Silver Hill, until she had an affair with another patient, a Harvard grad who she lost her virginity to, and which resulted in a pregnancy. She was able to get an abortion due to her psychiatric care, but again it placed further emotional confusion and trauma on her. As she told David Weisman, director of *Ciao! Manhattan*, her last movie, "it wasn't too good a first experience with lovemaking. I mean, it kind of screwed up my head, for one thing."[16]

Released from the hospital, she swept into Cambridge, Massachusetts, in the fall of 1963 in her gray Mercedes, as if she was straight out of a fashion commercial. As an art student at Radcliffe, she spent her days molding clay sculptures with her elegant, nicotine-stained fingers, and developing a reputation as the prettiest, and richest, girl in town. Reeling from the trauma of her abortion and childhood abuse, she surrounded herself with a safe circle of gay men, which included Ed Hennessy and Chuck Wein, a Harvard student who dressed like an English teddy boy.[17]

She found Cambridge too stifling, and instead she was drawn to the gleaming mecca of insomniacs, New York City, with a plan to become a model. It was the summer of 1964, and having just turned twenty-one she could now access her trust fund and moved into her grandmother's apartment on Park Avenue. This was no slum-dwelling arrival in the city; it was uptown luxury. She went on spending sprees draped in her leopard-skin fur coat worth tens of thousands of dollars, and which must have been paid for by her parents, and she arrived by limousine at the city's new youth-focused discotheques that were replacing the café society hubs like El Morocco and the Stork Club.

She hit the nightspots in the same outfit she wore to dance training—a black leotard and T-shirt worn with tights, with a white mink or leopard print coat thrown over the top; the ballerina of the gutter meets WASP socialite. She had long chestnut hair, she lined her eyes with dark kohl and layers of spidery eyelashes, and she always finished the look with a pair of chandelier earrings. Whenever Edie walked into a room, or took to the dance floor to perform the twist, everyone turned to watch.

The date was March 26, 1965, the event was Tennessee Williams's birthday party at producer Lester Persky's loft, and the star attraction was Edie, sucking up the attention as she danced her fusion of ballet and rock 'n' roll, made even more dramatic because her leg was in a cast after having crashed her Porsche. When Andy Warhol arrived with his entourage, he was immediately struck by her, pronouncing all the syllables of "beautiful" for dramatic effect. The meeting had been a setup; Persky thought Edie could be the next superstar that Warhol had been looking for.

The artist, born Andrew Warhola to a working-class Slovakian family in Pittsburgh, had long been fascinated with celebrity and the construction of the "It" girl. Andy suffered illness as a child, and so his overprotective and widowed mother confined him to his room. To entertain himself he pored over movie magazines, sketching the adverts and glossy glamor portraits of stars like Hedy Lamarr.

After graduating from Carnegie Institute of Technology in 1949 he moved to New York to make his name as an artist and commercial illustrator. In

1962 he was taught silk screen printing, and he was drawn to the idea that the repetition of printing could turn an ordinary household product into an icon.

The Campbell's Soup Cans exhibition in July 1962 was his breakthrough, closing in Los Angeles the day before Marilyn Monroe was found dead. With foresight that her death would make her even more famous as an object, he immortalized her with his series of silk screen prints, "Marilyn Diptych" and "Gold Marilyn Monroe" from 1962 and "Shot Marilyns," in 1964, all based on the *Niagara* still. Andy's Avant Garde expressionism was attracting a coterie of bohemians who latched onto him and helped with his prints. He created a studio in a loft on East Forty-Seventh Street which, as the Factory, would be a notorious gathering place for artists, models, musicians, and hangers-on.

Warhol liked to bring a charismatic young woman into his circle and turn her into his "Girl of the Year." Baby Jane Holzer had, for a time, been the one. Like Edie, she came from privilege but liked to slum it among the downtown artists, and under Warhol's tutelage, the word "Superstar" was invented for her. She was a glittering, lion-mane blonde, and Tom Wolfe profiled in her in the *New York Herald Tribune* as a new celebrity, one who shaped what was fashionable for a lightning-bolt moment. "To the magazine editors, the newspaper columnists, the photographers and art directors, suddenly here is a single flamboyant girl who sums up everything new and chic in the way of fashion."[18]

Baby Jane was drifting away from the drug-fueled craziness of the Factory, where speed was the narcotic of the moment, and Andy was losing interest. Impressed by Edie's energy, Warhol invited her to the Factory the next day, and immediately drew Edie into his fold. In return she mimicked his look by chopping off her brunette hair, bleaching it and spraying it silver, as if they were now two fashionable freaks for the Space Age.

Warhol saw a reflection of Edie in his Marilyn screenprints. She had the translucent skin, the smoky eyes, and the alluring smile that masked "more problems than anybody I'd ever met." He found her to be "so beautiful but so sick. I was really intrigued."[19]

Buoyed by the French New Wave, Andy Warhol experimented with filmmaking by producing underground movies that starred his followers. Rather than a narrative, he aimed to "find great people and let them be themselves and talk about what they usually talked about and I'd film them for a certain length of time and that would be the movie."[20] It was an early prototype of reality television where he believed "everyone will be world-famous for fifteen minutes." Baby Jane had been the reality star for a moment, but Edie was now the focus. She "didn't need a script," he said, "if she'd needed a script, she wouldn't have been right for the part."[21]

He understood that a true star was never fully the character they played, rather the audience wanted to see their real self on screen. To be Marilyn, he said, "was to be a star, incandescent and otherworldly, but also to be Norma Jean Baker, a human being, ordinary and dull, trapped inside a star. This is the predicament of all stars, of course, only Marilyn was the first to reveal it."[22]

Andy's new movie *Vinyl* (1965), an adaptation of Anthony Burgess's novel, *A Clockwork Orange*, featured an all-male cast, but for one scene set to Martha and the Vandellas' "Nowhere to Run," he couldn't resist bringing Edie into the shot. Her movements were understated; all she did was smoke and dance while sitting on a couch, but the blonde in the background with the leopard print belt was captivating.

Next he cast her as the star of *Poor Little Rich Girl*, designed to be a day in the life of a socialite. Filmed in her own apartment, she wakes up, drinks coffee and smokes, puts on her makeup and knocks back pills. In *Beauty No. 2*, she lies in bed in her underwear with the actor Gino Piserchio kissing and stroking her, as Andy asks her intrusive questions, as if he's scrutinizing her position as an overexposed "It" girl and wishes to shatter her surface.

Edie Sedgwick and Andy Warhol arrive at Vidal Sassoon's New York launch party in 1966. *ANL/Shutterstock.*

In April 1965, Lester Persky held a drug-fueled party for "the Fifty Most Beautiful People," which went on until 5 p.m. the next day. The guest list included Montgomery Clift, William Burroughs, and Tennessee Williams, who arrived with Judy Garland on his arm, but, according to one of the Factory regulars, Robert Olivo, also known as Ondine, no one paid any attention to Judy, even when she was doing the twist with Rudolf Nureyev. The only one they wanted to see was Edie.[23]

She had achieved celebrity in such a short space of time that she was featured in *Vogue* in August 1965 to demonstrate the new "youthquakers"—an expression that had been coined by the magazine's editor-in-chief Diana Vreeland to capture the sweeping youth movement that was shaping fashion, art, and music. It was fabulous to be young, and in the editorial, Edie, described as "white-haired with anthracite-black eyes and legs to swoon over," was photographed in her apartment, performing arabesques in her leotard, while balancing on her leather rhino footstool.

There was also a feature in *Life* magazine in November 1965 which dubbed her "The Girl with the Black Tights," and declared:

> This cropped-mop girl with the eloquent legs is doing more for black tights than anybody since Hamlet. She is Edie Sedgwick, a 22-year-old New York socialite, great-granddaughter of the founder of Groton and currently the "superstar" of Andy Warhol's underground movies. She used to wear her tights with only a T-shirt for a top but lately has taken to wearing them with mid-thigh-length dresses—"the simplest, stretchiest ones I can find." Her style may not be for everybody, but its spirited wackiness is just right for lively girls with legs like Edie's.[24]

On October 7, 1965, Edie made a brief, and late, entrance to the private view of Warhol's first solo exhibition of his work at the Philadelphia Institute of Contemporary Art. There was a heavy rainstorm that night, and by 8 p.m. the VIPs had still not arrived. The other guests had been waiting for three hours, consuming cocktails as they studied the Marilyn, Elvis, and Jacqueline Kennedy prints, blocks of wood painted as Brillo pads, apple juice, and cornflakes, and a reproduction of a newspaper photograph of a car crash, which was impossible to look away from. Eventually Edie and Andy sailed in at 8:15 p.m. and only stayed for fifteen minutes.[25]

For the official opening the next night, the crowd waiting outside roared in appreciation, chanting "Edie and Andy! Edie and Andy!" as the stars rolled up again. Andy did little in front of the camera, but Edie, described as the artist's "deb disciple," shrilled "*Foufou*," French for "Crazy," as she surveyed the cheering crowds who jostled for their attention as if they were the Beatles.[26]

She may have been doused with stardust, but she was struggling with her demons. Eighteen months after Minty killed himself, another brother, Bobby, who also had a history of mental illness, fatally crashed his motorbike into a bus, either by accident or on purpose. The grief consumed her, and her only relief was the special vitamin shots administered by a doctor who followed the same modus operandi as Max Jacobson, or "Dr. Feelgood." The notorious medic to the stars in Hollywood created an energy-boosting formula loaded with methedrine. The shots weren't cheap, and Edie and her Factory cohorts waited in line at the doctor's office for their injections. She had dabbled in acid, but the speed gave her orgasmic energy and she never wanted to come down. She forced herself to sleep with downers, and then, when she woke up in the late morning, she would take some amphetamines in her coffee, do balletic exercises in her leotard while listening to *La Traviata* and the Beatles, until she came alive. She would then get ready, putting on her earrings and applying heavy black lashes like batwings, and taking phone calls to set up photo shoots. For this brief spell, Edie was on top. As she glittered under the lights from the gold dust she applied to her face and body, the idea of pure stardom, like that of Marilyn Monroe and Greta Garbo, thrilled her.

At the same time, her life was chaos. The speed addicts who were supposedly her friends stole her jewelry, expensive furs, and designer clothing. She was consumed with fears that she wasn't good enough, and having flown into the flames of fame, she was destined to destroy herself.

She made eleven films with Andy in four months, including *Lupe*, which explored the life of tragic Mexican Lupe Vélez, but the relationship was becoming strained, and it would reach a breaking point with the introduction of Bob Dylan in December 1965. The folk singer had been told he should meet this "terrific girl" and they arranged a date at the bar upstairs at the trendy Kettle of Fish on MacDougal Street.[27]

She sought anyone who could temporarily fix the pain, and there was a fleeting affair with Dylan, and all sorts of promises around making a film together. The folk singer couldn't stand the speed freaks of the Factory scene and persuaded her to distance herself from the crowd. To her devastation, their relationship couldn't go any further because he had secretly married Sara Lownds just months before.[28] Warhol cruelly broke the news to her, and as the color in her face drained, she walked out of the artist's life. Bob Dylan wrote the unflattering "Leopard-Skin Pill-Box Hat" about Edie, along with other songs supposedly inspired by her on his album *Blonde on Blonde*.

To further spite Edie for leaving him, Andy Warhol also found a new girl, Ingrid von Scheflin, and after shearing and dyeing her hair blonde like Edie's, he named her Ingrid Superstar. But Ingrid's worship was only fleeting. Instead, Warhol's next "Girl of the Year" was the German singer Nico, whom he put in his 1966 movie *Chelsea Girls* in place of Edie, and which proved to be his first commercially successful film.

After splitting from Andy, and the plans to work with Dylan's manager fell through, Edie focused in on fashion work. She worked as a fittings model for Betsey Johnson's boutique Paraphernalia, which sold hip fashions that followed the youthquake trends for futurism and psychedelia.

At *Vogue*, editor-in-chief Diana Vreeland gave her a makeover for a photo-spread in the March 1966 edition. Her hair was long and blonde, her makeup softer, and she laughed naturally as she posed in a black slip and black chemise worn with Givenchy stockings.

"She had a little dance step in her walk; she was so happy with the world. She was charming. She suggested springtime and freshness," Vreeland remembered.[29]

She was also profiled in *Women's Wear Daily* in April 1966 as a fashion revolutionary alongside Baby Jane Holzer and troubled socialite Tiger Morse. But if Edie was going to be protected as a *Vogue* regular, the idea was dropped when it was realized there was too much negative gossip and that her deep involvement in the drug scene would reflect badly on a magazine that propagated wholesome values.

In March 1967 she began work on the film *Ciao! Manhattan*, which was conceived by Chuck Wein and Factory regulars John Palmer and David Weisman as a semi-autobiographical, avant-garde account of Edie. She played the semi-fictional Susan Superstar, and spoke to the camera about her own life as it spiraled. She was now living in the infamous Hotel Chelsea, where Warhol had filmed her for the deleted scenes from *Chelsea Girls*. In the grips of her addiction, she would often be so out of it that her lit cigarettes would spark fires. One evening the blaze was so severe that she was badly burned and her cat, ironically named Smoke, was killed. The incident led to her hospitalization, and given her mental deterioration, work on *Ciao! Manhattan* was suspended.

Meanwhile, Warhol's Factory was coming to the end of its halcyon days. After being evicted from the building because it was scheduled for demolishment, the group moved into a loft at 33 Union Square. Here, on June 3, 1968, he was shot by Valerie Solanas, a fringe member and radical feminist who responded violently when he rejected her script. At the same time as he lay in hospital in critical condition, Senator Robert Kennedy was also being treated for gunshot wounds in Los Angeles. Kennedy died, and Warhol pulled through, but both these moments of violence were an awakening; that the youthful sixties dream of peace and love was tarnished.

Jean Seberg had been nominated for a Golden Globe Award for *Lilith*, and it marked a turning point for her to be taken seriously in Hollywood. As part of her Hollywood comeback, she won the female lead in *Paint Your Wagon* (1969) the western musical starring Lee Marvin and Clint Eastwood. Rex

Reed interviewed Jean while filming in the wilderness of Oregon, where she told him "I feel like an American again for the first time this summer, being here near the farm country." She was, he said, the "golden sunflower girl from Marshalltown, Iowa, who was a star at 18 and an unemployable has-been at 20" and was now "very much back indeed."[30]

Jean had been re-created as an angsty and intellectual adopted Parisian, and now, back in Hollywood, it was important for her to be seen as the all-American girl. Highlighting her credentials as a bona fide Midwesterner, he wrote: "If you expect a jaded, bonne vivante who leads philosophical discussions in the innovational techniques of Jean-Luc Godard, forget it. She gets handwritten letters from Andre Malraux, wears Yves St Laurent to eat hamburgers, beats Francoise Sagan at poker and is married to Romain Gary, but the darling of Breathless is American as a boysenberry."[31]

Paint your Wagon was a box-office disappointment, but she followed it with the smash hit ensemble movie *Airport* (1970). Yet this new turn as a Hollywood star was set to come crashing down on her. In 1968, Jean was seated next to activist Hakim Jamal on a flight to Los Angeles. He was closely associated with the Black Panthers, and after hearing about the community work the group were involved in, including providing meals for students at Compton schools, she was moved to donate money. The social consciousness of her Lutheran childhood had stayed with her as an adult, and now that she had money, she wanted to put it to good use. Some of her altruism included providing loans to filmmakers in Europe and buying a house for Black students to live in Marshalltown while attending Iowa Valley community college, although it had caused alarm among some of the city's white residents. She was one of the first Hollywood activists to speak on major civil rights issues, although she would downplay it by ruefully calling herself "the poor man's Jane Fonda."[32] Jane had also moved to Paris, married a French man, director Roger Vadim, and actively protested the Vietnam War and the civil rights movements.

Jean's donations to the Black Panthers were flagged to the FBI, and they began monitoring her actions. The agency's director, J. Edgar Hoover, who took a particular interest, wrote that she "should be neutralized."[33] When they found out, through bugging her home, that she was expecting a second child with Romain Gary, they came up with a plan to feed gossip to the papers that the child wasn't Gary's but had been fathered by a Black Panther.

The FBI sent a cable from its Los Angeles office to Hoover on April 27, 1970, that "the possible publication of Seberg's plight could cause her embarrassment and serve to cheapen her image with the general public."[34]

On May 19, 1970, *Los Angeles Times* columnist Joyce Haber wrote a blind item about "Miss A," the beautiful blonde who was "the current 'A' topic of chatter" because she is "expecting," and "Papa's said to be a rather prominent Black Panther."[35]

Newsweek, in an article in August 1970, outright named Jean when sharing the scandal, and the stress to Jean was so overwhelming that she overdosed on sleeping pills. She went into premature labor and her baby girl Nina died a few days later. She buried her back in Marshalltown, where she insisted that the public view the body in a casket to show that she was white.[36] It was later revealed that Nina was the daughter of a Mexican revolutionary, Carlos Ornelas Navarra, whom she had an affair with while filming *Macho Callahan* in Durango over the winter of 1969.

"It's hard to keep track of the leading ladies on the pop scene—they come and go so fast that nobody ever stops to wonder what happened to last year's girl. Or even last week's girl," wrote the *New York Post* at the beginning of May 1968. "Like, who has lately thought 'Whatever happened to Edie Sedgwick?'"[37]

She wasn't on many people's minds because she was a patient at the private, Upper East Side Gracie Square Hospital after having a drug-induced breakdown. She was still an inmate when her father died and by the time her mother brought her back to California in late 1968, she could hardly walk or speak. There were spells in Santa Barbara, where she fell in with a hippie group, and after being caught by the police with drugs she was put on probation for five years and placed in the town's Cottage Hospital.

Fellow patients remembered that Edie kept a notebook full of photographs and newspaper clippings of herself, so that she could prove to the others that she was *the* Edie Sedgwick. She always had to be the star of the hospital, doing outrageous acts such as shrieking loudly or gorging down multiple meals at once.[38]

By 1970 she felt well enough to pick up work on *Ciao! Manhattan*. Her once cropped silvery hair was now long and brunette, and having felt self-conscious of her flat chest, she had breast implants put in. To excuse the difference in the footage from three years before, she explained that she was eating better, but in reality she could barely deliver her lines. In one scene in *Ciao! Manhattan* she receives electric shock treatment, and in a case of art imitating life, she ended up back in hospital receiving the treatment for real.

While at Santa Barbara Cottage Hospital she had met actor Michael Post, who believed he could save her from her drugs and alcohol addiction. They married at the Sedgwick's Rancho La Laguna in July 1971, her hair long and loose as a bohemian bride in white. They spent the summer on the beach in Santa Barbara, nude sunbathing as she dreamed of her future, of having babies and making movies. But still, she relied on drugs to help her sleep, often pretending she'd lost batches of pills to get further prescriptions.

The night of November 15, 1971, had seemed like a regular evening. Edie attended a fashion show at Santa Barbara Museum of Art, but at the after-party, she was visibly drunk and got into an argument with another guest who called her a drug addict. She phoned Michael to collect her, and back at the apartment, he administered her usual prescribed dose of pills, and she fell into a deep, rattle-breathed sleep. The next morning, unable to rouse her, Michael realized she had died in the night. It would be recorded as an acute barbiturate overdose.

Her death didn't make the news until over a week later, but in a piece in the *Boston Globe*, David Weisman, producer of *Ciao! Manhattan*, described her as "the predominant life-style of the youth of the nation. Few kids today even know who Edie was, but they'd be completely different if she hadn't lived."[39]

Her name recognition may have faded by the early seventies, but her death would place her in the tragic realm of Marilyn Monroe and Clara Bow, whose candid honesty exposed their personal traumas. Edie's name symbolized not only being an "It" girl, but a manufactured superstar who exposed herself on camera as the first reality celebrity.

Her sister Alice insisted Edie was not a victim. She was "more like a feral creature springing out of captivity," who had been spoiled by her huge trust funds. And just as Warhol had predicted, her status as an "It" girl was heightened by an increase in media consumption and a worship of celebrity, as she scrambled for meaning through fame and drugs.[40]

In April 1971, Jean Seberg and Romain Gary brought libel suits against *Newsweek* and two French publications for spreading the gossip about the paternity of her daughter, and she was awarded $8,333 in damages. But it was too late to fix the harm to her mental health. In a 1974 interview with the *New York Times*, she said she had "cracked up" after her baby's death, and Gary would later claim that "every year on the anniversary of this stillbirth, she had tried to take her own life."[41]

The trauma was too much for their marriage, and after their divorce she married director Dennis Berry in 1972, before separating in 1976. As she struggled to maintain her emotional stability, she spent her nights in Paris's nightclubs, drinking heavily and dancing, and bantering with people, "don't you know who I am?" There was a pseudo-marriage to a nineteen-year-old Algerian actor, Ahmed Hasni, whom she clung to as her keeper and companion against her extreme loneliness. When he persuaded her to sell one of her Paris apartments and then kept the proceeds for himself to open a Moroccan restaurant, she claimed to friends that he was abusive and that she wanted to get away from him. On August 30, 1979, forty-year-old Jean was reported missing from her apartment. [42]

Her car was located eleven days later, with her decomposing body in the backseat, naked and covered by a blanket. Having gone unnoticed for many days in the baking sun, a suicide note was clutched in her hand, and she lay next to a tub of barbiturates and an empty bottle of water. As her biographer David Richards wrote, "It was a macabre ending to a destiny that at one point appeared to have been charted by the fan magazines . . . a miraculous incarnation of the American dream." A year before she had lamented to Dennis Berry's mother, "I used to be a little princess. They'd come and get me in black limousines. They don't come anymore."[43]

Romain Gary held a blistering news conference in Paris where he railed against the collusion of the FBI and the press. "Jean Seberg was destroyed by the FBI," he said, as he outlined the full story, which hadn't been made public before.[44] Gary killed himself fifteen months after her death, leaving their son an orphan at eighteen.

Ed Seberg, who had been so protective of his daughter and the gossip around her personal life that had been splashed across the tabloids in his drugstore, only learned she was dead when tuning into the radio to hear a football game. Despite her family wishing for her to be returned to Iowa, she was buried at Montparnasse Cemetery in Paris, on Gary's insistence. Her father released a statement to the press: "Jean attempted all her life to help and comfort any who were in need. She lived her convictions until the people in our world showed they did not understand her convictions. Then she gave up."[45]

Her hometown, who had wrapped a collective protective arm around her when they saw the open casket, felt great sympathy as to how tough the celebrity world could be.

Her peers, Larry Nichols, a forty-year-old factory worker who had once played her son in a high school drama, spoke to the *Los Angeles Times* shortly after her death: "I can see now that she should never have left Marshalltown. It was familiar, it was friendly." And Shirley Borton, a thirty-eight-year-old waitress, agreed. "You take a small-town girl out into that kind of world and you know what happens? It ruins her, that's what happens. This time it was the government."

It was hard not to see the parallels between her own tragic life and the martyred heroine of her film debut, and it was also impossible not to make a connection between the "It" girls who had come before. As another local told the press, "I guess she was one of those people who comes all unhinged when their star starts to fade. You had Marilyn Monroe, and now you have Jean Seberg."[46]

12

Twiggy, Jean Shrimpton, and the Mod Look

Twiggy photographed in 1967 by Zdenko Hirschler. *Zdenko Hirschler/Shutterstock.*

Walking down Fifth Avenue over the Easter weekend in 1967 was a young woman with skinny legs poking out from under a white fur coat, a short sweep of blonde hair framing a freckled face and huge spider-lashed eyes. She was so different from the other women in their Jackie Kennedy suits and bouffant hair that passersby turned to gawp.

"Bambi meets ET" was how Twiggy would later refer to herself, and the seventeen-year-old model, straight out of Swinging London, had arrived in New York to a whirl of publicity, as she dominated every newspaper and magazine as the biggest British import since the Beatles. She was named as "The Girl of 1967" and "The Paper Girl," because, as Twiggy recounted, "She's like fashion. The big thing of the moment, but you'll be able to crumple her up and throw her away like a piece of paper."[1]

Those whose heads swiveled at the sight of her couldn't believe how startingly *thin* she was, and it was this thinness that was so synonymous with the look of the sixties. She would stick out her tongue, cross her eyes, move her angular body to the backbeat of the mod sound, and her voice sounded every bit the Cockney "bird" that she was.

Twiggy's discovery coincided with London being named the hippest city in the world by *Time* magazine in April 1966. In the now legendary "Swinging City" feature, with colorful images of youthful fashion on Carnaby Street, it said: "Ancient elegance and new opulence are all tangled up in a dazzling blur of op and pop. The city is alive with birds [girls] and beatles, buzzing with mini-cars and telly stars, pulsing with half a dozen separate veins of excitement."[2]

The secret was out that London was the epicenter of switched-on style, but the look that was now dominating the world with the introduction of its latest "It" girl was brewed in the previous, less "swinging" decade. In 1955 Mary Quant and husband Alexander Plunkett-Greene threw open the doors to London's first fashion boutique, Bazaar, located in the heart of Chelsea. Quant was part of a wave of young Brits taking advantage of the grants to study at art colleges, and she honed a fresh style that offered a nod to the bohemianism of the Arts and Crafts movement and to the freedoms of the flapper.

Conditions in Britain were desperate as the country struggled to recover from the sacrifices of the war. With food rationing still in place up until 1954, there was a scarcity of essentials like butter, eggs, and meat, there was limited hot water and electricity due to coal shortages, and London's foggy streets were still blitzed out with piles of rubble due to a lack of money in being able to rebuild.

"Young people had nowhere to go to keep warm except the cinema, and nothing to do," said Quant. "We dreamt of America. We knew we had to do things ourselves, or nothing would happen at all."[3]

The American culture of the fifties had worshipped the voluptuous—a push for femininity with the comfortably maternal body of large breasts and hips, but young Brits were waif-like due to the food restrictions. As founder of fashion label Biba, Barbara Hulanicki recalled: "The postwar babies had

been deprived of nourishing protein in childhood and grew up into beautiful skinny people. A designer's dream. It didn't take much for them to look
outstanding."[4]

By 1959 the economy was strengthening, employment was low, and the
country was entering into a period of affluence. With the end of National
Service in 1960, and with increased leisure time and disposal income, the
Baby Boomer generation was freer than ever before. The Mod subculture
had emerged from London's rubble as a provocative, style-conscious
movement created by, and for, young people, and they chose to express
themselves through art, film, fashion, photography, and music. The Mods
thought the height of insolent cool was French films, Italian espresso bars,
American jazz, and Mary Quant's "Chelsea Look," which was a poptastic,
colorful celebration of active youth. Her customers became known as "dolly
birds" and as they paraded in their shorter skirts and colorful tights, out-
raged Mayfair gentlemen in bowler hats would beat on the shop windows
with their umbrellas shouting "Immoral!" and "Disgusting!"[5] The clash
between traditional morality and the new permissiveness was exemplified
by model Christine Keeler and her scandalous affair with politician John
Profumo, which shook up the establishment when it hit the headlines in
1963.

The first model and "It" girl for this new London was Jean Shrimpton, after
her fawn-like beauty caught the attention of David Bailey, a charming East
End wide boy who was making a name for himself as a maverick fashion
photographer.

"If the world of the mid-60's belongs to the young she is their symbol and
fashion-plate," stated the introduction to her 1964 autobiography. "She is the
one they identify themselves with. Gamine or goddess, she is the one they
wish to be."[6]

Jean Shrimpton, known as "The Shrimp" for her slim figure (a term she
hated), became the world's highest paid model and the face of this new era.
The Mods honored the most stylish leaders of their pack as "a Face" and
now she was "The Face of the moment," the "It" girl, and, according to one
weekly magazine, "the 'with-it' girl who welds pop groups and mini-skirts
into the new image of Britain: morally shy, economically disintegrating, but
fun."[7]

Born in High Wycombe in 1942, Jean's was a quintessentially English
childhood: she was raised in comfort on the family farm with her sister Chris-
sie, who dated Mick Jagger in 1967. Even after becoming one of the most
famous faces in the world, she preferred to muck about on her parents' farm
"in old clothes and no makeup, far away from the artificial life in the West
End."[8]

She arrived in London in August 1959 to enroll at secretarial college. She
was only seventeen, fresh from convent school, and after a year of training,

"I still couldn't type and was pretty depressed at the thought of spending my life in a 9 to 5 job. Then someone noticed I had a 34-23-35 figure and suggested I try modelling."[9]

Jean had the type of face that would stop people in their tracks, and as she enjoyed her lunchtime sandwich in Hyde Park she was often approached by men who suggested she model or act. One of these was *Zulu* director Cy Endfield, and he gave her the name of a modeling agency who trained her up for advertising work. She was working on an ad for Kellogg's Cornflakes when David Bailey arrived at the same studio for a *Vogue* magazine shoot. Struck by her wide-eyed beauty, he asked for an introduction and then invited her to do a shoot with *Vogue*.[10] "What attracted me to her was that she genuinely didn't care how she looked. She honestly never understood what all the fuss was about. That was very attractive to me," he told *British Vogue* in 2010.[11]

As her lover and manager, Bailey insisted she do fashion editorials rather than advertising to ensure her exclusivity, and when they both arrived in New York in 1962 as the first wave of the new British invasion, they caused an immediate stir.

"He made a lot of money out of me," she later contended, and she was "irked" by it because "Image rights didn't exist back then."[12]

Despite the intensity of their time in New York, their relationship ended when she left him to be with Terence Stamp, the devastatingly handsome actor who chilled audiences in the cult movie *The Collector* (1965). The two shared a flat in Mayfair while being the toast of Mod London. "We were two pretty people wandering around thinking we were important," she said in 2011. "Night after night we'd go out for dinner, to the best restaurants, but just so that we could be seen. It was boring. I felt like a bit part in a movie about Terence Stamp."[13]

She may have been an "It" girl, but she wasn't a partier, and she didn't care for the press intrusion. "I've hated publicity all my life. I didn't even like it when I was a model," she told the *Guardian* in April 2011.

In 1965 Richard Avedon paired Jean with Steve McQueen for the February 1965 edition of *Harper's Bazaar*. He was the rugged, all-American actor and she was the willowy Modish English girl with the large eyes, and this contrast was also put to effect in the 1990s Calvin Klein campaign featuring Kate Moss and Mark Wahlberg. But unlike the latter, McQueen respected her and spoke in wonderment at how she could turn it on for the camera. "I told him it was just my job, and it was. The ability to turn on and off again until the photographer is happy is what all the best models have. It's an automatic reflex."[14]

If Mary Quant had introduced the thigh-high miniskirt by 1964, and Cathy McGowan set it as a national trend on the hugely popular British music show *Ready Steady Go!*, it was Jean Shrimpton who took it global. In spring 1965 she and Stamp arrived in Australia, where she was due to present a trophy at the Melbourne Cup. When her dressmaker realized he was short of the white fabric needed for her shift dress, he instead created a miniskirt. She wandered onto the member's terrace two hours late and on the arm of Stamp, exposing her stockingless legs, and without the customary gloves and hat that ladies were expected to wear to the races. It triggered a fashion shockwave in a conservative country that wasn't used to the hip, modern styles coming out of London. Photographers clamored to record the moment, crouching low so that they could capture even more leg in moves reminiscent of those upskirt paparazzi shots of noughties stars. Her controversial clothing knocked the winning horse off the front pages of Australia's newspapers.

As the miniskirt sparked a cultural revolution, being thin was in, and young British women exemplified the new look of the decade—the Bambi-eyed waif. Twiggy's look was in such synergy with the times that it appeared as if she was factory-made to wear the baby-doll dresses and miniskirts.

Born Lesley Hornby in Neasden, a suburb of northwest London in 1949, Twiggy became one of the few icons who are recognizable by a single name. The youngest of three daughters, she was raised in a tight, humble family where the domesticity was at times interrupted when her mother was admitted to a psychiatric hospital for what would now be considered bipolar disorder.[15]

As a fashion-conscious teenager she adored Jean Shrimpton, ripping out images from magazines to stick on her wall alongside the Beatles, but, like her idol, she had never considered that she could be a model. At five feet six inches tall and weighing 84 pounds, she felt she was far too skinny, despite the cod liver oil and malt her mother gave her to feed her up. She was also working class and these things just didn't happen to someone with an accent like hers.

She fell in with a gang of fashion-conscious Mods and they would go to all-night dance parties to jam to the sounds of the Small Faces and The Who. She refused the purple heart amphetamines that were so prevalent but wore a big rain mac to look "with it."

Still, she knew she was the wrong shape, and at school she was nicknamed "Olive Oyl" because of her stick-like legs. "All the boys laughed at me. Their name for me was Oxfam. The only girls they were interested in were ones with boobs. Preferably big ones."[16]

She played around with makeup, copying the eyes of her rag dolls by applying three layers of eyelashes above the eye and painting on the lashes underneath. She began shopping at Biba, a treasure-trove of ever-changing fashions, where the clothes were modeled by girls that shared her same body type.

While still at school, she took a Saturday job washing hair in a salon and it was here, in spring 1965, that she met the rakish Nigel Davies, a hairdresser for Vidal Sassoon who also had a stall at the Chelsea flea market. Thinking Nigel wasn't a name for someone who was going to make it big in the fashion business, he changed it to Justin de Villeneuve and dressed like a foppish dandy in his velvet jackets and handkerchiefs.

He was ten years older than her, married with a daughter, but they began dating. Reflecting on the age gap in her memoir, she acknowledged she now considered it wrong for a twenty-five-year-old to date a fifteen-year-old. His nickname for her was "Stick," and this evolved to "Twigs" because of her skinny legs and the false lashes painted on her bottom lids. He could see there was something special about her, a quality like Jean Shrimpton or Pattie Boyd that made her stand out. With her father's blessing, he became her manager and arranged for her headshots to help along her career. Still not convinced she had the right looks, she agreed to have her hair cut into a new crop by the hairdresser Leonard Lewis, whose salon, Leonard of Mayfair, was one of the achingly hip London hotspots. He tried out a new angular cut with a side sweep parting, photos were taken, and by chance Deirdre McSharry, fashion editor of the *Daily Express*, came across them and was struck by her sweet face which, she said, offered a contrast to the horrors of the world.

Deirdre arranged for Twiggy to do an exclusive photoshoot with the *Daily Express*. The next day her dad rushed out to buy a copy of the paper, but after scanning every page, she wasn't there. Nor was she in the next edition, or the one after that. It was three whole weeks until she appeared, but when it did, she was shocked that she was named as "The Face Of '66."

She was described in the copy of the February 23 edition as "The Cockney Kid with the face to launch a thousand shapes. And she's only 16. . . . This is the look that from this moment will launch thousands of clothes, a craze for freckles, dozens of hairpieces and will cause a sell-out in eye pencils."

Twiggy was now the most in-demand model in the UK, supplanting Jean Shrimpton, and the next month, she achieved the pinnacle for a model, an offer from *Vogue*. "Within a month, I was all over the newspapers, I was getting offers to go to Paris. I can't say I didn't like it. I loved it, it was brilliant."[17]

By March 1967, when she arrived in the United States to take the country by storm, she had appeared in thirteen different shoots for *Vogue*'s international editions. Landing at JFK airport with Justin, she was greeted by a mob of paparazzi and fans in the biggest welcome party for a Brit since the Beatles touched down in February 1964. It further reinforced the all-conquering British invasion, and Edie Sedgwick, who had been named the "Girl of the Year" for 1965, accused her of stealing her look.

Before her arrival, a profile in *Life* magazine helped to drum up further interest in this young girl with the "thick Cockney accent," whose "fence-picket contours—90 pounds, 31-23-32 led schoolmates to call her 'Sticks.'"[18]

Twiggy's schedule included more photoshoots for *Vogue*, *Seventeen*, *Mademoiselle*, *Ladies' Home Journal*, and *McCall's*, with the world's top photographers, Richard Avedon, Helmut Newton, Guy Bourdin, and Norman Parkinson all scrambling to capture her angular moves.

Bert Stern, renowned for his "last sitting" of Marilyn Monroe, filmed her arrival in Manhattan for a documentary called *The Twiggy Story* and as part of it, she was interviewed on camera by Woody Allen, then a stand-up comedian. Perhaps to undermine her as an airhead model, his first question was "Who's your favorite philosopher?" She cheekily turned it around on him, but she felt burned at his attempt at humiliation.

Life magazine had asserted that "in the swift-moving teeny-mod-mini world of British fashions, Twiggy now strides far ahead of the pack," and as the "Face of 1967," she was now successor to the celebrated Jean Shrimpton. She hated the insinuation that she was leaving her idol in the dust. "It's plain horrible to say I'm Jean Shrimpton's rival—her successor," she told *Life*. "She's so perfectly beautiful and I'm not even pretty. No one will ever take from her. The woman I really love is the big one with the fuzzy hair. What's her name? Jean Harlow, that's it! Leonard who cuts me hair is doing me a wig like her."[19]

Twiggy was such a phenomenon that with her father and Justin's instruction she set up her own corporation, Twiggy Enterprises, under which she launched a fashion line aimed at teenagers. The clothing line was a flop, but there were fake eyelashes, wigs and hosiery, notebooks and pens and paper dolls, and Mattel also produced a Twiggy Barbie-style doll which was dressed in a series of bright Pop Art clothes.

Some of the American reporters weren't exactly kind about her body, insinuating she was more like a boy, and they painted her as a child who pulled silly faces and answered "dunno" to many of their questions. *Look* headlined their article with "Is it a Girl? Is It a Boy? No, It's Twiggy," while veteran reporter Inez Robb believed she needed a decent feed. "Even a decade ago any editor or photographer would have advised Twiggy to invest in falsies and go on a diet of whipped cream and baked potatoes. Innocent bystanders of both sexes would have given her a brief look and said, 'Poor kid.'"[20]

In the *New York Times*, Charlotte Curtis sneered that the "mini-bosomed fashion model of the year, just looks like your next door neighbor, if he happens to be a skinny 12-year-old boy, and when she arrived in New York yesterday, she was dressed accordingly—in short pants."[21]

She may have disliked the Jean Shrimpton rivalry, but in the world of celebrity, and particularly in fashion, there was always a younger model threatening to usurp. Twiggy only modeled for four years, and by the early seventies was focused on acting. She won a Golden Globe for her performance in Ken Russell's *The Boy Friend* (1971), she performed on Broadway, worked as a television presenter, and designed her own collections for British high-street label Marks and Spencer. She had been levelheaded about her meteoric rise to fame, eschewing the drugs and alcohol that many stars in her position succumbed to, and she was able to survive the peaks and troughs.

Throughout her career, Twiggy's body had always been up for discussion, and like her 1990s equivalent, Kate Moss, she was criticized for encouraging an unhealthy aesthetic. In a clip from an ITN interview in 1970, she responded to a question about curvier figures being back in fashion. "The bosom has never been out. That would mean that women have been out, which is ridiculous, innit?"

Just as Twiggy was bowing out of fashion, along came the next "It" girl. Jane Birkin was very much a product of the collision between Mod fashions coming out of Swinging London and France's groundbreaking New Wave filmmaking, as she became the quintessential cool girl of the free love era.

Jane Birkin carrying her signature straw basket at London airport in May 1966. *Wallace/ ANL/Shutterstock.*

With her tousled hair, toothy smile, and a well-bred English demeanor, she was both a tomboy and a sexual sophisticate for her relationship with Serge Gainsbourg, the nude photoshoots, and the recordings of her orgasmic sounds.

Born in December 1946, Jane was the eldest of three children to Chelsea-dwelling bohemians. Her mother, Judy Campbell, was a famous actress and muse to Noël Coward, and her father, David Birkin, also an actor, came from a line of wealthy Nottingham lacemakers.

Growing up in a fêted celebrity family, she was surrounded by actors and producers, and the icons on the screen affected her immensely. When she and her younger sister Linda saw Jean Seberg in *Saint Joan*, she wrote in her diary that she found it "terribly good and I cried a lot." She was also devastated on hearing the news that Marilyn Monroe had died. "I told myself that it wasn't possible, not her, she made us laugh so much. Garbo OK, but not her!"[22]

Growing up, she never felt beautiful. Rather, she was awkward and shy, and after being bullied at boarding school because she was skinny, she was desperate for her breasts to develop. "The others said I was half boy, half girl. I had no breasts, not even a developing bosom. It was horrible."[23]

Through her father's connections, she auditioned and won the part of a deaf-mute girl in Graham Greene's *Carving a Statue*, staged at London's Haymarket Theatre in September 1964. She followed it with *The Passion Flower Hotel*, which introduced her to composer John Barry. Jane was seventeen and a shy virgin, and he was thirty years old, and despite her father's pleas that she was too young, they married.

During this time, she began to develop her unique sense of style. At Berwick Street Market she found a straw basket for sale, and using it in lieu of a handbag, it became her signature. She was so eye-catching that a director her mother was working with realized he had been sitting next to Jane at the theatre. He was struck by her "funny black smoky eyes and long legs and black tights," that she looked like a child yet had a wedding ring, and with "the most enormous basket under the seat" which had a ticking sound coming from it. He said, "I realised who she was by your description of her, slightly mad, very young, with an enormous basket."[24]

She auditioned for Italian cult director Michelangelo Antonioni's *Blow-Up*, set within the Mod subculture of Swinging London, and was cast alongside Gillian Hills as two teenagers who are so desperate to be fashion models for David Hemmings's photographer that they strip naked for him.

With her thick fringed hair and sullen sexuality, her small role in the Cannes Film Festival's Palme D'Or–winning movie made a huge impact. There were stories that projectionists were slicing out the negatives of her nude scene to keep for themselves.

She gave birth to her daughter Kate shortly after the film was released, yet her marriage imploded on her discovery that Barry had been in Rome with another woman. She and her baby temporarily moved back in with her parents, and now that she was a single mother, she needed to focus on her career. She heard about an audition for a French film, *Slogan*, which was attracting top models like Marisa Berenson, but she struggled with her imperfect French during the script reading for director Pierre Grimblat. This wasn't helped by the moody sarcasm of the film's lead, Serge Gainsbourg, who was acting the scenes with her.[25]

Despite breaking down in tears at her audition, she won the part, and the film, and her introduction to Serge would change her life. The French-Russian actor, renowned for his courting of sexually sophisticated women, had just separated from Brigitte Bardot, with whom he had a successful musical partnership. Revolution was in the air in Paris 1968, and he and Jane hit the town, visiting the city's vibrant nightclubs and drag shows, and by the time dawn broke, and they were wandering through the bloody meat markets of Les Halles drinking champagne, they had fallen for one another.[26]

Establishing herself in France and moving into Serge's all-black apartment in Paris with Kate, Jane blossomed from being a copy of Jean Shrimpton to her own "cool French girl" style, with big doll eyes defined by spidery lashes, her bangs, and wide gap-toothed smile. It was a uniquely chaotic Parisian chic, where she displayed a naïve sexuality, combining English reserve with French passion. She adored Serge, found him witty, clever, and sexual, and she was incredibly open in the way she confided to reporters about her terrible jealousies around the attractive women who flocked around him.

"It's amazing what Paris can do to a girl," she told the *San Fransisco Examiner* in 1969. "In France they don't seem to have girls like me around. It's kind of a mutual effect we've had on each other. Sometimes I wake up in the morning and look at myself, and I'm quite surprised at the way I've turned out. It's as if I'd been in a cage all my life, and now I've broken out and I'm living the way I always wanted to live without knowing it."[27]

The image of the saucy Parisian style icon would go global on the release of her and Gainsbourg's first single together, "Je T'Aime . . . Moi Non Plus." He had originally written it for Bardot, but when he heard Jane singing in the bathtub, to her relief, he asked for her to duet with him.

In the wine cellar restaurant of the exclusive Hôtel des Beaux Arts, Serge quietly put the record on the turntable, and as it played, the diners put down their forks and listened intently. "I think we've got a hit record," he whispered to Jane. And he was right.[28]

Not only was "Je T'Aime . . . Moi Non Plus" a smash hit, selling three million copies in just over a year, but it was one of the most controversial songs of all time. It was banned in France, Spain, and Britain, even after it got to number one on the BBC's flagship music show *Top of the Pops*, and was denounced by *L'Osservatore Romano*, the Vatican's official newspaper.

When the *Sunday Post* asked whether it was true that she and Serge were really making love while recording it, she replied, "Unfortunately, we were not. We went to London for the recording session and were sitting in glass cages at opposite ends of the room, wearing ear-muffs. There was absolutely no physical contact between us. It couldn't have been less sexy."[29]

They followed it with the album "69 Année Érotique," with Jane as the cover star and with their reputation as the couple whose currency was sex.

"We must have represented a form of freedom," she told *French Vogue* in 2017. "The twenty-year age gap, our lifestyle, we went out at night and came home to wake up Kate and Charlotte before school, and then slept in the daytime. That was my fantasy, our lack of taboos . . . Serge used to say: 'We are not an immoral couple, we are an amoral couple.'"[30]

She was no society princess in haute couture; instead, her crochet dresses unashamedly skimmed the top of her horse-riding toned thighs, and she teamed scruffy jeans with sheer tops that revealed her nipples. She always carried her childhood toy monkey and her Portuguese straw basket which "did not leave my side. If I was denied entry to Maxim's because of my basket, I didn't care. I had this assurance."[31]

In one famous image, taken at the Riviera's Whisky a Gogo nightclub, in January 1972, she dances, barefoot, her back pressed against Serge, his handing clasping her body just under breasts, and with her micromini Paco Rabanne so transparent it reveals her panties. "This is the flash effect of the photographers' camera," she later said. "If I had known, I would not have put knickers on!"[32]

For Jane, Serge would unveil a new side of her that had always been there but masked with shyness, and in her miniscule dresses, it helped create the image of the sexually voracious sex kitten for the seventies. The murder of Sharon Tate in 1969 by Charles Manson and his dangerously brainwashed hippie followers marked the end of the flower power innocence and the air of youthful freedom, and instead the following decade was grittier, sleazier, and more hedonistic.

Jane further pushed boundaries with a spread in *Lui* magazine, the French equivalent of *Playboy*, which led to accusations of pornography.

She laughed at the suggestion of being the sex symbol of the seventies. "A few years ago I was considered skinny, bandy-legged and flat-chested and I don't see why people have changed this opinion. I suppose there are a lot of kinky old men after schoolgirls. They call Raquel Welch a sex symbol she does have a big bosom and all that—but she has no humor. I like people to be funny and laugh at themselves. Marilyn Monroe had sex but she was also humorous. There will never be another sex symbol like Marilyn Monroe."[33]

The sex symbol she was most frequently compared with, and whom she was accused of replacing, was Brigitte Bardot, who was now treated as an aging star. But rather than competing, the two were put in bed together in 1973's *Don Juan*. In her diary, she revealed that before filming this scene, she and Serge had had a huge fight, and after crying all night she arrived on set with shiny eyes. "That's why I'm so pretty in that scene, because for once, I wasn't covered up with the typical make-up of the sixties."[34]

She and Serge's love affair was hot and dramatic, with stories of her pushing a lemon pie into his face during a row at a Paris nightclub, and then throwing herself into the River Seine and having to be rescued by the river patrol.

All the while, Serge considered her his own creation who would always obey him. "I can make any number of them and better and younger but they're nothing without me," he boasted.[35] She and Serge had a daughter together, Charlotte, in 1971, and even after ten years together, they chose not to marry. Still, she fretted about approaching forty, but by this point, she'd had enough of the relationship, of his drinking and his moods and violence, and she left him in 1980 and moved in with the director Jacques Doillon. They had a daughter together, Lou Doillon, in 1982.

It turned out that she could be a style icon with or without Serge. On a flight from Paris to London she was seated next to Jean-Louis Dumas, chief executive of Hermès, and as she placed her basket in the overhead locker, all its contents spilled out onto the aisle. She explained to him that she hadn't been able to find a good weekend bag, and so he reworked a bag in their atelier to suit her needs, and the Hermès Birkin bag was born.[36]

As for Jean Shrimpton, she became disenchanted by the fashion industry, loathing her nickname "The Shrimp" and the approaches by lotharios like Warren Beatty and Jack Nicholson who treated her as a trophy to be won. She was much more comfortable studying art and reading American literature, preferring that to the celebrity circuit. After relationships with photographer Terry O'Neill and poet Heathcote Williams, she settled with writer Malcolm Richey, moved to Cornwall, and opened an antiques shop. She was happy to give up the glamor of international travel to embrace the rural living that she had enjoyed so much as a child.[37]

"Fashion is full of dark, troubled people," she told the *Guardian* in 2011. "It's a high-pressured environment that takes its toll and burns people out."[38]

Supermodels, Pretty Babies, and Studio 54

Margaux Hemingway and Brooke Shields

Margaux Hemingway at an event in London in 1979. *Armando Pietrangeli/Shutterstock.*

Margaux Hemingway's friends and neighbors were worried because they hadn't seen her for days. It was July 1996 and she'd recently moved into a new apartment in Santa Monica with its calming Pacific Ocean views. She'd hoped that her new role as host of *Wild Guide*, an outdoor adventure series to air on the Discovery Channel, could boost her flagging career. But when friends met with her for dinner, she sounded forlorn and confessed that she hadn't been feeling very good.[1]

By Monday morning, she had not returned any phone calls all weekend, and one of her friends, Judy Stabile, decided to drive past her house. She saw Margaux's white Ford Bronco parked outside, and when she received no response after knocking on the door, she climbed a ladder to look in the window, and spotted Margaux on the bed. She asked two construction workers to break down the door, and it was then that they made the grim discovery. She had been dead for several days. Some friends thought she may have died from an epileptic fit, others that it was linked to her public struggles with alcoholism and bulimia or to the "Hemingway curse."[2] The Los Angeles coroner's office was final in their ruling—she had killed herself with an overdose of barbiturates.[3]

Margaux hadn't been able to recover her career to anywhere near the stratospheric levels it had been when she was billed as the world's first supermodel. Yet the woman who was once described as the face of a generation,[4] who represented the glitz and glamor and excess of the 1970s, was now a warning that extreme, fleeting fame was a poisoned chalice.

The tragic ending would never have been imagined when she held the fashion world at her fingertips, signing the first million-dollar contract ever given to a model. She was six-foot tall and strong, with caramel hair framing sculpted cheekbones, a button nose, and a wide smile that broke out into spontaneous laughter. She was that perfect blend of athletic goddess and corn-fed wholesomeness, the type that photographers scrambled over in the seventies.

This decade was an exciting one for fashion and celebrity; not only were exclusive contracts being given to models, but it was also a transformative period of sexual freedom and revolution on the back of women's liberation and Gay Pride. It was a glossy, chaotic, and hedonistic time, yet there was also a darkness under the glittery surface as the free-flowing drugs and alcohol could be a temptation that broke the most vulnerable.

Born in Portland, Oregon, in 1955 as Margot, she was the second of three daughters to Byra Louise Whittlesey and Jack, the oldest son of Ernest Hemingway. When she discovered that her parents were drinking Chateau Margaux on the night of her conception, she changed the spelling of her name—an early indication of her impulsiveness and a desire to weave magic through storytelling.

Her family spent a few years on their grandfather's farm in Cuba, and then to Ketchum, Idaho, in 1967, a small town surrounded by pine forests and mountains, and the place where Ernest had killed himself six years before. The shadow of the Hemingway curse, of a family history of depression and suicide, hung over the family. As little sister Mariel said: "It was kind of like the Kennedy family. The Kennedys had these horrible tragedies and we were the other American family that had this horrible curse."[5]

Margaux was a sports enthusiast, taking advantage of the awe-inspiring outdoors of Sun Valley by skiing in winter, riding horses and swimming in the rivers over summer. The Hemingway girls were local celebrities in the area for their athleticism and their charisma, and Margaux in particular possessed a starry imagination and an ability to spin a good yarn, just like her grandfather.

Yet they also struggled with their own mental health. Margaux was afflicted by epilepsy, and undiagnosed dyslexia left her with insecurities around her own intellect. It worsened her anxiety and depression, triggering bouts of bulimia which reoccurred during periods of stress. In the documentary *Running from Crazy* (2013) Mariel revealed that both her older sisters were abused by their father, and that they grew up in a house where their parents had blazing, violent rows. There's a pattern with "It" girls, that those who have suffered childhood trauma are often desperate for validation, and stardom becomes a tool to gain acceptance from as many people as possible, to compensate for what they lacked when younger.

After high school Margaux drifted between jobs, smoking marijuana and drinking at the local cowboy bars, but she was restless for more in life. Knowing that she had the qualities that would make her appealing for show business, she sent out modeling shots to agencies. When she didn't receive any responses, she approached a local talent agent and together they decided to set up their own PR firm for sports events. As part of this, Margaux arranged a business trip to New York to meet a boxing promoter.

She arrived in the city like the overexcited teenager she was, in cowboy boots and clicking her gum as she cried out, "Yippee!" She found the forward approach of the men in New York unnerving, but then her height and her bawdy language proved an effective defense system. "When a girl looks like me and talks rough, it blows their mind. They just sort of scurry away like the rats they are."[6]

Sipping tea in the Palm Court of the Plaza Hotel, nineteen-year-old Margaux attracted the attention of Errol Wetson, heir to the Wetson's hamburger chain. He wooed her by sending a rose and a bottle of champagne to her hotel suite, and then brought her as his date to a party which was attended by models, agents, and photographers who all wanted to know who this exuberant but wholesome country girl was.

Four months later she moved into Wetson's Manhattan apartment, and by 1975 they were married. He was now controlling her like a Svengali, instructing her on what colors to wear, and criticizing her legs because he felt they were too heavy. He transformed her from a naïve country girl from Idaho to a sophisticated model, not just bringing her to the right parties, but also introducing her to fashion designer Halston and influential fashion photographer Francesco Scavullo.

By the mid-seventies, the doll-like waifs were passé, and instead, as American fashion brands like Ralph Lauren and Halston had taken over from the French to dominate fashion, the all-American girl was now the sought-after look. As opposed to the strung-out hippies, this new woman was tall and strong, with long glossy hair, tanned skin, big eyes, and a toothy smile.

At first, Margaux was criticized for her swimmer shoulders and unplucked eyebrows and it was suggested she lose forty pounds. She refused—they could take her as she was or not at all. Her unaffected personality was infectious among the jaded fashion and society people, and six months later, in March 1975 she had reached the pinnacle of modeling with a *Vogue* cover shot by Richard Avedon. She had also signed the world's first million-dollar modeling contract as the spokeswoman for the Fabergé perfume Babe. Soon her face was on every glossy magazine and news publication, including the June 16, 1975, issue of *Time* magazine, which captioned her glamorous image with "The New Beauties."

"It's hard to imagine anyone more All-American than the big girl standing over there, head above the crowd," wrote the *Montreal Star*. She was described as the girl who refused to pluck her eyebrows, and "who came out of the land of milk and corn 18 months ago toting only her grandpapa Ernest Hemingway's name and her own wholesome good looks," and who, in 1976, was "the Girl of the Year."[7] Later, she would confess that she never really liked the smell of Babe perfume, but, she conceded, "it was fun and it did make me one of the most famous faces in America."[8]

At a Fabergé press conference in June 1975, as she sipped her birth date vintage Chateau Margaux 1955 wine, she spoke of her stratospheric rise. "It's like magic, like angel dust sprinkling all over me. I'm not a model, I'm an athlete. I just freaked everybody out. It's all unbelievable, like a movie. I'm just having the best time."[9]

In 1974 Warhol's close friend Bob Colacello started a new column, "Out," for the artist's *Interview* magazine. He often wrote about the new "It" girls on the scene, although they weren't named as such, but included Nicaraguan jet-setter Bianca Pérez-Mora Macías, who married Mick Jagger in 1970, and fashion designer Diane von Furstenberg. And as the sensational "It" model, Margaux was a regular at Manhattan's pulsating disco scene, in particular Studio 54 when it opened in April 1977.

Studio 54 was a melting pot of celebrity culture and hedonism, with beautiful people of all races and sexual orientation coming together to have a good time. As Colacello said, "New York was cheap, it was open. It was in crisis financially, crime was everywhere. But it was very creative. And we, the baby boomer generation, were just coming out of college. We just wanted to have fun. And any kids who had a bohemian slant came to New York."[10]

Regulars at Studio 54 included Grace Jones, the model Iman, and Pat Cleveland, the African American model who was one of the most in-demand on the Paris catwalks. Marc Jacobs came with his high school textbooks so he could leave the nightclub in the morning and go straight to class. "It gave me an unhealthy curiosity about subcultures and anonymous sex," said the designer.[11] It became a place where the antics of a core group of celebrities, including Andy Warhol, Liza Minnelli, and Halston were all splashed on Page Six of the *New York Post*. When Halston held a birthday party for Bianca Jagger, she climbed onto a white horse that had been brought into the club and the photos were splashed across international publications.

"I was in awe of that whole Halston-Liza Minnelli crowd," Margaux said in an interview with *People* in 1988. "To me they were the real celebrities, and I was just a girl from Idaho."[12] Pat Cleveland was also regular at Studio 54, often a familiar sight on the dance floor in shimmering Halston designs. The Harlem model, who had an African American mother and Swedish father, often struggled with the double prejudice of being too light-skinned and not dark enough. At sixteen she had traveled with *Ebony* magazine on one of their pioneering fashion tours into the deep south, and then signed with Wilhelmina Models, a new agency established by Dutch model Wilhelmina Cooper, which was more inclusive.

Every time Pat was photographed for the cover of American *Vogue*, her hopes were dashed when it was given to a white girl instead. Wilhelmina advised her that she should make a name for herself in Europe first before building her career in America.[13] Pat promised that she wouldn't live in the States again until a Black woman appeared on the cover of American *Vogue*, which Beverly Johnson achieved in August 1974.

She was invited to Paris by Antonio Lopez, a trailblazing illustrator for *Vogue*, and she became part of his group of American fashion creatives that included Juan Ramos and model and former Warhol superstar Donna Jordan who spent their afternoons in Café de Flore and their evenings touring the city's nightclubs.

She said, "We came out of America like wild, crazy people. We had grown up with movies and movie-star attitude and we were there to be stars, superstars. We wanted to shine day and night."[14]

Just as Wilhelmina had predicted, Europe was much more accepting of Pat, and by 1971 she was traveling between Paris, Milan, and London, and was a favorite for Karl Lagerfeld for Chloé, who dressed her as Marie Antoinette ("She said let them eat cake, but my dear, you look like the cake")[15] and introduced her to Andy Warhol. As she remembered, "we would flirt and throw kisses, dance on tables. We were the ultimate glamor girls."[16]

Back in New York, it was Pat who was one of the first guests at Steve Rubell's new nightclub Studio 54, after he invited her to come along with friends. "It just so happened that one night, Halston called me up and asked if I would like to go over but that we weren't staying in—I was going to take him somewhere. I took him over to Studio 54. The place was empty: it was just me, Halston and Steve." Halston was so impressed with the place that he vowed to bring all his friends, and soon it was the wild VIP venue where scandal hit the gossip columns the next day.[17]

There was a freedom to disco in the way people could be uninhibited on the dance floor. "What was interesting is that women felt secure enough to dance nude in the place," Swedish photographer Hasse Persson recalled. "This is after the feminist movement of the 70s: if a woman wanted to be nude that was her privilege, no one would ever touch her or say anything. They were like queens on the dancefloor."[18]

Also at Studio 54 was another supermodel who would likely be targeted as a "nepo-baby" if she were carving out a career today. Marisa Berenson was the granddaughter of Elsa Schiaparelli, the Italian surrealist fashion designer. As one of the top models of the decade, she graced the cover of *Vogue* and *Harper's Bazaar* and was name-checked in the gossip columns as a regular on the New York nightclub scene.

Marisa and Berry Berenson were compared to Jackie and Lee Bouvier, as two well-connected sisters at the center of society. They established themselves in their "Halcreations" by "getting their names in the columns and their faces in the Vogue-Harpers Bazaar, Town and Country circuit," wrote the *New York Times*. "They might have made it on their own (in fact, they both insist they would have) but there is no denying they had some powerful clout."[19]

Berry was short-haired, blond, athletic looking, makeup-less, while Marisa had long auburn hair, was willowy, and seemed shyer than her sister. Berry was on one side of the camera as a photographer for *Vogue*, and Marisa was on the other side, as Yves Saint Laurent's "girl of the Seventies."

Marisa's childhood was immersed in Hollywood and fashion history—she had been taught to dance by Gene Kelly; Greta Garbo was a friend of her parents, Gogo Schiaparelli and US diplomat Robert Berenson; and her grand-mother's friend and collaborator, Salvador Dalí, wished to paint her. It was *Vogue* editor Diana Vreeland who encouraged her to be a model after spotting the sixteen-year-old at a New York society ball in 1963.

Under the guidance of Vreeland, she moved to New York as a teen model and her beloved father died shortly after. His death "gave me all the more incentive to go out and live on my own."[20] Grandmother Schiaparelli was afraid of her living in New York alone. "I was a little bit outrageous too," she told the *Guardian*. "I did the first nude in *Vogue*, and things like that, and she was horrified."[21]

She also had a knack for being in the right place at the right time—she modeled for some of Coco Chanel's last collections, she was a devotee of the ashram of Maharishi Mahesh Yogi in India at the same time as George Harrison, and Andy Warhol splashed her in his *Interview* magazine in 1975. She was such a regular on the nightclub circuit that she was named "Queen of the Scene" by *Newsweek*.

The decade may have been marked by successful drive for equality under the women's liberation movement, but there was also a troubling response to these feminist gains. Teenage girls were too young to stand up for their rights in the same way as adult women were doing, and as they were appreciated, and exploited, for their undemanding simplicity, there was an uneasy depiction in popular culture of the precocious Lolita figure.

New Year's Eve 1978, and the dance floor at Studio 54 was a mass of shimmering glitter and strobe lights as Grace Jones made a dramatic entrance under a giant cobra. Wrapped in gold lamé and surrounded by ten male danc-ers wearing nothing but G-strings, she mesmerized the crowd gathered on the sidelines as she gyrated through her disco set.

Huddled together watching the performance were teenagers Brooke Shields and Margaux's little sister Mariel Hemingway. In their demure floral dresses, their hair worn naturally, they giggled as they watched the suggestive performance in the early hours of the New Year. They were clearly far too young to be up at this time, let alone to be surrounded by such decadence, but for two teenage "It" girls in the seventies, normal rules didn't apply.

From the age of thirteen, Brooke was a regular at the hottest nightspot in town. Accompanied by her mother Teri, she would pose for the photographers by the famous red rope, then would hit the dance floor. In her autobiography, Brooke stated that she was usually home by 11:30 p.m., and never witnessed the debauchery and drug abuse, as she eschewed alcohol and other stimulants, having seen the effect of alcoholism on her mother. In the newspapers at the time, Brooke's young age was commented on, but her nightclubbing was never treated as unusual—she was a star, and therefore belonged to the prime celebrity space.

Brooke was only thirteen when she played a child prostitute in *Pretty Baby* (1978) and fifteen when she was a stranded beachcomber discovering her sexuality in *The Blue Lagoon* (1980). Similarly, in Woody Allen's *Manhattan* (1979) Mariel Hemingway played his forty-something writer's teenage girlfriend. She may have earned an Oscar nomination for Best Supporting Actress, but the casual way this relationship was depicted, with her character Tracy as a naïve but sexually eager and experimental young woman, is uneasy. When Tracy is encouraged by him to give up her dream of studying in Paris, her own goals and ambitions are overlooked, and instead, she is treated as a pure ego-soother for a man who can't get on with women his own age.

Brooke Shields's mother Teri was convinced her daughter was the most beautiful girl in the world when she was born in 1965, and she put her to work as a child model from the age of eleven months. She was in high demand for commercials and catalogues including Macy's, Sears, Bloomingdale's, McCall's, and Butterick. She was even cast as Jean Shrimpton's daughter in one advert, which only made her mother more convinced that Brooke's perfect face could make her famous too.[22]

Her mother may well have envisioned Brooke as the future of European cinema when she agreed for her to act in such a risqué film as Louis Malle's *Pretty Baby*, which she auditioned for when she was just eleven. When it premiered at the Cannes Film Festival in 1978 and received the Palme d'Or, the attention it was given, Brooke wrote in her memoirs, "would scar me for life." At the film's premiere she was crushed by the frenzied crowds who pulled her clothes and grabbed at her hair, as if they wanted a physical piece of her.

Pretty Baby made her a star, and while her young age was acknowledged, she was still sexualized. A report in the *New York Daily News* in June 1978 stated: "Brooke Shields is now an older woman, having attained the age of 13 last Wednesday. . . . Brooke has been in front of cameras since appearing in her first nude shot—for a soap ad when she was 11 months old."[23]

At the same time, her mother came under attack for allowing her daughter to be exposed in such a way. Teri struggled both as a single mother and as an alcoholic, and having a famous daughter, described as the most beautiful girl in the world, not only helped to secure their financial future, but also gave her the validation and pride she always wanted.

In 1980, Brooke became the youngest model to ever grace the cover of *Vogue* magazine, and she was cast in the biggest movie of her career, *The Blue Lagoon*. The movie catapulted fifteen-year-old Brooke to icon status for teenage girls. Her face was splashed on the cover of every magazine, and her fans wished to know everything about her; what shampoo she used, what her aspirations were, whether she had a boyfriend.

Teri insisted her daughter reply to every fan letter, to sign every autograph request at appearances, and to pose for photographers. "Because of her hyper-vigilance toward my public, I felt as if the world owned me. It was the feeling that everybody wanted to take a piece," Brooke wrote.[24]

When Calvin Klein approached the fifteen-year-old to appear in ads for their jeans, the concept, she was told, was to tease with the wordplay of genes and jeans. When the commercials shot by Richard Avedon aired in 1980, the blatant double entendre was shocking, as she whispers into the camera: "You want to know what comes between me and my Calvins? Nothing." It was so controversial the ad was pulled from the air, and Teri Shields was again attacked for allowing her daughter to be exposed.

Endless Love (1981) was another story of sexual awakening, but working with Italian director Franco Zeffirelli was an exciting prospect for her mother's plan for her to become a European-style actress. Her love scenes used a body double, but still, there was a difficult dichotomy between the sexually precocious girl on screen, and the modest, possessed girl in the preppy outfit who appeared on television defending her mother.

What came back to haunt them was a photoshoot for the *Playboy* publication, *Sugar and Spice*, that she took part in when she was ten. It's hard to believe that child pornography would be so openly available in the 1970s, and that Brooke's mother would allow for her to pose nude, oiled, and made-up. Teri and Brooke took the photographer Garry Gross and Playboy Press to court to wrangle the rights back, but the New York courts ruled in the photographer's favor after his lawyer argued Brooke was "no Shirley Temple" for the risqué films she had made.[25]

By 1981 her image was a commercial property that could generate money for whatever projects were dreamed up. There was a Brooke doll, where the body was altered to reflect her real-life figure, and which came with leggings and sweaters and a prom dress. There was the Brooke Shields Glamour Center, which was a replica head with a similar mane of caramel hair which could be styled in different ways.

"The most poignant part of all was how disassociated I was with my own body," she later recalled. "As a model, I was primarily a cover girl. I was labeled 'The '80s Look' by *Time* magazine. People said I had the most beautiful face in the world. Well, that seemed ridiculous to me. It didn't register as true. 'Most beautiful' was an arbitrary concept and I was afraid to buy into it."[26]

Margaux loved her celebrity life as it allowed her to escape the depression and torment that haunted her, and she sought release in the fizz of champagne. "I did the whole New York scene. I took the disco life seriously," she said in 1979. "It was one party after another. Party time over and over and over again. And I was exhausted." She learned through all those late nights and always having to be on, that "the party life takes and takes. And it doesn't give anything in return."[27]

She was also driven by a fascination with the hard-drinking mythology of her grandfather, and she wanted to "live my life to the fullest, with gusto. I always thought alcohol would give me the strength and courage to do whatever I wanted."[28]

After conquering modeling, Margaux turned to acting after being promised by Italian producer Dino De Laurentiis that he could turn her into a star. She went to Hollywood to make *Lipstick* (1976), in which she played a model who is violently raped. When her attacker is acquitted, and then rapes her younger sister, she embarks on a mission of revenge.

It was a typical 1970s exploitation movie that took advantage of her supermodel status and featured real-life snapper Francesco Scavullo in scenes set in a photographer's studio. On Margaux's suggestion, fourteen-year-old Mariel was cast as her younger sister. The film was panned, but gallingly, Mariel took the limelight, and it led to her being cast by Woody Allen in his next movie. As Mariel won rave reviews for *Manhattan*, including an Academy Award nomination for Best Supporting Actress, Margaux fell further into drugs and alcohol, and the humiliation of being overshadowed by her little sister marked the beginning of her downfall.

As Mariel wrote in her memoirs: "People said I was a star, while Margaux's acting was hurtfully panned. She intensified her self-destructive behavior, and the distance between us began to take on adult dimensions."[29]

She had tired of Wetson's controlling nature and they divorced in 1978, and in 1979 she married Venezuelan film director Bernard Foucher. They moved to Paris, where she spent too much money, drank too much, and was overheard gushing about her sex life in too loud a voice.[30]

In 1981 she planned to make a documentary with Foucher about her grandfather, but even after several trips to Cuba and interviews with people who knew him, the project struggled to get off the ground. In 1985 she called off the project, divorced Foucher, and after injuring herself skiing in Austria, gained seventy-five pounds and spent her days drinking to try to numb the insecurities and depression.

"I drank more and more and was slowly killing myself with alcohol," she recalled. "My thoughts were erratic, and I had trouble with my memory. I thought about suicide periodically, especially when I was drinking heavily."[31]

She credited a twenty-eight-day stay at the Betty Ford Center in 1987 with saving her life. Emerging refreshed and healthy, she threw herself into running, yoga, painting, and singing to help soothe the negative thoughts. Still, she remained isolated from her family, lashing out at her mother whom she blamed for her painful childhood, and she was intensively competitive with Mariel whom she felt had only succeeded in acting because of her influence. Margaux struggled to pick up her acting career, and agreed to pose nude for *Playboy* in May 1990, which helped her pay off the almost $1 million she owed in taxes.

She turned to alternative health and healing, learning about the shamanic art of the Northwest Coast Indians, and Hawaiian huna philosophy to try to get to grips with the dyslexia, epilepsy, and bulimia she had struggled with since she was a teenager. She went on a spiritual odyssey to India in 1994, but when she returned to the States her shaved head was covered in sores and a further breakdown led to her hospitalization and treatment at a private clinic in Twin Falls, Idaho.

"I needed to go inside and clear the blockages," she told *People* in 1994, "because nothing was coming to me, no jobs, no work." Only a few years later she would be dead—her obituaries heralding both her status as the first supermodel, and her fall from grace. *The Guardian*'s headline, "America's First Babe," was followed by a description of those two sides of her. "One was the fashion icon who flitted effortlessly through the social hothouse of mid-seventies Manhattan. The other . . . was a swollen, failed actress, enslaved for much of her life to alcohol and eating disorders and, perhaps, the legacy of her famous surname."[32]

For Marisa, despite the pressures of her life, of the instant fame, the money, the parties with musicians, and the easy access to drugs, she was protected from falling into a destructive path by the old-fashioned values of her family. She was also spiritual rather than bohemian, choosing, she said, "orange juice and meditation" over drugs and sex.[33]

Despite the huge fame and the possibilities open to her, Brooke wanted to follow the stages of a normal teenage life and she was accepted into Princeton University in 1983. There was no let-up from the demands of the media even as she took a break from celebrity; the paparazzi snuck onto campus dressed as college students to try to capture photos of her. The other students were protective, refusing bribes when they were asked to take a camera into the communal showers.

Her life was still so aspirational that she agreed to write a book, published after her freshman year, which was called *On Your Own*, and was more of a lighthearted lifestyle guide for other girls going to school. In its pages she was open about her plans to save herself for marriage, and this confession was pounced upon by the media, making the nineteen-year-old the most famous virgin of the time as she went on dates with John Travolta, Leif Garrett, Scott Baio, and John F. Kennedy Jr. It was the same obsession two decades later when Britney Spears made a similar declaration of chastity.

After graduation Brooke assumed a successful career in acting and modeling would be there for the taking, but now that her fame had eclipsed her perceived talents, no decent movie roles came her way. She'd also put on twenty pounds on college, and she was not "the skinny, exotic woman-child I had once been," she said.[34]

Instead of movies, Brooke was offered commercials for instant coffee and for a weight-loss campaign in Japan, and by the 1990s her name was tinged with nostalgia for those who remembered her teen movies and the Calvin Klein commercials. Her career was eventually saved by a guest appearance on *Friends*, and then her sitcom, *Suddenly Susan*, which first aired in 1996.

She reevaluated her position as a child star and teen "It" girl in a 2023 documentary, *Pretty Baby*, which also examined the power dynamics that bred this objectification. What was eye-opening was the intrusive and inappropriate questions she faced as a young teen by interviewers on television. She believed that the bar of what was acceptable was so low at the time. "Whether it's asking me my measurements on nationwide television, asking me to stand up. Barbara Walters did that and compared herself to me, and just the approach that they had in asking me questions as a twelve-year-old was really just unconscionable," she told *The Kelly Clarkson Show* in April 2023.

It was the same misogynistic systems that Britney Spears faced as a young pop star; not only was her virginity up for discussion but she was also roundly criticized for being too sexual. She was a "Lolita" figure men lusted over, while at the same time facing hostile questioning by interviewers like Diane Sawyer who moralistically blamed her for "getting burnt by the fire she lit herself."[35]

14

Kate Moss, Tara Palmer-Tomkinson, and the Champagne "It" Girls of the 1990s

Tara Palmer-Tomkinson arriving at her Bond-themed party in December 1998. *Shutterstock.*

In December 1998 socialite Tara Palmer-Tomkinson made such an unforget-
table appearance at her own twenty-seventh birthday party that it was the talk
of the British press the next day. Sashaying into London's Tramp nightclub
in a big sheepskin coat, she cast it off to reveal a white bikini in the style of
Ursula Andress, worn with a pair of heels, a knife belt around her thigh, and
a mask and snorkel on her head. It was the type of attention-grabbing antics
that Tara was known for, often made more controversial given her godfather
was Prince Charles, the future king.

The theme for her party was James Bond, and while fellow London "It"
girl Tamara Beckwith wore a black leather jumpsuit to mimic Pussy Galore,
the *Daily Mail* asked the question, "Could Tara be trying a little too hard?"[1]

Before Kim Kardashian, before Paris Hilton, Tara, or "TPT" as she was
often known, was famous for being famous. Everyone wanted her at their
party, she received brand endorsements because of her skills at promotion, and she wholeheartedly embraced the perks of private jets, holidays
on yachts, and love affairs with millionaires. Rather than Instagram, Tara
influenced the old-school way: with her photo splashed in the tabloids and
celebrity magazines like *Hello*.

Tara's fame in the nineties coincided with a national reawakening as Britain emerged from a recession into a period bubbling with excitement and
confidence. The country was on the brink of an economic boom and Tony
Blair's New Labour was earning a celebrity following for the hope his party
offered after a long spell of Conservative rule.

The thriving Britpop indie music scene helped make London the new party
town, as politics, high society, rock 'n' roll and fashion collided together at
the "supernova" places like the Met Bar and the Atlantic Bar and Grill, just
off Piccadilly Circus. Supermodels and Turner Prize artists knocked back
espresso martinis with the socialite circle of Tara, American-born oil heiress
Normandie Keith, and Tamara Beckwith.

As journalist Shane Watson said: "We were still very much about fun then.
This was the Cool Britannia moment, the era of Britpop, when the London
scene made the cover of *Vanity Fair* ("London Swings Again!") and Ab Fab
was the comic mirror of my life. No one had yet heard of a wheatgrass shot
let alone non-alcoholic alcohol; you could still smoke in restaurants or at a
bar with your second or third martini and find a place to dance until 3am."[2]

It was like the swinging sixties all over again, and these socialites were
out for a good time. Reminiscent of the ultra-fashionable celebutantes of the
1930s, they were rich, thin, and desirable, and didn't have to worry about
making it to work after a night of partying. The *Sunday Times* named them
"Bollinger Babes"—the youthful daughters of aristocrats who were shaking
up traditional events of the season like Royal Ascot, and were only too happy

to be splashed in the pages of *Hello* and *Tatler*. For Ascot 1995, Tara and Tamara pulled up in a white stretch limo, leading to gasps from the inherited wealth corner that it was terribly new money.[3]

Tara and her ilk were like mischievous debutantes from a bygone era, but Kate Moss was the quintessential Brit girl of the 1990s, wild and glamorous, a cigarette in one hand and a martini in the other.

The next generation "It" girls crossed over from high society into the new "ladette," a phenomenon that celebrated women who downed pints and stumbled out of the Met Bar, swore and gave the finger to the paparazzi, and were just as prone to bad behavior as the men. On the other hand, Tara and Kate Moss didn't drink pints; rather their stimulants of choice were champagne and cocaine.

There was a naughty wink about Kate, as if she was in on the joke, yet she was decadently bohemian in her lifestyle, worshipping at the altar of 1970s excess, complete with friends like Anita Pallenberg, Marianne Faithfull, and David Bowie.

At a time when London was the epicenter of cool, Kate was "It." She mixed vintage and designer for a completely unique but accessible look—a leather jacket and a floaty skirt, a slash of red lipstick. Her enigma at the peak of her celebrity, with her refusal to do many interviews, only enhanced her appeal. Yet she was omnipresent, crossing from high fashion to art and rock 'n' roll. Over the course of her modeling career she appeared seventy-two times on the cover of the "Big Four" editions of *Vogue*, she sat for eight portraits for the National Portrait Gallery in London, and as a rock star favorite, she performed in music videos for Oasis, Primal Scream, Marianne Faithfull, Johnny Cash, and Paul McCartney.[4]

Journalist Shane Watson first met Kate for an interview for *Elle* magazine, when she was twenty-one and in an all-consuming relationship with Johnny Depp. Staying in a suite in Claridge's, and having been at an event the night before, he had taken scissors and cut off the bottom of a long satin John Galliano gown. Asked what her life might be like after thirty, "she wrinkled her nose and looked appalled at the prospect. She couldn't bear to think what it would be like to be that old."[5]

As fabulous as her life would be, her beginnings were mundane. She was born in the London suburb of Croydon in January 1974 to Peter, a travel agent for Pan Am, and Linda, a barmaid, who divorced when she was thirteen. The perk of her father's job was travel, and it was after a holiday in the Caribbean, having waited on standby at JFK airport for days, that the fourteen-year-old was spotted by Sarah Doukas, founder of the modeling agency Storm Management, on the flight home. Kate and her parents didn't think she was "model material," but Sarah saw something special in her. She slogged around London going to bookings in her school uniform but her mother only accompanied her for one day. It was pointless, she said, and so Kate did it on her own.[6]

She was forced to navigate the dangers of being a young model, including fighting off predators. During a casting with an underwear catalogue photographer, he asked her to take her bra off, and feeling uneasy, she "got my stuff and I ran away."[7] A more successful audition was for John Galliano in 1989, who was the first major designer to cast her in his show.

Kate had no plans for her future. She didn't feel particularly talented, and she just enjoyed hanging out with friends, going clubbing, drinking, and smoking. Modeling would help bring her some money while she was let loose on London's nightclub scene.

In 1990 the sixteen-year-old met photographer Corinne Day and stylist Melanie Ward, who both worked closely with British street style magazine *The Face*. Corinne Day was drawn to Kate because she was the opposite of what models were expected to look like. Kate was a scruffy waif rather than a glossy Amazonian whose otherworldly beauty didn't reflect youth culture. The swinging days of Twiggy and Jean Shrimpton were long gone, and Corinne wanted to return to that youthful, edgy sparkle.[8]

Corinne was commissioned to do photos for a "Third Summer of Love" theme for *The Face*, to capture the mood of rave culture. Acid House had emerged in the late eighties, with warehouse parties in London fueled by the new chemical drug, ecstasy. It created a sense of euphoria, and as disparate groups of people, from football hooligans to middle-class students, connected, they danced all night in sweaty warehouses or in fields in the middle of nowhere as a respite from the excessive eighties. Like the grunge movement coming out of Seattle, it was the opposite of glamorous, but it was real and hedonistic and fun.

For the photoshoot at Camber Sands, East Sussex, Corinne snapped Kate mid-conversation, laughing and smoking cigarettes, yet the young model also found it distressing because she didn't want to take her top off.

"It was painful because she was my best friend and I really loved her, but she was a very tricky person to work with. But the pictures are amazing: she got what she wanted and I suffered for them, but in the end they did me a world of good. They changed my career."[9]

With her natural freckles, the snaggle-tooth smile, and waifish body, she was the grungy, barefoot antithesis of Cindy Crawford and Linda Evangelista, and the photos defined the new look for the next decade.

The Face photographs were soon appearing on fashion moodboards on the other side of the Atlantic. Marc Jacobs, the young head designer at Perry Ellis, was so inspired by Kate that she would shape his controversial spring

1993 grunge collection, which took the disaffected style coming out of the music scene in Seattle and turned it into high fashion.

Grunge rejected beauty and worshipped drug use as a way of disassociating from the concerns around the recession and a lack of jobs. It was a nihilistic anti-fashion, of stringy hair and plaid shirts from thrift stores, and Kate was its poster girl. On the runway in November 1992, alongside supermodels Christy Turlington, Helena Christensen, and Carla Bruni, Kate Moss was the only one who looked like she belonged in Jacobs's designs.

After Kate was photographed by Patrick Demarchelier to relaunch *Harper's Bazaar*, she came to the attention of the Calvin Klein office, whose team included creative director Fabien Baron and Carolyn Bessette, a Grace Kelly blonde who understood the downtown New York scene. Calvin Klein was in a slump and to regain his popularity he needed to tap into the youth market. Previous successful campaigns, including those with Brooke Shields, were overtly sexual, and this time he wanted to capture the grungy mood while facing up to the threat of AIDS.

When Kate arrived for her casting in a pair of his jeans, she confidently plopped herself down on the studio floor, which at once grabbed the attention of Klein, who saw that she would appeal to fellow teens—"What is less than perfect is sexy."[10]

Also signed up by Klein was Mark Wahlberg, then an overconfident rapper famous for his muscled body, and the two were filmed together for an advertisement shot by Herb Ritts in gritty black and white. Having to press herself against him was incredibly stressful, particularly when he was so hostile and arrogant.

"It didn't feel like me at all. I felt really bad about straddling this buff guy. I didn't like it," she later said. "I couldn't get out of bed for two weeks. I thought I was going to die."[11]

She told BBC presenter Lauren Laverne in 2023 that she felt objectified. "And vulnerable and scared. I think they played on my vulnerability. I was young and innocent, and Calvin loved that."[12]

Her eight-year contract with Calvin Klein, £2 million a year at one point, was the biggest modeling contract of the day, and while he dropped Wahlberg, Kate continued to be the face of his underwear, fragrance, and jeans in commercials and on billboards in major cities. The simplicity of the plain cotton underwear, the long hair and makeup-free skin shot in stark black and white ushered in a new era of fashion photography that featured wafer-thin models who appeared to survive on coffee, cigarettes, and stimulants, and which would be dubbed "heroin chic."

In 1993, Corinne Day shot Kate for an eight-page spread for *British Vogue*, where she posed in underwear with fairy lights strung up on a wall behind her. These photos would spark a huge controversy and Kate would be roundly blamed for encouraging drug use, anorexia, and pedophilia. She was nineteen at the time, and the photos were bright and colorful, yet there was something about her young looks, that it looked like a girl's bedroom, that was offensive to many.

The *New York Times* compared the photos of Kate to that of the dead Laura Palmer in the TV series *Twin Peaks*, and placed them in the context of a new fascination with the "Lolita" figure.

"Are they, as the photographer insists, an attempt at documentary fashion? Are they just part of the waif continuum? Or are they an attempt at not just child pornography but some sort of class porn, that is to say, the eroticizing of the low-rent girl?"[13]

The controversy severed Corinne Day's relationship with *Vogue*, and Kate was advised by her agent that she should cut ties with her friend to protect her own career. Billboard photographs of Kate were being spray-painted with graffiti such as "feed me," and her body was roundly up for debate in the press, in the same way that Sarah Bernhardt and Twiggy had been mocked for their supposedly unnatural thinness. Kate was more than a model at this point, she was an "It" girl, and with the enormous interest in her life and the influence she wielded, girls looked up to her as their inspiration. Continually described as a "superwaif" and "stick-thin model," the negative influence over young women and disordered eating stayed with her, renewing the controversy in a 2009 interview with *Women's Wear Daily* when she claimed her motto was "Nothing tastes as good as skinny feels."[14]

It was the night of the CFDA Fashion Awards in 1994, and Kate had been the guest of Calvin Klein, who credited her with pushing his label back into the black. After the show she and Naomi Campbell swept into Café Tabac, the East Village bar that was a favorite of the fashion crowd. Journalist George Wayne grabbed Kate by the hand and led her into a back room, where actor Johnny Depp was having dinner with friends. "Kate, this is Johnny. Johnny, this is Kate." The sexual attraction was immediate, and it was the start of a three-year love affair that placed them as the grunge version of the "beautiful but damned"—painfully cool, successful, and with a taste for mind-altering substances.

They were the sharp cheek-boned, glittering version of Sid and Nancy with their notorious rows in hotel rooms, including one that caused $10,000 worth of damage to the presidential suite at The Mark Hotel, New York.

Kate lived the "sex, drugs and rock 'n' roll" lifestyle, attending Rolling Stone Ronnie Wood's fiftieth birthday party in June 1997 in a cowboy hat and tiny shorts as she cozied up to Anita Pallenberg and Oasis's Noel Gallagher.

With Britpop having pushed out grunge, and heroin chic declared over in 1997 following the shocking death of model Davide Sorrenti from an overdose, Kate was now one of the faces of the Cool Britannia movement. When she wore a Clements Ribeiro Union Jack sweater, it was immediately coveted. She and Johnny even took part in the recording of a charity record, *War Child*, performing on Oasis's contribution to the album, and they promoted it together on the UK's most popular morning show, *The Big Breakfast*.

Kate had a voracious appetite for drugs, allegedly able to consume three grams of coke and a bottle of vodka in a night, and earning the nickname "the Tank."[15] It was too much even for Depp, and she was paranoid that he was cheating on her and would phone to track him down wherever he was on set. When they broke up, Kate was devastated and it triggered "years and years of crying."[16]

If Kate's decadence was compared to Zelda Fitzgerald diving into a fountain in a slip dress, then Tara's voice full of money was straight from the pages of *The Great Gatsby*. Born in 1971, Tara grew up on her family's 1,200-acre Dummer Grance, a Grade II–listed country pile that neighbored that of the childhood estate of Sarah Ferguson, later the Duchess of York.

Her father, Charles Palmer-Tomkinson, was a close friend of Prince Charles's and served as his ski instructor, having represented Great Britain as a skier at the 1964 Winter Olympics. Her mother Patricia was severely injured and almost died in a 1988 avalanche that killed a royal aide. Tara's childhood followed the pattern of those born into aristocratic families. There was the spell at Sherborne boarding school in Dorset, in which she was proficient in piano, viola, and tennis, and ski trips with Prince William and Prince Harry.

When one of her boyfriends landed a helicopter on her parents' lawn, blowing all the petals off the flower beds, "Mummy was furious. . . . So from now on it has to be landed in the orchard."[17]

After boarding school, she moved to London to flat-share with her sister Santa, who worked in public relations for Ralph Lauren. The Chelsea flat was a base for extensive partying, as she spent her days at Rothschild's bank, then as a fashion stylist for glossy magazines, and her nights on the social circuit.

Even though she was given a generous allowance from her parents, there was no car for her twenty-first birthday. Instead, she saved up her proceeds from modeling to buy a red Mazda MX5. It was the first thing she had bought for herself, and she adored zipping through London with the top down, even when it was raining.[18]

In July 1995 she was arrested for speeding and suspected drunk driving when she careened across Chelsea Embankment in her Mazda, with Emily Oppenheimer in the passenger seat. She escaped the drunk-driving charge after a six-week wait for the results of her blood test, but the incident made it into the tabloids, where she was described as "Prince Charles' kissing pal."[19]

When paparazzi captured a fleeting moment of her being kissed on the cheek by Prince Charles while skiing in a pair of Ray-Bans, her name and image was splashed across the tabloids. Charles and Diana had just separated, and she was forced to deny the uncomfortable rumors she was more than a close family friend. On the back of the photo, Ray-Ban hired her to model for them, and she was soon signed up by other brands for her privileged, celebrity lifestyle—Mazda, Prada, Chanel, Versace, and Dolce & Gabbana.[20]

By 1995, a new movement called Britpop, with bands including Oasis, Blur, Pulp, and Suede, had pushed out the disaffected grunge movement in favor of something brighter, poppier, and very British. The sound meshed a sixties swing with themes around rave culture, football, and eating chips on a Saturday night, and the clothes combined thrift-shop vintage, Mod revival, and football casual. There were parties every night of the week in London and public relations experts were securing the most-demand "It" girls for their product launches. These PRs were part of the scene themselves—Meg Mathews would marry Oasis's Noel Gallagher, and party planner Fran Cutler was close friends with Kate Moss.

"The good times have never been so good, London is cool, champagne is flowing, recreational drugs are as casual as cashew nuts the party scene is powered as never before, by publicity and celebrity," wrote Victoria Mather in the *Evening Standard* in 1999. "You're an international designer/hotelier/ nightclub guru/restaurateur and you want to launch your new shop or eaterie, boutique, hotel or groovy bar and so you employ a PR empress, like Aurelia Cecil or Meg Mathews, to create the launch party at which famous people will be seen, and most importantly photographed, in order to generate the whirl of publicity that alerts a waiting world to the cool virtues of your product."[21]

Tara had the reputation as "the toff-about-town" and a "Trust Fund Babe" and every brand wanted her at their party.[22] She was a favorite among the glitterati for her sparkling personality and her sense of fun. "Why am I famous? That's the question I'm always asking," she laughed in that signature rapid machine-gun-fire manner.[23]

However she had achieved it, she was one of the most in-demand faces in the "It" crowd. Through 1995 she was a guest at Elton John's AIDS benefit at London's Versace store and at Jemima Goldsmith's wedding of the year to Imran Khan; her twenty-fourth birthday was hosted at Monte's, an exclusive private members club, and she was a fixture at the hottest new restaurant in Chelsea, Daphne's, because she was dating its owner, Danish millionaire Mogens Tholstrup. Her relationship with Tholstrup sparked a scandal because he was married. In a report in the *Sun*, Prince Charles was said to have given his approval to her relationship with Tholstrup when he was allowed to join Tara in the Royal party at Klosters.[24]

Her parents disapproved of her regular appearances in the tabloid news-papers in skimpy clothing. "It could be just a cashflow thing," one friend explained, as if they were straight out of the movie *Saltburn*.[25] Tara joked that whenever anyone asked her mother how she maintained her slim figure, she would get out the scrapbook of her newspaper cuttings and say, "read this, this is how I keep thin: my youngest daughter."[26]

In November 1996, Jane Procter, the editor of society bible *Tatler*, splashed Tara on the cover of the magazine alongside Normandie Keith, naming them as the new "It" girls. "What does it say about us that we care so much about them?" asked the coverline.

In this one cultural moment, Tara's reputation was sealed as one of the filthy rich private jet-setters who bronzed themselves on yachts moored at St. Tropez and sipped cocktails in Monte Carlo. Tara even proclaimed that she never left home without her passport in case lunch in Windsor ended up in Rome. There was one billionaire friend who was known to fly his guests to Venice for a decent coffee, which she described as "like going to Starbucks for me."[27]

"The more I heard about Tara, the more she sounded like the girl of the moment—the girl everyone wanted to be—so we revived that Twenties mon-iker and decided to call her the It girl," Procter remembered. "It was simple, really. The headline to a fashion story was written and a phenomenon—'the It girl'—was reborn, with Tara as its poster girl."[28]

By this time, Tara was already penning a weekly column for the *Sunday Times*, which was partly ghostwritten by the Style section's deputy edi-tor, Wendy Holden. With celebrity columnists coming in guns blazing and then only lasting a short time, she was skeptical that Tara would be able to hold readers' attention. "Little did I suspect what was coming," she later reflected.[29]

"The Social Diary of Tara Palmer-Tomkinson" poked fun at her jolly silver spoon background, complete with her trademark "Yah!" as the headline.[30] Originally, she was supposed to write it herself, but with her inability to fol-low deadlines, it was done over the phone. In the days before mobiles, trying to locate wherever Tara was in the world was, according to Wendy, a "weekly challenge worthy of MI5. I would invoke the help of her mother, her sister and her agent, before Tara herself would call (once from a car wash) and announce that she was ready to 'do the column.'"[31]

It was such a hit that posh friends would beg to be mentioned—when Lord Frederick Windsor and his friends bumped into her in a burger bar, she gave them a name-check.[32] *Tatler*'s Victoria Mather was at a house party in Ireland where she observed the guests fighting over the Style section of the *Sunday Times* to read her column (the butler was dispatched by bicycle to the village to buy extra copies). She may have been dismissed as silly and frivolous, but they were all desperate to read her.[33]

Tara was well aware that her column's appeal was to play up to the "It" girl label as a super-posh, and privileged, party girl. And she fizzed with personality—witty, kind, and with the ability to laugh at herself, she also appeared fragile because of her genuineness. This made her much more adored than the other "It" girls like Caprice and Normandie Keith, who may have been beautiful but took themselves seriously.

Underneath the glittering surface and party-loving demeanor, she felt most at home in the countryside, taking the dogs for a walk in her Wellington boots. There were two versions of Tara that conflicted with one another. "One was a sweet, country-loving girl who relished her weekends at home with the family; the other was the one you'd see in the gossip columns, hogging the limelight," she said in 1999. "In the end, the two Taras blurred into one, and I hated her."[34]

Despite all the attention from the fawning PRs who bestowed her with luxury goodies and party invites, she felt lonely, often dipping into melancholy around her failed love affairs and the fair-weather friends who turned up when it suited them.

Sometimes all the media attention and the nightly battles with the paparazzi was overwhelming, particularly when the British press only wanted to tear her down; to use the photos where she was blurry-eyed and stumbling out of a bar.

"I'm not necessarily crazy about being an It Girl anymore," she told the *New York Times* in an interview that took place in April 1999. "But I don't mind continuing to use it. Besides, I love my diary. I plan to keep on writing it until I'm 80. And Mummy and Daddy are very proud of me."[35]

Beneath the confidence and the air-kissing, she harbored a dark secret, and after three years as a party columnist she was burning out. As she told the *New York Times*, "I'm emotionally bankrupt. Then again, who wouldn't be with my schedule?" Her evenings were crammed with three cocktails parties a night as she schmoozed with the crème of London, and she was terrified of being exposed for her serious cocaine habit, which had become more pronounced the more famous she got. After trying coke for the first time at the age of twenty-one it became a crutch to provide energy and confidence "when faced with rooms full of strangers and flashing paparazzi lights."[36] Cocaine was as readily consumed as the canapes at a nineties party, and her addiction was said to cost up to £400 a day. She took the edge off the restless jitters after every line by washing it back with copious champagne.

She was lean and tanned, always dressed in Dolce & Gabbana, Versace, or Ben de Lisi, with glossy hair that attracted a rotation of rich playboys, yet still felt inadequate, particularly "when I'm in the sack with someone," she said. "You want to be this fantastic Venus temptress, not concentrating on lying on your side to make your boobs look bigger."[37] She struggled to manage her money, with her credit cards removed from her at one point, and despite being engaged several times, her high-profile relationships would implode. Journalist Victoria Mather described her as a "frail bunny" whose "innocence is there to be taken advantage of," and that "Being good at partying isn't always good for good girls. And the Tara I know is a good girl, not just an It Girl."[38]

By the time her interview had been published in the *New York Times*, she had already checked into the Meadows clinic in Arizona. The major wake-up call had been when she was a guest on the British comedian Frank Skinner's talk show that same April and was plastered across the papers the next day because she was clearly on something. The headlines shamed and embarrassed her into seeking help.

After breaking up with Depp, Kate found solace with even more hedonism, as she partied with London's notorious Primrose Hill Set, which included Sadie Frost and then-husband Jude Law, Pearl Lowe from indie group Powder, and her husband Danny Goffey of Supergrass. Kate was both a high-end fashion model and catnip for the tabloids, and there were salacious reports of drug-fueled partner-swapping and threesomes among this notorious set.

Anyone who ventured out with Kate could expect to be "Mossed"—she would drag them to the hottest bars and then to the after-parties, where they would inevitably stay out until 7 a.m. or later.[39]

When she found out that Depp was expecting a child with Vanessa Paradis, the first choice for the Calvin Klein campaign, it caused her to spiral further into a drug haze to hide her loneliness. In August 1998 she went on a bender in Ibiza and at a rave on a beach she met Diana Dors's son Jason Lake. In a kiss-and-tell in the papers, he revealed that he had been introduced to her through mutual friend Jade Jagger, daughter of Mick and Bianca, but given he'd been traveling in Goa for an extended period, he claimed never to have heard of her. After partying for forty-eight hours, he woke up with Kate next to him in his bed.

"Awright, Jason? Shall I make us some tea and toast?" he remembered her saying. His impression was that she was "really down to earth, but I'm hearing this voice, this Croydon accent, and I thought, 'Is it just me, or is she a bit rough?' . . . I looked at her and thought, "Yeah. She's really pretty and she's fucking sexy. She's got a bit of a gob on her, but she's lovely."[40]

Looking back on that summer of 1998, Kate was pushing herself to the limits. Why bother sleeping when there was so much more to do, and so many places to go?

"I was working, I was travelling a lot. I was playing and I didn't stop. It got to the point where it wasn't much fun anymore. It all became unbalanced. I was not very happy. I was doing things that weren't good for me. I had tried to stop certain things before; I had tried to get focused on other things. But I always ended up back in the same place and it wasn't making me happy. It is quite amazing what I didn't feel after a while. I didn't really want to feel things, probably."[41]

In November 1998 she checked into the Priory for five weeks, and when she came out, she cleaned out her home of alcohol, attended regular Alcoholics Anonymous and Narcotics Anonymous meetings, and saw a psychiatrist once a week. She began dating Jefferson Hack, the magazine publisher of *Dazed and Confused*, and in September 2002 she gave birth to their daughter Lila.

Over the next few years, Kate's value as a cultural icon, an "It" girl to modern muse, was captured in a number of art projects. In late 1999, *British Vogue* commissioned seven of the Young British Artists to create pieces inspired by Kate to be shown at the Tate Modern in May 2000. Kate's timeless beauty and appeal went beyond being the girl of the moment; she was compared to Marilyn Monroe, the Roman goddess Venus, and even the Virgin Mary. This was reinforced when she struck up a close friendship with the artist Lucian Freud, and as his muse, he painted her nude when she was pregnant.

Kate's undone style was part of her appeal—she wasn't perfectly groomed like Victoria Beckham, and in paparazzi photos her hair was tousled and messy, as if she had just rolled out of bed. Entire clothing lines and look books were created on the back of what she was snapped wearing one day, such as a slip dress that she had trimmed with a pair of scissors. By the 2000s, with the rise of celebrity gossip magazines, her outfits were analyzed and reproduced in the rising internet fashion brands like ASOS, as well as High Street favorites Topshop and Zara.

She selected vintage slips and forties and fifties cocktail dresses from specialists such as London's Steinberg & Tolkien. Girls coveted everything she wore—from the Vivienne Westwood pirate boots to Alexander McQueen's skull-print scarf and her ballet flats. After being snapped at Glastonbury festival in 2005 in tiny shorts, a waistcoat, and Hunter Wellington boots, she single-handedly reformed muddy festival fashion as well as reviving a heritage fashion brand.

Kate Moss setting the festival fashion aesthetic at Glastonbury in 2004. *Tim Rooke/ Shutterstock.*

She may have gone to rehab at the tail-end of the nineties, but she was just as wild in the 2000s, the glue to her group of Primrose Hill hedonists. Kate's thirtieth birthday party in January 2004 was themed "The Beautiful and the Damned," after F. Scott Fitzgerald's 1922 novel, as she connected deeply with Fitzgerald's destructive, decadent characters. The after-party was held in a suite at Claridge's, and served up with the champagne and cocaine were stories about group sex with Sadie Frost and Ronnie Wood. She was still making headlines, but there were also questions as to whether Kate was being usurped as an "It" girl by Jude Law's new girlfriend Sienna Miller, who had set a mass boho chic trend, and was named "Girl of the Year" by *Vogue* in December 2003. On the back of rumors that Chanel had severed her contract, there were digs in the press that it was her age and bohemian lifestyle, and in further bitchy asides, there were reports she had been knocked back for dates by Alex Kapranos of Franz Ferdinand and Sergio Pizzorno of Kasabian.[42]

In January 2005 Mick Jones of The Clash brought Kate to watch Pete Doherty rehearse with his band Babyshambles. She invited him to play at her thirty-first birthday party and from there they became the next rock 'n' roll couple. He was a heroin addict who had been imprisoned for burglary, but Kate considered him a modern-day Lord Byron. And even though columnists wondered what she saw in him, their hedonistic odd-couple relationship was catnip to the newspapers and gossip magazines. With the dirty fingernails and the wane complexion, he wore his drug addictions on the outside yet their association didn't do harm to her modeling career. It only served to enhance her cool factor.[43]

That was until photos were splashed in the *Daily Mirror* that appeared to show her snorting cocaine. One September evening in 2005, Kate had come along to watch a Babyshambles jam session, and dressed in shorts and knee-high boots, she carved out lines for the others in the room while knocking back vodka shots. Someone at the session secretly recorded it and the exposé sparked a scandal that caused her to lose over £4 million worth of modeling contracts, including for H&M, Chanel, and Burberry. The *Daily Mail* gloated on its September 22, 2005, cover—"Cocaine Kate's Career in Ruins."

Once again she was chastised and shamed for being a bad role model for teenage girls and there were false reports that social services were considering taking her three-year-old daughter away from her, as if the media were actually willing for this to happen. She checked into rehab in Arizona to appease her critics. "I felt sick and was quite angry because everybody I knew took drugs. For them to focus on me and try to take my daughter away was really hypocritical," she later told the *Times*.[44]

Despite the initial loss of contracts, the fashion world formed a protective circle. At the conclusion of his fall Paris Fashion Week show, Alexander McQueen bowed to the audience in a T-shirt saying "We Love You Kate," and youthful makeup brand Rimmel refused to pull their new campaign with Kate, which was themed around how to "recover" after a wild night of partying with their "anti-fatigue" technology. After a cooling-off period, she was hired once more by Calvin Klein, and new contracts flooded in, including for Stella McCartney, Nikon, and Virgin Mobile. Later she became the face of Coca-Cola and Diet Coke, almost asking for her to make the inevitable joke, "I've always loved Coke." From her early days as a teen model, Kate's charm and her "never complain, never explain" mantra was her silence, and this allowed her to bounce back. If there had been stories before the cocaine shame that her career was on a downward spiral, then her currency had doubled.

As the *Guardian* explained, Kate was "shorthand for the biggest ongoing celebrity drama of our times. She now officially embodies all kinds of newsworthy qualities: danger, sleaze-edged glamour, decadence, sex, corrupted youth and ineffable beauty, addiction, money and fashion."[45]

Kate gave up drinking as she approached fifty, moving from Highgate, North London to the idyllic Cotswolds region. She was bored of partying, and instead focused on woo-woo therapies—transcendental meditation, healing crystals—and growing her own vegetables. "I like to go to bed, get up early—do my meditation before anyone is up. And I like to be in control."[46]

Emerging from rehab in the noughties, Tara firmly embraced the new era of reality television which had been sparked by the huge success of *Big Brother*, first launched on Britain's Channel 4 in 2000 after the original Dutch series the year before. There were new shows that combined the access-all-areas filming with the addition of celebrities being shown in their natural states. In 2002 Tara was a surprise hit on the British television show *I'm A Celebrity… Get Me Out Of Here!* in which a group of recognizable names were placed in a camp together in the Australian rainforest. She followed it with further television appearances on prime-time shows, and other 1990s "It" girls also played up to the new fashion for slumming it on reality television. Caprice was on *Celebrity Big Brother* in 2005 and Tamara Beckwith took part in shows like *Dancing on Ice* and *Celebrity Scissor Hands*.

Tara had maintained her sobriety from drugs, but by 2006 she required cosmetic work on her nose to repair the damage. Given Kate Moss's scandal, the press salivated over the photos that showed her looking her worst, as if she was being shamed by the newly puritanical media for all her excesses. In 2011 she hit the headlines again when new pictures of her damaged nose appeared just before she was due to attend the royal wedding of Prince William and Kate Middleton.[47] She had to work hard to keep herself clean from drugs and she blamed British journalists for trying to make her relapse with their intrusive articles that would feed into her feelings of self-worth. What was the end game, she seethed. "Because the end game was going to be Amy Winehouse."[48]

Tara's love life had been well documented, but by the time she had reached forty, she had all but given up on it. "But no one will ever love me again, I look like Quasimodo," she told one friend, and she really struggled with aging. It was tough for someone so beautiful and vibrant to accept that they were now treated differently.[49] Instead, her group of friends were "a lot of gays," including the actor Rupert Everett. She and Rupert would joke, "We're dying to die, so that people can be upset at our funeral."[50]

As much as she had carved a famous-for-being-famous persona, it was frustrating that she was dismissed for being a dim party girl. "Being called talentless, that is the worst," she said. "I can recite every line of Shakespeare. I've got a really good brain. Of course, I haven't earned [fame] and I didn't feel I was worth it, and going to all those endless parties, it made me feel worth a pile of shit."[51]

She reinvented herself as an author, first with *The Naughty Girl's Guide to Life* in 2007, and then the ghostwritten novels *Inheritance* (2010) and *Infidelity* (2012). As a classically trained pianist she also, like Paris Hilton, experimented with music, releasing an album of ballads in 2012.

In 2015 Tara received the shock diagnosis of a brain tumor, and she was terrified. After treatment she was given the all clear, but she continued to suffer from a rare autoimmune disease.[52] She shut herself away from all the attention she had once courted, and in February 2017 her name hit the headlines again. Tara had been found dead in her apartment at the age of forty-five.

At first it was suspected that her brain tumor had returned, but an autopsy later revealed her cause of death was a perforated ulcer. It was a tragic end for an "It" girl who had been so vibrant and fun, and who possessed that rare ability to laugh at herself and her privilege. She paved the way for reality stars, Instagram influencers, and the Kardashians, who became cultural fixtures for "being famous for being famous."

"I'm really glad I'm posh," she once said. "There are some nice holidays. And some nice princes. Holidays, princes and cashmere, those are the best bits. And the drugs are quite good with being posh, because you can afford better ones."[53]

15

Paris Hilton, Britney Spears, and the Noughties "It" Girls

Paris Hilton papped while arriving at an event on Melrose Avenue, November 2006. *Francis Specker/Alamy Stock Photo.*

There's a photo that perfectly encapsulates the celebrity culture of the mid-noughties. Sitting in the driving seat of her Mercedes-Benz SLR McLaren is Paris Hilton, with Lindsay Lohan and Britney Spears both squeezed in beside her, their giddy faces glowing from the flash of the camera.

It was the night of November 28, 2006, and they'd dashed from a Beverly Hills party and into the safety of Paris's car to escape a mob of photographers. The next day the *New York Post* splashed the snatched shot with the headline "Bimbo Summit"—a sneering insinuation that these were brainless women who were made to be exploited. The image, which Paris compared to *Charlie's Angels*, would later be mass-marketed on mugs, cards, bags, and laminated windscreen shades.

The "Bimbo Summit" photo marked the point before the downfall of these three women, with Paris soon going to jail for violating probation for a reckless driving case, Lindsay wrecking her career with her unreliable behavior on set and checking into rehab, and Britney's very public mental breakdown leading to an enforced conservatorship which took away her freedom for thirteen years.

All three—Britney, Paris, and Lindsay—have at times been compared with Marilyn Monroe as symbols of the tarnishing of the American Dream. Lindsay even styled herself like Marilyn in her "Golden Dreams" calendar for a spread in *Playboy*, and like the fifties icon, she was perpetually late to set, she struggled with addiction issues, and appeared to be on a path of self-destruction.[1]

Paris Hilton was the epitome of "famous for being famous," taking Tara Palmer-Tomkinson's model of celebrity and fully exploiting it by transforming it into a billion-dollar business. On the surface she was skinny and blonde, she loved to party, the definition of what she did for work was blurry, and she could turn on her sex appeal, and her little girl voice, for the paparazzi in an instant. The "Bimbo Summit" image was taken nine years after the death of Diana, Princess of Wales, whose last photo was under the glare of a camera flash. If her death had triggered sober reflection on the fervent pursuit of celebrities, then it was all forgotten by the millennium.

The 2000s was the new paparazzi age, fueled by the overwhelming popularity of weekly celebrity gossip magazines, the burgeoning internet ripe for online blogs like that of Perez Hilton's, which cruelly dissected young, famous women, and new technologies like digital cameras, which allowed an image to be downloaded in seconds, and cell phones that made it easier to track a starlet like prey.

The UK's *Heat* magazine, first conceived in 1999 as a culture magazine, was relaunched in 2000 by editor Mark Frith to specialize in celebrity gossip. If you look at the magazine's covers across the years, there's a clear shift in

how this gossip was reported from 2003. Initially cover stories were celebra-
tory; "Madonna and Guy's Wedding Secrets!" and "Posh's Dramatic New
Look" were splashed in 2001. But by April 2003 there was a sudden shift.
The garish covers now promised "stars without make-up," "boob jobs! Who's
had them, who hasn't," and "drunk celebs." At this point *Heat* introduced its
"circle of shame," as if it was highlighting with a red pen the cellulite, sweat
patches, and spots that were afflicting glamorous women. The *Mail Online*,
launched in 2003, followed suit with its "sidebar of shame." These outlets
argued they were just giving the public what they wanted. Paris Hilton called
it "the Chicken McNugget of the new information age: not especially good
for you but delicious. And irresistible. I was at the eye of that perfect storm."[2]

In the year 2000, the possibilities of the world wide web were only just
being discovered, but there was no social media, no camera phones, or You-
Tube to upload videos. The main threat was the paparazzi, whose digital
cameras made it so much easier to capture an unguarded moment; of a beautiful celebrity shoving a burger in their mouth, tripping up over the dog lead,
almost dropping their baby, and falling out of a nightclub drunk. A self-starter
with a camera and a shameless desire to pursue could earn tens of thousands
for the right picture.

These new "It" girls, which included, at times, the stars of *The O.C.* Mischa
Barton and Rachel Bilson, actress Tara Reid and Paris's best friend Nicole
Richie, were the culture of the time—mentioned in songs, from N.E.R.D's
"Everyone Nose (All the Girls Standing in Line for the Bathroom)," to Pink's
"Stupid Girls." The singer was scathing that little girls were being taught to
be as vacuous as Paris, when she preferred to celebrate the "outcasts and girls
with ambition." A *South Park* episode, "Stupid Spoiled Whore Video Play-
set" went further; denigrated the "It" girls of the time as it reflected the trend
to sexualize, insult, and harass young women.

It was at the turn of the millennium that Paris first arrived on the scene as
the "It" heiress. In an October 2000 article in the *New York Post* profiling the
"daring heiresses of New York's social scene" who were "young and sinfully
gorgeous with multimillion-dollar trust funds," Paris was named as the most
outrageous, with "a tendency to flash her thong."[3] And in a feature in the *New
Yorker* in 1999, Paris Hilton's blonde privilege was compared to other debutante "It" girls of the past, including Brenda Frazier, Jane Holzer, and Edie
Sedgwick.[4] It was these "It" girls that were on the mind of David LaChapelle
when he plotted out his boundary-pushing images for *Vanity Fair*'s September 2000 issue which celebrated the notions of being a modern "It" girl,
alongside a feature on Paris and younger sister Nicky titled "Hip Hop Debs."

Paris recollected how she and LaChapelle discussed "Edie Sedgwick, the
intriguing idea of the 'It Girl,' and how celebrity worship mimics religious

ecstasy."[5] He snapped her giving the finger while revealing her breasts through a mesh vest, spread out on her back on a beach while surrounded by surfers, and on a neon street with Nicky, both striking confident, arrogant poses in micro-miniskirts. For the accompanying feature, Nancy Jo Sales sat down with the Hiltons at their home in the Hamptons, as mom Kathy teased Paris with the nicknames "the Heiress," the "it girl," and "Star," because she'd known from a young age that she would be one. Her grandmother had even been told by a psychic that the adorable little blonde girl would one day be the most photographed woman in the world—bigger than Marilyn Monroe.[6]

"People think I'm just this party girl," Paris smiled. "Well, I'm not like that. I don't just go to parties. I wake up in the morning and go to auditions. I was going to go to college, but then I decided to take a year off. They were mad."

Despite her denials, the article launched Paris as the new spoiled little rich girl as she worked the party circuit with Nicky, dressed like "blonde Barbie twins," knowing that they were soaking up all the attention. "It's like all she wants to do is become famous," a friend revealed to Nancy Jo Sales, "to wipe out the past, to become somebody else."

Paris had only just reappeared on the party scene after disappearing during her final year of high school. When Nancy Jo Sales asked where she had been, Kathy disclosed, incorrectly, that she had gone to London to escape a stalker.[7] It turned out that Paris was holding on to a dark, painful secret.

The Hilton family had moved from Los Angeles to New York in 1996 for dad Rick's business and Paris fell into the club scene, sneaking out of her bedroom to go dancing all night. As her photos were splashed in the tabloids, her parents were increasingly fretful that their daughter was out of control. So, they made the terrible decision for her to be kidnapped in the middle of the night from their apartment in the Hilton-owned Waldorf Astoria and taken to a wilderness school that was supposed to kick wayward teens into shape. It was a traumatic, cruel experience of extreme endurance, hunger, isolation, and abuse from the teachers, which stole her teenage years.

Trapped there for over a year, despite desperate attempts to escape, she imagined a future where she would have enough money to be completely free and independent. She imagined a world where instead of a drab uniform and bloodshot eyes she would have "lush fake lashes, a seamless spray tan, and a touch of glitter on my cheekbones. Instead of shame, I would wrap myself in audacity, and I would make so much money and be so successful, no one could ever have control over me again."[8]

Paris adored Diana, Princess of Wales and was devastated when she died, but she didn't connect the early glimmers of celebrity lifestyle she had experienced with the fervent paparazzi who were blamed for Diana's death. The joy of the 1990s partly ended with a car crash in a Paris tunnel in August 1997, and then, two years later, with the death of another style icon. John F. Kennedy Jr. was flying his wife Carolyn Bessette-Kennedy, the willowy blonde who had once worked for Calvin Klein, to a wedding in Martha's Vinyard in July 1999 when he lost control of the plane and it plummeted into the sea.

Nine months earlier, a teenager from Louisiana was propelled to the top of the charts with her debut single, and it sparked a new wave of pop music, shifting from the indie sounds that had rocked the previous decade into something more fresh, precocious, and pop. Courtney Love, Kathleen Hanna, and Shirley Manson had been the strong and insolent rock stars of the nineties, but under this new pop banner Britney Spears and Jessica Simpson were girlishly pink and overtly sexualized.

Britney Spears's story was the American dream, of transforming from a Bible Belt innocent into a global pop icon and lusted-after sex symbol. She was the girl next door whose blonde perkiness was not just desirable, but relatable. Her gymnast-honed body with the washboard flat stomach revealed by low-rise jeans was hailed as perfection and for several years she was regularly named as the world's "Sexiest Woman" by magazines like *FHM*.

At first she was the precocious virgin, but then, following her split from Justin Timberlake, she was the harlot who broke his heart. As Britney struggled with her identity and the immense pressures of fame she faced, she expressed her wild side, she got married, she had children. When Britney revealed her true self it was often too much—and as authentic as it was, she was dismissed as white trash.

The noughties was a peculiar post-feminist landscape, where programs like *Sex and the City* empowered women to have sex like men, yet it also placed an awful lot of pressure on young women to be "sexy." They were expected to have Brazilian bikini waxes, to wear thongs with the strings visible above their hipsters, to be adept at pole-dancing, and to be as skilled in bed as a porn star. Sexy was everywhere—in music, film, and art, in fashion and sport, with Olympians even being encouraged to strip off for magazine spreads. Being "Hot" was the way to be popular; and Britney and Paris were the women to emulate. It was a period that Ariel Levy, in her book *Female Chauvinist Pigs*, named "raunch culture," as "Girls Gone Wild" became a cultural phenomenon as the Y2K version of *Playboy*. Its founder, the since-disgraced Joe Francis, encouraging real women, rather than models, to strip off for the cameras. They were often college-age or younger, so drunk they could hardly consent, and would be mortified the next day to realize they'd been filmed flashing their breasts, making out with their friends, and performing sex acts. It also had a narrow lens of female beauty: blonde, blue eyes, skinny limbs.[9]

"This was a time when feminism could not have been more needed. And yet, perversely, it was a time when women's liberation had been declared prematurely redundant," wrote Sarah Ditum in *Toxic*, her book about the period which she dubbed "the Upskirt Decade." "Things that the second wave of feminism had worked hard to make socially unacceptable—pornography, sexualisation, painful beauty standards—now made a resurgence."[10]

The initial charm of Britney Spears was her American every-girl quality and a childhood that was painted as humble and ingrained with the southern values of her hometown, Kentwood, Louisiana. In her 2023 memoir she revealed the reality—that her father was an alcoholic, her parents were always arguing, and her mother Lynne, who had penned the memoir *A Mother's Gift*, in 2001 on the back of her daughter's fame, would give thirteen-year-old Britney alcoholic cocktails on car journeys.

From an early age, Britney discovered that singing made her feel confident and in control, and her mother latched onto her talents by sending her tape to agencies and television shows in the hope she might be able to harness it as a career. She competed in the *Star Search* television contest and was then recruited for *The Mickey Mouse Club*, alongside future stars Justin Timberlake, Christina Aguilera, and Ryan Gosling. At the age of fifteen she signed with Jive Records and moved to New York to record her first album.

Britney was more in control of her image and her sound than credited with in the beginning. To get into the right mind for recording her first single, ". . . Baby One More Time," she stayed up all night so she could sound more mature. She also rejected the label's concept of a futuristic animation for the video, instead suggesting it be set in the classroom, with Britney as a bored schoolgirl who starts dancing as soon as the bell rings. She knotted the shirt of her Catholic school uniform around the waist, wore her hair in bunches, and unleashed a new look and sound for the new millennium.

Thrown into the limelight, and named as the Princess of Pop, her Lolita qualities were reinforced with her cover feature for *Rolling Stone* in April 1999, with the headline "Inside the Heart, Mind & Bedroom of a Teen Dream." David LaChapelle arrived in Louisiana to photograph her in her family home, positioning her surrounded by dolls, and lying on satin bed-sheets in polka-dot underwear as she talked on the phone. Britney was treated as a precocious teen who was both innocent and sexy at the same time. Her body was analyzed and critiqued, and there was a particular fascination as to whether she'd had plastic surgery on her still-growing chest. Watching the clips of older male interviewers ask these questions, it's like the treatment of Brooke Shields all over again.

At a time when abstinence was being pushed as the only form of birth control, much was made of Britney's own vows of celibacy, and her relationship with Justin Timberlake only further served to pique interest. MTV's host Kennedy was even quoted as saying "Britney is a perfect example of the contradictory feelings people have about virgins. It's kind of lame to act slutty and not follow through."[11]

Britney expressed her disgust at being offered £7.5 million by an anonymous businessman for her virginity. Given the Lolita fantasy, there was always a question of her suitability as a role model. Just as parents winced at the breathy lyrics, the cover of the February 14, 2000, edition of *People* magazine asked if she was "Too Sexy Too Soon?"

At the 2000 VMAs, she performed a mash-up of The Rolling Stones' "(I Can't Get No) Satisfaction" with "Oops! . . . I Did It Again," beginning in a suit and fedora, and stripping off to a sparkly flesh-colored bra for an athletic, strong routine. Britney, in her memoirs, recounted how MTV sat her in front of a monitor to watch as members of the public critiqued her performance, that it was too sexy and a bad example for children. "Did I do something wrong?" she asked herself. "I'd just danced my heart out on the awards show. I never said I was a role model. All I wanted to do was sing and dance." She described it has her "first real taste of a backlash that would last years."[12]

Paris emerged blinking into 1999 from Provo Canyon School, the Utah youth treatment center, to find that Britney was the number-one star and there had been huge changes in technology. Cell phones were becoming ubiquitous, people communicated by email, and the new iMac came in a range of colors. With her focus on being a model, her starved body was a fit with the heroin chic trend of the times, and she dyed her hair back to "Barbie platinum," bought rave outfits at Hotel Venus, owned by Patricia Field, the costume designer for *Sex and the City*, and hit the nightclubs in L.A. Now that she was eighteen, no one could stop her from drinking and dabbing MDMA to help her shut out the painful memories. She adored feeling like a star on her nights out, and she embraced the paparazzi to relish every moment of attention, shifting her vocal register to a girlishly soft sound. She felt like Marilyn Monroe even when she was shopping at Kitson or buying frozen yogurt.

Ron Galella, an old-school paparazzo, described her in 2005 as "a phenomenon." He praised her as "sexy, smart, gracious, and kind, and there's no one like her in the past, and I doubt there will be another one like her in the future. She's always giving us variations on the red carpet, posing this way and that way, and this is what a photographer wants: variety, you know, moving around. Because that's what life is about: movement."[13]

The David LaChapelle photos proved to be Paris's access point to A-list fame, and as she walked the runway at major fashion shows and turned up at the most exclusive parties every celebrity magazine wanted the latest gossip tidbit. Barron Hilton would say: "Most of my life I was known as Conrad Hilton's son. Now I'm Paris Hilton's grandfather."[14]

Paris was turning herself into a brand, as she embraced her image as the perma-tanned, Barbie blonde with the desirable flat stomach that was designed for the low-rise hipster jeans that were normally so unforgiving. Tara Palmer-Tomkinson had been in demand as a brand representative and party guest, but now Paris was collecting fees for every appearance. She may not have concentrated well at school, but she was instinctual when it came to business. She could party hard, but at the same time she was savvy about how to capitalize on every moment of her celebrity.

She would further exploit this character in her own reality TV show *The Simple Life*, alongside her best friend, Nicole Richie, daughter of the singer Lionel Richie. Reality television was a phenomenon of the 2000s, fulfilling audiences' voyeuristic desire to see into people's lives under the guise of psychological insight. Shows like *Big Brother* and *American Idol* not only gave ordinary people their chance to achieve their Warholian fifteen minutes, but also celebrities could now expose themselves to young audiences in fly-on-the-wall shows. The success of *The Osbournes* kick-started this new trend, and now, in their series, Paris and Nicole acted as spoiled Beverly Hills princesses as they were sent to stay and work with Midwest farming families.

Paris told the BBC's *The One Show* in 2023 that creating the character of "this Barbie doll, fantasy life" was a trauma response, "so I didn't have to think about what I went through. And then I got *The Simple Life*, and then I had to continue playing that character season after season, and then I almost got stuck in it because I was so used to doing it. And I'm naturally a shy person, so I feel like it was sort of a mask, to just be able to deal with all the pressures."[15]

Just as the show was about to air, there were rumors that there was a sex tape of Paris with an ex-boyfriend, Rick Salomon in circulation. Paris, who was now dating "Girls Gone Wild" founder Joe Francis, was about to become the ultimate prize of exploitation in a world where real sex was selling. By November 2003, mainstream publications were reveling in the tape's existence, and the full version, available for purchase, received free advertising on the late-night shows that made jokes at her expense. Rather than sympathy, Paris was slut-shamed and chastised for her own indecency in allowing it to happen. "Funny, no one mentioned the decency of people who watch creepy sex videos of teenage girls," she wryly commented in her memoir.[16]

Paris was painted as a spoiled brat who got everything she wanted, and deserved; she was too pretty, too rich, and not apologetic enough, and therefore she needed to be brought down. A woman's career could be destroyed by the hint of a sex scandal. Vanessa Williams, the first Black woman to be crowned Miss America in 1983, was stripped of the title when *Penthouse* magazine published nude photos without her consent. Just over a year after Paris's sex tape, Janet Jackson suffered a wardrobe malfunction at the 2004 Superbowl halftime show, and the resulting scandal impacted negatively on her career (while Justin Timberlake emerged unscathed). YouTube was launched on February 14, 2005, as a response to millions searching for Janet Jackson's "nipplegate" video.

With double standards around race, maybe it was easier for a white woman to be forgiven, and Paris looked to her icon Marilyn Monroe as her guiding light in how to handle a scandal designed to humiliate her. Rather than denying she was the girl in the nude calendar, Marilyn had owned it. And Paris chose to do the same for her sex tape. Even though she was still a teenager when it was filmed, and the tape was released for profit against her will, rather than sinking her, it would propel her to new levels of fame. Instead of hiding away, she chose to make a surprise appearance on *Saturday Night Live*'s "Weekend Update" with Tina Fey and Jimmy Fallon in June 2003, demonstrating that she could laugh at herself.

When *The Simple Life* aired on Fox on December 2, 2003, it was a hit, partly driven by the curiosity around Paris and her love her/hate her marmite personality. If "It" girls of the twentieth century had been created through the movies, then fame in the new millennium was found in reality television.

She launched her own perfume and jewelry range, she modeled for *Vogue* and Guess jeans, and in 2005, she appeared in an advert for Carl's Jr., chowing down on a burger while sexily washing a car. "That's hot!" was the tagline, matching her own trademarked expression. She tried acting, with a role in the 2005 slasher film *House of Wax* (advertised with the slogan "See Paris Die!"), and released her first single, the reggae-infused "Stars Are Blind," in June 2006.

In an interview with the *New York Times* in May 2005, she declared her role models to be the empire-creating Sean "Diddy" Combs and Donald Trump, two billionaires whose reputations haven't aged well. Paris was commanding up to $200,000 for a twenty-minute appearance at a party, or more if she was in Japan, and she was even opening her own nightclubs, Club Paris, in Orlando and Las Vegas.

There was a book, *Confessions of an Heiress*, a huge success when published in September 2004, which was aimed at teenage girls but drew in readers from a wide demographic.

With her unashamed ability to profit from her fame, Paris was one of the first influencers of the internet age. This new capitalist term, "influencer," came into being around 2015, but Paris was the self-proclaimed OG, or original, who was a promoter for the burgeoning cell phone industry in the early 2000s. She clipped her clamshell phone to the waist of her Juicy Couture tracksuit, then updated it to a rhinestone-encrusted Nokia. In 2004 she and Snoop Dogg were the face of the Sidekick, the first smartphone that included a phone, camera, email, and text, and she credited herself with inventing the selfie when she and Britney turned the camera phone on themselves in November 2006. Although this claim was refuted by those who pointed out there were much earlier examples, such as the Swedish couple using their homemade selfie stick in 1934.[17]

Britney's schedule in 2002 was tireless, with album promotions and tours, and it was coupled with a devastating breakup with Justin Timberlake that marked the moment when things began to fall apart. The former boy band singer was trying to build his reputation as a solo star, and his first single, "Cry Me a River," was designed to propel him to serious R&B artist status. The music video featured a woman who looked just like Britney, even wearing the same baker boy cap she often sported, and in the media she was slut-shamed as the cheater who broke Justin's heart. Although, according to Britney, it was he who had been cheating on her. The double standard, that men "are encouraged to talk trash about women in order to become famous and powerful," was something she felt bitterly.[18]

In the reassessment in the 2020s of how Britney was treated during this time, her 2003 interview with Diane Sawyer, planned as publicity for her new album, *In the Zone*, was used as an example of the double standards. She informed Britney of a comment by the Maryland governor's wife that the singer should be shot for being a bad role model to children. But rather than condemn this threat of violence, she insinuated it was justified for Britney's scantily clad photoshoots. "What happened to your clothes?" she chastised.[19]

Britney would describe the interview as a turning point, the moment that she felt herself switching from good to bad girl. There was the sensational kiss with Madonna at the MTV Video Music Awards in 2003, dressed in virginal white alongside Christina Aguilera, and in the music video for the dark ballad "Everytime" she played a superstar who dies in a bathtub, as if she was destroying her own persona. On a trip to Las Vegas she spontaneously married a childhood friend, until her parents swept in and forced it to be annulled.

If she was at the peak of her career, then it would slide further into chaos when she met dancer Kevin Federline. One of Britney's naïve mistakes was to follow Paris's example by taking part in her own reality show, *Britney and Kevin: Chaotic*, filmed with handheld camera footage while backstage on the 2004 The Onyx Hotel Tour. The format may have worked for *Madonna: Truth or Dare*, but it was too exposing of her raw lifestyle as she drank heavily, swore, and discussed her sex life. "I'm real, I'm just going to tell you like it is," she said, but people didn't want to see the gloss removed.

There was a wedding to Kevin, and she had two babies in quick succession. It was tough on her body and on her mind as she struggled with postpartum depression while also being stalked by paparazzi. Pictures were splashed in magazines of Britney with messy hair and without makeup, and with the normal body of a woman who had just given birth. She didn't have the gym-toned abs that she was once celebrated for, but, as she wrote in her memoirs, "At what point did I promise to stay seventeen for the rest of my life?"[20]

After a much-publicized and relished split with Kevin, Paris Hilton reached out to Britney, who she could tell was struggling, and invited her out to have some fun. The tabloids were quick to label Britney as an irresponsible, out-of-control mother who was drunk, on drugs, and flashing her naked crotch to the cameras.

To gain full custody, Kevin rehabilitated his own image while painting Britney as an unfit mother and the stress of the situation led to candid shots of a "crazed" Britney. In February 2007, she was captured shaving off her long mane at a hair salon and as she attacked a photographer's car with an umbrella, like a wild animal unleashed. These incidents were played as jokes, but, she wrote, "nobody seemed to understand that I was simply out of my mind with grief."[21]

Part of her appeal had been her hair, and so by shaving it off she was making a statement—she wasn't going to be the pretty, good girl anymore, the one who tried so hard to be liked, and who was supposed to be America's dream girl, even as she was leered at and criticized as a bad influence. Her fourth album *Blackout* was released in October 2007, and it was an angry, pointed skewering of the culture she was at the center of. The single "Piece of Me" tracked her as "the American Dream" whose derriere is exposed in the magazines, who is given the finger by the paparazzi, and who is both too fat and too thin. She was invited to perform "Gimme More" at the VMAs, but it was a disaster as she was ridiculed for the hair extensions and stomach that wasn't as flat as it had been before she birthed two children. Whatever she did was now trashy and slutty, and her opening line of "Gimme More," in which she utters "It's Britney, bitch," placed her as a new, monstrous Britney.

Eventually the mocking, the harassing, the public's willing for her to fail came to a dramatic conclusion following a disturbance at her home. On January 3, 2008, as the cameras flashed around her, she was strapped into a stretcher and taken by ambulance to hospital to undergo an emergency psychiatric evaluation.

For the next thirteen years she was placed in a conservatorship by her father, who controlled her finances, her diet, and her career. Despite her mental health issues, she was put back to work—releasing albums, going on world tours, and providing a steady source of income for all those who worked for her. Britney's fans began to realize something was wrong, and the grassroots #FreeBritney movement spent years campaigning for her to be released from this conservatorship.

She just wanted to be normal, but in this pressurized world, the young woman who was suffering from postnatal depression was exploited until she broke. There was a classism to it, as the good southern values she was at first praised for were used against her as she was now considered white trash. As Jennifer Otter Bickerdike writes in *Being Britney*, "Fans did not understand (or want to understand) that the very 'ordinariness' they so loved in Britney was actually a reflection of themselves—a reflection that they did not like as much when it was mirrored back at them."[22]

Paris's starry ascent almost crashed when she was handed a forty-five-day jail sentence in May 2007 after being caught behind the wheel on a suspended license, following a drunk-driving plea the year before. There was a collective appetite to punish her, not just for the crime, but for all her transgressions as a supposedly vacuous party girl. Rather than being placed under house arrest, as had been expected, she was sent to maximum security, a place usually reserved for violent offenders.

Once released, she took part in a mea culpa interview with Larry King, where she vowed never to drink and drive again, and during an appearance on David Letterman in September 2007, he relished her discomfort at being asked about her time in jail. The interview was designed to humiliate her and all the other rich and beautiful trainwrecks who deserved their fall from grace. The interview resurfaced in 2021, at a time when the #FreeBritney campaign brought about a new reckoning for how the noughties "It" girls had been treated.

The glamorous lifestyle that Paris embodied was an escape for everyone who lapped up the gossip and bought the celebrity weeklies. Naomi Wolf described the mid-2000s as a time when the American population was "hypnotized" by affluence and consumerism. "We're in the most aggressively anti-intellectual, anti-literate, anti-middle-class discourse," she said.[23]

Alexis Neiers said she had been drinking with Nick Prugo at a trendy bar on Hollywood Boulevard on July 13, 2009, when his friend, Rachel Lee, came to meet them. Both Lee and Prugo had been robbing celebrity homes, having used the tools of the internet, such as Google maps and *Gawker*'s "Gawker Stalker" feature to find out a celebrity's current location. The teenagers knew that Orlando Bloom was in New York making a movie and so, under the cover of darkness, they broke into the home he shared with Miranda

Kerr, stealing up to $500,000 in Rolex watches, Louis Vuitton luggage, clothing, and artwork.[24]

Across a ten-month period from October 2008 the gang stole over three million dollars' worth of jewelry, purses, and clothing from the homes of the current crop of "It" girls, including Paris Hilton, Lindsay Lohan, Audrina Patridge (from the reality show *The Hills*), and Rachel Bilson.

Rachel Lee called the robberies "going shopping," as they grabbed a suitcase and filled it up with Chanel, Prada, Marc Jacobs, and Dolce & Gabbana. Paris Hilton's was the first home they tried, because they thought she was too "dumb" to notice, and they were able to enter with a door key found under the mat. As well as designer clothing, they also claimed to have stolen Grey Goose vodka, five grams of cocaine, and crumpled cash from her wallet. It wasn't until months later that Paris realized two million dollars' worth of jewelry had been taken.

In August 2009 they targeted Lindsay Lohan's Hollywood Hills home, stealing up to $130,000 worth of clothes and jewelry. Through the LAPD, the actress used TMZ to release her surveillance tapes of the suspects, and with tips pouring in, the gang were soon apprehended.[25]

Neiers, a former pole-dancing instructor, was taking part in her own reality show, *Pretty Wild*, with her best friend and *Playboy* model Tess Taylor, and was followed by the "E!" network crew as she arrived at Los Angeles Superior Court to be charged with burglary of Orlando's home. Their nickname, "the Bling Ring," quickly caught on as it had all the ingredients of a juicy story—it was an audacious crime carried out by celebrity-obsessed Millennials, and Neiers was said to have worn six-inch Louboutins to her court appearance. The burglars were now the celebrities, with *Good Morning America*, *Dateline*, and TMZ all waiting to film them.

"They wanted to look like celebrities, and wear things that made them look good. They wanted to be able to go up to the door at certain nightclubs in LA where the celebrities were hanging out, and to walk in and look . . . styled and beautiful," said Nancy Jo Sales in a documentary for the DVD release of Sofia Coppola's 2013 *The Bling Ring* movie. "Why do kids want to look like celebrities? Actually doesn't our culture promote that idea. We have something that we never had before. A twenty-four-seven celebrity news media."

The lifestyle of the noughties "It" girls had rubbed off on impressionable teenagers who believed their lives wouldn't be complete unless they lived the life of the rich and famous— "papped" at nightclubs, possessing the latest bag and shoes. The celebrity style section of magazines and online fashion brands like ASOS taught how to get the look of celebrities, but imagine owning the exact sparkling dress Paris had been photographed in, or the sunglasses and

Birkin bag? Fame was the currency of millennials, and this emulation culture would only become more pronounced with the advent of the Instagram age.

One actress whose image and personal life fed the celebrity culture of the 2000s was determined to stand up and fight. By 2005 she had become a focus of tabloid attention for her relationship with Jude Law, her co-star in 2004's *Alfie*, coupled with her status as a poster girl for bohemian luxury. Sienna Miller was "the biggest tabloid target in Britain," according to the *Observer* in June 2005, and an "actress and model who has been traded like pork belly on the celebrity market."[26]

As she acted in a London West End production of *As You Like It* over the summer of 2005, the twenty-three-year-old was faced with a very intrusive article in the *Sun* that revealed she was pregnant. Performing on stage eight times a week, she felt completely exposed, and looking back on it in 2022 she described it as "hell." She was in the public eye while feeling "extremely heartbroken. Trying not to break. All the while being mocked and ridiculed."[27]

Sienna was born in New York to an American banker and art dealer father and an English–South African mother who was a former model and PA to David Bowie. There was a sparkle of stardust to her childhood; her mother went into labor while watching *The Nutcracker Suite* in a New York theatre.[28]

She attended an English boarding school from the age of eight, and with her sunny and expressive personality driving a desire to be an actress, she returned to New York to study at the Lee Strasberg Institute.[29] She took jobs as a model, including for a prestigious Pirelli calendar, before being cast in two 2004 movies, the gangster flick *Layer Cake* and *Alfie*, both of which required her to be nude.

Sienna's global fame happened almost instantaneously, before those movies had even been released. She was first linked to Jude in the *Mail on Sunday* at the end of September 2023, with a gossipy article about how Jude, going through a divorce with Sadie Frost, was spending more time with twenty-one-year-old Sienna, and they had enjoyed drinks together at London's the Met bar.[30] Then there were the snatched photos of their first recorded kiss, splashed in the *News of the World* on October 12, 2003. From then on, every moment in their relationship would be salaciously reported in the media.

She described meeting Jude as "the most incredible experience," telling *British Vogue*, "I started working in film, I was travelling around the world, I was in love, my circle of friends expanded. I love how my Glastonbury years evolved. I started off in a grimy tent on a hill and ended up in a Winnebago. I don't look back on that time as negative at all. And I came out perfectly all right on the other side."[31]

The more her photos were splashed in celebrity magazines like *Heat*, the more she became known as the "It" girl with the unique and covetable wardrobe. There were the floaty dresses worn with cowboy boots, the fur gilets, and coin belts that sparked a global "boho chic" trend. In one letter to the *Sunday Times*'s "Wardrobe Mistress" a reader begged to find out where they could find a wide, studded belt like the one Sienna was wearing.[32]

She was disappointed to see that much of the vintage clothing that she had collected from a young age was now mass-produced. "I remember feeling saddened, like, 'Oh, these little, treasured pieces are replicable.'"[33]

By summer 2004 she was said to have ousted Kate Moss as the world's number-one global style icon, and that she had inspired Matthew Williamson's London Fashion Week collection.[34] As much as she was celebrated for her aspirational lifestyle and her Glastonbury appearances, she disliked being called an "It" girl, because "it wasn't celebrating anything that I wanted to celebrate. People would come up to me and say, 'I love your clothes!' I'd be like, '*Aaaaaargh*, I'm trying to do Shakespeare!'"[35]

She told *The Guardian* in 2007: "I don't even know what an It girl is. As far as I'm concerned, an It girl is somebody who doesn't do anything except go to parties and get her photograph taken. Everyone I've worked with on any film will say I'm the hardest worker."[36]

All she wanted was to be taken seriously as an actress, in the same way Jude Law was given respect for his talents. She was considered an empty fashion vessel, so she was delighted to be cast in the challenging role of Edie Sedgwick in a biopic of her life, *Factory Girl* (2006). There were similarities between Sienna and Edie—both came from a wealthy background, they were labeled "It" girls, and they were famous through their connections with a man: Andy Warhol in Edie's case, and Jude Law in Sienna's.

To further link the two together, there were stories about how Sienna was losing weight and experimenting with drugs to tap into Edie's mindset. She immersed herself in the self-destructive character and "sometimes it was upsetting," she said. "It's not like I sat there talking like Edie and making people call me Edie, but I didn't want to take the black tights off and I still don't."[37] She was even criticized in the tabloids for wearing black tights and a top to the launch party of the movie at the Chelsea Hotel, as if she had forgotten her skirt, when it was clear it was a tribute to Edie's look.

Factory Girl was the first film she made after the pregnancy story broke and filming also coincided with news reports that Jude had cheated on her with his children's nanny. It marked the end of their relationship, but still the attention was relentless as she was linked with other actors, including *Factory Girl* co-star Hayden Christensen, who had been a "shoulder to cry on."

Sienna was very open, often too open, in interviews, and this landed her in trouble, like when she jokingly called Pittsburgh "Shitsburgh," and when she told a *Guardian* interviewer that people did drugs "cos they're fun."[38] She described the barrage of attention that she and other young female celebrities were subjected to as "just so toxic. Those days—the frenzy of it, the madness of what women, specifically, were subjected to."[39] She was chased by paparazzi whether by car or on foot, spitting at her to provoke her, and given how the misogyny around her relationships was reported, she even had "slut" spray-painted on her front door.[40]

Sienna was determined to fight back against the intrusion, and from 2008 she took the tabloids and paparazzi to court. She was a key witness in the UK's Leveson Inquiry in November 2011. In a statement to the inquiry, she described how, as a twenty-one-year-old, she would find herself "at midnight, running down a dark street on my own with ten big men chasing me, but the fact they had cameras meant it was legal. Take that away and what you got? A pack of men chasing a woman, and obviously that's a terrifying situation."[41]

She won an injunction against the worst of the press agencies who trailed her and accepted £100,000 in damages from News International in May 2011 over the *News of the World*'s hacking of her phone. In 2021 she reached a settlement with the *Sun*, and she was allowed to read a prepared statement where she alleged that the paper discovered her early pregnancy by "blagging" her medical records.

The noughties' intrusive tabloid culture was forced to change as they lost their power to social media, which allowed celebrities to have their own voice. Now, when we watch Britney Spears documentaries and see how singer Amy Winehouse was hounded while suffering from drug and alcohol addiction, it's incomprehensible.

In the 2020s the maligned "It" girls of the noughties would reemerge triumphant as they used the power of their own voices to explain what it had really been like during that frenzied, misogynistic time. Paris has continued to be an innovator, embracing cryptocurrency and the market for the digital artwork of NFT or "non-fungible tokens." She married American author and entrepreneur Carter Reum and had two children via surrogacy. Britney was finally able to speak for herself—first in court, as she sought to remove the shackles of her conservatorship, and then in her own best-selling memoir. Paris's memoir came out just six months before Britney's, and in it, she also sought to reclaim her story, by revealing the trauma that shaped her career. She said that by trying to shed the character with the baby voice to reveal the real "her," she could be "the woman Marilyn never had a chance to evolve into: It Girl gone Influencer."[42]

The Kardashians and the Instagram Influencer

Kim Kardashian in November 2007, enjoying her newfound fame as she's mobbed by photographers while shopping in Beverly Hills. *London Entertainment/Shutterstock.*

For her headline-grabbing moment on the red carpet at the New York Met Gala in 2022, Kim Kardashian squeezed into one of the most famous gowns of the twentieth century—Marilyn Monroe's "Happy Birthday Mr. President" gown. The risqué dress caused a sensation in 1962 for the illusion of nudity with its flesh-toned fabric studded with rhinestones.

Sixty years later, Kim created a similar uproar, but this time it wasn't so much for the nude effect, and more the allegations that she had caused irreparable damage to the priceless gown, borrowed from the Ripley's Believe It or Not! museum in Florida. There was something so audacious about Kim using her money and influence to step into Marilyn's shoes, with many feeling as if she was exploiting the actress's memory.

The way Kim wore it—with her own branded shapewear underneath, and her hair bleached and slicked back rather than a platinum cloud—was considered a poor imitation.

She explained her decision-making on her reality TV show *The Kardashians*, in an episode titled "What's More American than Marilyn Monroe?" Kim spoke of how Marilyn "transformed herself into this complete icon, and now everyone on the planet knows who she is. Much respect."

Kim's career followed a similar vortex. Driven by a desire for fame, she made sure she was photographed at every event she attended with her famous friends, she used her body to market herself as a brand. When a sex tape threatened to derail her career (as a nude calendar had threatened Marilyn's), she was unapologetic in using it to her advantage. What's more, they both represented the beauty ideals of their era; Marilyn was the voluptuous blonde whose soft, helpless womanhood suited the regressive 1950s. Kim's beauty appeared impossibly manufactured, as she brought plastic surgery mainstream, encouraged the phenomenon known as "Instagram face," and used extreme dieting to shed sixteen pounds to be able to fit into Marilyn's dress.

If Marilyn was the "It" girl of postwar consumerism, Kim was the "It" girl of the internet age. From a reality show joke to billionaire entrepreneur; a glossy-haired, caramel-contoured queen whose pout-and-peace-sign signature pose has been mimicked in a million Instagram selfies. She rose from relative obscurity to becoming one of the most famous, and wealthiest, women in the world, and always with the question—what was she actually famous for? Her response—"Well, a bear can juggle and stand on a ball and he's talented, but he's not famous. Do you know what I mean?"[1]

When Marilyn wore the dress at Madison Square Garden, her experience was only shown from a few backstage shots and the grainy recording of her on the stage, breathing into the microphone as if she was making love to the president. For Kim, the Met Gala was a multimedia performance with 360-degree access for her fans. She shared photos on social media of before and after the event, posting on Instagram Stories her doughnut and pizza after-party, and with the cameras that were filming her reality show, we were able to see the complete journey, from bleaching her hair to squeezing into the gown and posing for photographs, and her interactions with her boyfriend in her car on the way to the gala. We had to apply our own assumptions to Marilyn's experience, but Kim showed us everything, from every conceivable angle.

Kim was, for much of her twenties, fame-adjacent rather than a celebrity in her own right. She first arrived on the scene as the new nightclub buddy of Paris Hilton's. The most famous Kardashian in 2006 was her late father, Robert, who died of esophageal cancer in 2003. He hit international headlines as one of O. J. Simpson's lawyers during the most infamous criminal trial of the 1990s, and had another major pop culture connection, having dated Priscilla Presley in the late seventies.

Kim held a deep desire to be a celebrity from a young age, with a dream of appearing on MTV's first reality show *The Real World*.[2] She was fourteen during the O. J. Simpson trial, and it was a first tantalizing taste of exposure. Her parents had divorced just a few years before the trial, and her mother Kris was remarried to Olympian Caitlyn Jenner, further placing the family on the periphery of celebrity. She had a wealthy, privileged childhood, but she claimed her father made her work hard for what she was given; she had to sign a contract for her car, promising she would wash it every week, fill it with gas, and pay for any repairs.

When MySpace launched in 2003 as one of the first social media sites, celebrities could connect with their fans, and unknowns could find an audience by uploading their own music or sharing images. Kim, whose profile was "Princess Kimberly," used it as a means of launching herself as a face and personality. There was something of a blank slate about her, although she was clearly positioned as a "queen bee" and a daddy's girl, with the subhead, "I'm a PRINCESS and you're not, so there!"

Her first job was in a clothing store to help pay for the car, and it inspired her new ambition to be a celebrity stylist, beginning with her friend, the singer Brandy. As a self-professed neat freak with an eye for fashion, she curated the wardrobes of Brandy and Paris Hilton, selling the unwanted items on eBay and then splitting the takings, with some of the profits going to charity. Once word-of-mouth was out, her business expanded to the wardrobes of Cindy Crawford, Nicole Richie, and Serena Williams. Using the tools of the internet while it was still in its infancy—MySpace, eBay—it was prophetic to how she would further push her celebrity.

In her first interview with *E!*, as she described her work as a celebrity stylist, she also expressed interest in having her own reality show. "I would totally do a show," she said. "I really want to do some kind of show that shows my life and what I do and my closet stuff, and all of that would be really fun for me."[3]

If it sounded vague, her early press coverage in 2006 was similar. She was referred to intermittently as a stylist to the stars, as Paris's sometime friend, and for her dates with media personalities Nick Lachey and Nick Cannon, where paparazzi were miraculously on hand to capture her with them. Kim's first magazine photoshoot and cover was in the February/March 2007 edition of *Complex* magazine, where she was billed as a celebrity stylist, "it girl" and "the way hotter friend of (insert A-list Hollywood chick here) in tabloid photos."

Paris's slim body shape was the desirable look of the noughties, at a time when size zero was heavily promoted, and with her curves, Kim was the antithesis. She learned from Paris some of the tricks to building a brand—tipping off the paparazzi as to where she would be and building up good relationships with gossip magazines for advantageous coverage. According to Kevin Dickson, editor of *In Touch Weekly*, Kim would offer him stories, but he told her she would only be given coverage once she had been on television—and so she made a very brief appearance on Paris's *The Simple Life*, and "that was enough for us to start putting her in *In Touch*."[4] Did she also learn from Paris that in the age of raunch culture, when women were expected to be both sexy and chaste, being unapologetic was the only way to navigate the double standards?

In early 2007, rumors were building that there was an intimate recording of Kim with an ex-boyfriend, Ray J (Brandy's brother), which was taken in 2003. She had denied it to *Complex*—"There is no sex tape!" she insisted—although she later explained her denial was because of the wild (and false) rumors about what the tape contained.

By February 2007 its existence was confirmed when *Kim Kardashian, Superstar* was released through a porn company, Vivid. Kim sued to try to prevent its release, but settled for $5 million, which paved the way for her homemade tape to become the most-watched X-rated film of all time. In the sleazy 2000s, there was little concept of invasion of privacy or of revenge porn, and instead, the media coverage of Kim was gleeful. She had even told *Complex* "I'm not gonna lie—when someone has one out I go look it up on the Internet. Everyone does."

The author Karrine Steffans, who once dated Ray J, claimed he believed the tape would "finally make him white-girl famous. It's a different kind of famous. White girls can do anything and be famous; a white girl could slip and fall in the middle of Rodeo Drive and all of a sudden she's a star. Black women can't do that, and certainly Black men can't do that, and white men can't do that."[5]

He would also later accuse Kris Jenner, acting as Kim's manager, of orchestrating its release as a means of building up publicity to help her with her plans for a new reality show.[6]

Having seen how an MTV show had made Ozzy Osbourne's family house-hold names and boosted their fortunes, Kris pitched her blended family as a show to Ryan Seacrest at the E! network. He saw the potential with this extended family—of the Kardashian daughters Kim, Kourtney, and Khloe, son Rob, Kris's two little daughters with Caitlyn Jenner, Kendall and Kylie, and Caitlyn's sons from her first marriage, with Brody Jenner already appearing in the reality show *The Hills*—and imagined that audiences would find a favorite that they identified with.

Debuting on October 14, 2007, *Keeping Up with the Kardashians* was an access-all-areas insight into the chaos of this extended Calabasas family who hovered on the outskirts of fame. The most newsworthy subject up for discussion was Kim's sex tape, and in the first episode, Kris informs Kim that she has been requested to appear on *The Tyra Banks Show*, on the proviso she'll talk about the tape. Kim looks downcast at the thought but concedes it will allow her to "set the record straight."

As Kris speaks to the camera, when she first heard about the tape she "wanted to kill her. But as her manager, I knew that I had a job to do, and I really just wanted her to move past it." As Kim rehearses her answers to potential questions with her sisters, she explains why she made the tape: "Because I was horny, and I felt like it."

In the first season, the Kardashians further placed themselves within raunch culture, by helping to promote "Girls Gone Wild" bikinis, and with Kris persuading Kim to pose topless for *Playboy*. By season two, Kim was relishing the celebrity dream, having become the most-searched term on Google and AOL. Kim replaced Paris as reality "It" girl—and she was firmly in control of her own image and celebrity. She didn't crack up under the pressure, she rarely drank—there would be no photos of her stumbling out of nightclubs or looking anything less than immaculate. Among the TV gold of family fights and luxury trips to Paris and Mexico, *Keeping Up with the Kardashians* would also be a gateway to open conversations around the Armenian genocide, trans rights, revenge porn, beauty standards, and how social media impacts mental health.

Following the 2008 economic crash, the worst financial downturn since the Great Depression, millions struggled with job losses, inflation, and foreclosures. The lifestyle that the Kardashians pushed offered an escape from reality, letting cash-strapped audiences live vicariously through their plush existence. The Bling Ring had tried to steal the "It" girl lifestyle for themselves, but for the less brazen, there were opportunities to mimic the Kardashian's L.A. sexy style.

The Kardashian sisters' boutique, Dash, which opened a New York branch in 2010, was a mecca for their teenage fans who wanted a selfie and a souvenir to take home—often choosing one of the more affordable items, such as the branded water bottles and key chains, alongside the successful perfumes, makeup lines, and jewelry collections. If there were any grounds for accusations of exploitation of their fans, it was an ill-advised credit card in 2010 that was aimed at teenagers and came with exorbitant fees.

Kim told the *Guardian* in 2012 that her fans were "a younger girl, like 15 or 16, who loves fashion, loves to be a girly girl, loves beauty, glam," and as a role model, she said she wasn't "your stick-skinny typical model," although her weight-loss endorsements, such as diet teas and waist trainers, seemed contrary to any claims of body positivity.[7]

At the same time, Kim's impossible body spoke of expensive high-maintenance, with her hourglass figure, the full lips, shining dark hair, and almond eyes. She was smooth and hairless, having undergone an IPL procedure to remove every part of her body hair.

As she became more famous, her butt was a focus of gossip—it seemed almost too plump and round that some argued it could only be an implant. Kim defended her figure, stating her Armenian heritage was responsible for the bigger breasts and butts that ran in the family. Not one to shy from a publicity opportunity, she even had it x-rayed during one episode of *Keeping Up with the Kardashians* to prove it was real.

In 2011 Kim's much publicized, no-expense spared marriage to the NBA player Kris Humphries lasted for just seventy-two days. It seemed far too convenient, and skeptics wondered if it had all been a big publicity stunt, as Kim would do anything to commodify her life. As much as she was idolized by teenage girls, Kim provoked strong feelings around her vacuousness, particularly among white men. Actors Daniel Craig and Jon Hamm both called her a "fucking idiot," with Hamm adding that "stupidity is certainly celebrated."[8]

In response, Kim insisted that being a reality star involved real skill. "But to be able to open up your life like that and to be so . . . if everyone could do it, everyone would."[9]

By April 2012 Kim was dating Kanye West, and with his help she became a serious contender in fashion and business. Their 2014 wedding earned her a first *Vogue* cover, and together they were courted by major fashion brands, flying in by private jet to attend fashion weeks around the world, and with major events like the Met Gala and the Grammys now open to her. As *GQ* wrote in a 2016 profile: "Her curves remained the same, but under Kanye's exuberant insistence, they transmuted from porny to arty. Her provocative selfies were no longer just attention-seeking; now they were also body positive."[10]

When she appeared on the cover of *Paper* magazine in 2014, with her naked, oiled butt in one image, and balancing a champagne glass on it in the other, the images were hailed as "Breaking the Internet." Photographer Jean-Paul Goude was inspired by his own 1976 photo of Black model Carolina Beaumont, and there were accusations leveled at Kim that she was not only appropriating Blackness, but eroticizing it. It would be just one example of this type of accusation in the years that followed.

The key to her promotion was her savvy use of social media. After MySpace died, she moved onto Twitter, and by 2012 had sixteen million followers, making her the ninth most popular in the world, just one place behind Taylor Swift and three behind President Obama. She learned its value as a free marketing tool when she designed her first perfume bottle and asked for feedback on which shade of pink it should be. "Light pink won by so much. These are the consumers that are going to be buying it, and they felt like they were involved."[11]

In 2010, a new photo-sharing app called Instagram was launched as part of the app boom triggered by the release of the iPhone in 2007. There was a desire, and a demand, to create more apps that would enhance social connections and become a part of everyday life. Instagram's ethos was to be aspirational and escapist, with vintage polaroid-style filters to fix poor quality camera phones.

The Instagram look, referred to in Japan as "Insta-bae," changed everything, from the minimalist interior design of cafés with their plants against pink, to the proliferation of artfully plated avocado toast, or indulgent ice creams and cakes loaded with candy bars. It also brought "selfie" culture, the desire to share a flattering portrait with followers, to the forefront, with the Kardashians as the de facto leaders. According to Sarah Frier in her account of the founding of the app, it was "like a constant first date, with everyone putting the best version of their lives on display."[12]

When Apple introduced the front-facing camera to its iPhone 4 in 2010 it was now easier to capture the perfect selfie, which could then be shared on Instagram or Snapchat. The selfie was such a phenomenon that it was named as the 2013 word of the year by the Oxford English Dictionary, and in 2015, Kim published a coffee table book, *Selfish*, devoted to her own selfies. She wasn't the first Kardashian to sign up to Instagram—Kourtney and Khloe were early users in 2011—but she shared her first post in February 2012, a selfie where she blew a kiss to the camera. As she recalled: "I'll never forget this . . . I was wearing a pink-and-white-striped robe from Victoria's Secret. My hair was in a ponytail. I always know my glam. I was sitting in my glam room and we took a picture on my BlackBerry, and I posted it, like, 'Hey guys. I'm on Instagram.'"[13]

A-list singers and Hollywood stars had been slow to realize the power of social media as they felt it would take away their mystery, and therefore devalue their performances. Instead, it was the women like Paris and Kim, representing a new type of self-made fame, who were the pioneers in how to exploit it to their advantage.

It was a powerful tool for celebrities to be able to curate their own image, while reclaiming it from the control of the paparazzi, whose unflattering snatch shots were devalued. As well as making it easier for her to pretend her life was a fairy tale, Paris found that "Since women like me and Kim made Instagram our bitch," it signaled the death knell of the type of paparazzi frenzy seen with Britney and Paris in the noughties. "There's still a market for candid pictures of celebs—especially if the celeb looks embarrassingly fat, skinny, ugly, drunk, or compromised in some way—so the paps are still out there, but it's nothing like it was in 2003," she wrote in her memoirs.[14]

At first social media was unpaid promotion, until influencers learned how to monetize it by following the Kardashian example. As members of the family accumulated millions of followers, Instagram became their main branding tool. Whatever they endorsed would sell out quickly, such as makeup, clothing, diet products, shapewear, and once Kim had reached an extraordinary level of fame, with over 300 million followers, she was able to make a million dollars for a single post.[15]

She ventured into her own app developments—there was her emoji and GIF app KIMOJI, and the "Kim Kardashian West Official" app, which offered beauty and fashion tips, exclusive photos, and her own status updates, and which generated hundreds of millions of dollars.[16] As *The Cut* wrote, "by filtering her own very particular reality through technology, she utterly changed not just the beauty business but also our idea of what a mogul is."[17]

"Kim Kardashian: Hollywood" was a free mobile game that was launched with Glu Mobile, who were looking for a celebrity face to attach to a game they already had in development. It generated $160 million by 2016, when *Forbes* magazine splashed her on their cover as a "Mobile Mogul."

Offering a modern commentary on the travails of being an "It" girl, players adopted the avatar of a celebrity, who they were tasked with climbing to the A-list and with Kim popping up to offer advice such as on how to date to get ahead, because—"Exposure, exposure, exposure!" It replicated the pressures of paparazzi, of creating strategies with publicists, and provided lessons on how one comment could backfire on the internet. Players could also buy energy boosts through the silver "K" stars which were paid for with real cash, helping the game to generate its revenue.[18]

Working in collaboration with Instagram, the September 2014 issue of *Vogue* featured the world's top models including Cara Delevingne, Karlie Kloss, Imaan Hammam, and Fei Fei Sun, under the headline, "THE INSTA-GIRLS! Models of the moment in the clothes of the season."

It described how Instagram, now with more users than Twitter, was an important tool for models to market themselves. They were expected to have a large social media platform before they were even hired for the job, and in turn the catwalk gave way to those who already had a following by way of a reality TV show or famous parents. It was no coincidence that the top models for the Victoria's Secret runway in 2015 were Kendall Jenner, who grew up on *Keeping Up with the Kardashians*, and Gigi Hadid, whose mother was a star on *The Real Housewives of Beverly Hills*. By opening up their lives to their followers on Instagram, they made some of the more unsavory aspects of the paparazzi redundant. And by curating their perfect lives, it negated one of the appealing factors of the "It" girl—her unfiltered chaos.

Instagram also brought opportunities for "It" girl wannabes who copied the aesthetic set by the Kardashian sisters—with their thick glossy dark hair, their bee stung lips, contour makeup to slim their nose and enhance their cheeks, and with plenty of cleavage on display.

"The explosion of the internet changed the market for 'It,' dramatically increasing both demand and supply," claimed an article in *The Cut* in 2023. "Suddenly, all an 'It' girl needed to do was to capture the attention of the multiplying number of party or street-style photographers and the blogs would take it from there. Once Instagram arrived a few years later, you didn't need even them; an 'It' girl could just do the chronicling herself."[19]

By 2015, with 50 percent of American teenagers now on the app, it was clear that social media was causing damage, from the bullying and trolling to the viral challenges that were leading to harm. In May 2017, the UK's Royal Society for Public Health named it as the worst app for young people's mental health, creating anxiety and feelings of inadequacy when users compared themselves to others.[20]

It was common knowledge that for years glossy magazines airbrushed photos of celebrities to create unrealistic beauty standards, and now it was possible for everyone to do it themselves on their phones. To help improve their selfies, and to compete with celebrities, there were apps such as FaceTune (released in 2013) and Adobe Lightroom, where its tweaks could smooth the complexion, whiten teeth, plump the lips, and slim hips and waists. But with this quest for perfection, what effect was this "tyranny of slenderness" having on teenage girls and young women?

The *New Yorker*, on the eve of entering a new decade, the 2020s, investigated "the gradual emergence," in the 2010s, "among professionally beautiful women, of a single, cyborgian face." The youthful face had "poreless skin and plump, high cheekbones," "catlike eyes and long, cartoonish lashes," and "a small, neat nose and full, lush lips." What's more, it was an ethnically ambiguous face that suggested "every American of the future were to be a direct descendant of Kim Kardashian West, Bella Hadid, Emily Ratajkowski, and Kendall Jenner." What she was describing was "Instagram Face."[21]

"I don't know what real skin looks like anymore," tweeted Chrissy Teigen in February 2018. "People of social media just know: IT'S FACETUNE, you're beautiful, don't compare yourself to people ok."[22]

With filters only a fix for photos, demand for real-life tweaks, such as Botox and lip fillers, increased exponentially. According to the American Society of Plastic Surgeons, in 2019 Americans received over 5 million neuromodulator injections such as Botox and almost 3 million filler injections. By 2022 that had increased by 73 percent and 70 percent, respectively.[23]

Kim denied that she'd had anything more than Botox and fillers, but it was her look that was setting the beauty standards of the twenty-first century. Beverly Hills plastic surgeon Jason Diamond told the *New Yorker* that "thirty percent of people come in bringing a photo of Kim, or someone like Kim—there's a handful of people, but she's at the very top of the list, and understandably so."[24]

Emily Ratajkowski posted her first selfie on Instagram on February 21, 2011. It was a grainy, vintage image of her fully clothed, with her dark hair hanging down and a closed-lip smile on her face. A year later, she would be catapulted to attention for exactly what she wasn't wearing in a certain music video for Robin Thicke's "Blurred Lines." While Thicke and his collaborators Pharrell Williams and T.I. were fully dressed, the models in the video were topless, as they cavorted and danced with various props, while the men tried to get their attention. The video transformed Emily into the next big thing, and she insisted it was empowering rather than misogynistic. "All women are objectified and sexualized to some degree, I figured, so I might as well do it on my own terms. I thought that there was power in my ability to choose to do so," she wrote in her memoir, *My Body*.

In this collection of essays, she explored how her body served her as a form of currency and questioned whether it was empowering. "They were the talent; we were more like props," she wrote of the video shoot, while also alleging that Thicke had groped her. She conceded, "how limited any woman's power is when she survives and even succeeds in the world as a thing to be looked at."[25]

Yet she was also complicit in the world that she was critiquing. Every time she posted a photo of herself in a bikini from her own swimwear line, the perfection of her body often triggered a sense of inadequacy in those who felt they couldn't live it up to it. She may have written about how she navigated a world as an object to be looked at, but she didn't reflect on how her images on Instagram impacted the self-esteem of other women.

My Body was an extension of an article Emily originally wrote in the *New Yorker*, "Buying Myself Back," the most read story of 2020, in which she described how her own image was rarely her own. She used the examples of a photographer who sued her for posting on Instagram a photo he had snapped of her on the street, and of spending $80,000 on a work by the artist Richard Prince, who had effectively just copied one of her Instagram posts and added a comment to it.[26]

In one essay, "Beauty Lessons," she comes close to acknowledging the different ways society treats women based on their looks, and that it "isn't kind to women who are overlooked by men." At the same time her own role as a sex object was a double-edged sword. She discovered she had been cast in 2014's *Gone Girl* after the director David Fincher had asked his star, Ben Affleck, to suggest a woman "whom men were obsessed with and women hated."[27]

As Eva Wiseman wrote in the *Guardian* in her review of *My Body*, "as activism, it's unsatisfying. Her commentary on the industry she's chosen is passionate and chilling, and yet at times rings hollow, in part because of her reluctance to subvert the male gaze she critiques."[28]

Kim Kardashian and Emily Ratajkowski's model of fame, using Instagram to promote their talents, influenced women around the world to use their looks and charisma to pull themselves out of poverty. While the "It" girl of the past had been created with the help of an artist or movie producer, a new generation of influencers sought fame for themselves, on their own terms. Rather than possessing the individuality which defined the "It" girl, they copied the template.

Qandeel Baloch was dubbed Pakistan's Kim Kardashian, a social media star who courted controversy with every viral video stunt and pouting selfie in a country ruled by religious piety. Keeping her true identity closely guarded, she used her online persona to transform herself into "Girl Power," a pro-vocative, sexy media star who danced and twerked, flashed her cleavage and challenged her audience of millions to judge her. The Kardashian connection was in some ways a misnomer, as she came from absolutely nothing, but she shared a real social acumen for gaining a foothold in Pakistan's media capital,

Karachi, and then doing whatever she could for attention. She was an inspiration to many for her unapologetic confidence in a country where women were expected to be subservient.

In April 2016, she was invited to appear on the comedy news show *Ajeeb Saa*, where over video link she would debate Mufti Abdul Qavi, an Islam scholar who was a frequent guest on television shows. Qandeel had provocatively promised to perform a striptease if the Pakistan cricket team were victorious over India in the Twenty20 International Cricket tournament. The presenter asked Abdul Qavi his thoughts on this stunt, but he chose to be diplomatic, instead mentioning he would like to meet her when he was in Karachi next time. In June, the outcome of that meeting was broadcast on Qandeel's social media channels. In one image, she poses with Qavi in his cap, her mouth opened provocatively in pretend shock. She also released a video to her millions of followers which showed a flirtatious exchange that was entirely out of keeping with how a woman should interact with a religious scholar. She would later claim that despite the pretense that he was offering guidance and coaching, they shared a soft drink and cigarette off-camera, when it was forbidden during Ramadan, and implied that he had sleazed on her. Accusing an Islamic scholar of unreligious behavior was one line that shouldn't be crossed.

Under a media scandal, reporters sought to uncover her true identity, which she had closely guarded for her own safety. There was one clue in the video of her meeting with the mullah—a mention that they were both from Multan, a city in southern Punjab. It didn't take long for a journalist to discover her real name, Fouzia Azeem, born in 1990, and that she was from a very conservative rural village.

Growing up in Shah Sadar Din, she was raised on a compound where women were expected to keep themselves hidden behind the walls. She was a free-spirited tomboy who loved running outside, and hated the idea of having to wear a burqa once she was married. Despite the strictness of her upbringing, her mother allowed some concessions with a television in the house, and by persuading her father that she should be educated. As she soaked up the Karachi-set soap operas, Fauzia dreamed of a celebrity life in the city where she could make money acting and singing. "She dreamed of becoming an independent girl and a model," her father would later tell a reporter for the *Guardian*.[29]

At the age of eighteen she was forced into a marriage to her cousin and soon after they had a son, Mishal. This restricted life of abject poverty was not what she wanted, and she would later say her husband was abusive to her. She snuck off into the night with her baby, seeking help at a crowded women's shelter in Multan. Her parents were horrified and cut off her support, and so she was forced to hand the baby back to her husband, who didn't let her see him again.

After being shunned by her family, she made her own living, working as a hostess on long-distance bus journeys, and by 2012, the twenty-two-year-old was now living in Karachi, earning money as a model. In December 2014 she appeared on *Pakistan Idol*, a vision of extroversion as she played up to the cameras and stumbled on her bright green platform heels. When her singing was mocked by the judges, she threw a fit, wailing and pleading until she was removed from the room, and her clip went viral.

Riding on the fame from the audition, she began posting selfies on Instagram and Facebook, posing provocatively in bikinis, and re-creating the type of Kim Kardashian identity that she wanted to cultivate for her ever-increasing number of fans. Rather than being truthful about her origin from the humblest of families, she said her middle-class parents lived in Islamabad.

Like the Kardashians, Qandeel worked with a digital and marketing team for her videos, bouncing ideas and writing scripts with the aim of making them trend. Some of her videos were simple in their provocativeness, lying in bed rubbing her eyes as if she just woke up, others posing in sky-high heels and shades as she danced. One of her viral successes was where she posed the question, "How I'm Looking?" to a man standing behind her. When he says "Marvelous," she challenges him—"Just marvelous?"[30] Brash and confrontational, it was the equivalent of a Beyoncé "I woke up like this" moment, but it was not how Pakistani women are expected to behave.

Social media was booming in Pakistan, and with 60 percent of the population under thirty, they were increasingly online and using apps on their phones. As well as men lusting over her images, she also had female fans who liked her cheeky personality and admired the boundary-pushing. "To become popular, you have to do a lot. It's necessary to do some bad things. You have to show yourself, take off your clothes," she once said. But she also spoke of how she was fighting for women in Pakistan to be able to say and do what they pleased without being condemned. And while it led to calls for her Facebook page to be banned, at the same time she was being invited on television to air her controversial views.[31]

She was, by 2016, one of the ten most googled people in Pakistan.[32] As the metrics reflected her success, she was offered sponsorship for posts, and the money she generated by advertising products on Facebook gave her enough money for a luxury flat and her own car, and to rent a home for her parents in Multan, allowing them to escape from the deprived compound. But her final stunt, of swaying on her bed in a bikini while offering to strip for the Pakistan cricket team, hit the headlines in India and Pakistan. Her Facebook page was bombarded with threats, she was called a slut, an ugly bitch who deserved to die, and with a campaign to shut down her social media accounts, Facebook suspended her. "No more videos on Facebook from today. Get lost, you perverts," she said defiantly. After the controversial meeting with Abdul Qavi, she would be silenced for good.

Once her identity was revealed, her family were exposed and shunned by the community, with Waseem Azeem, the youngest of Baloch's six brothers, receiving the brunt of the abuse for his sister having violated religious and cultural norms.[33] By the end of June she was terrified for her safety, but when she asked Pakistan's interior minister for police protection, she received no help.

She decided to return to Multan to be with her parents for Eid al-Fitr, as it felt too dangerous in Karachi, and she donned the niqab and hid indoors. One evening Waseem, who had berated her for the shame she brought on the family, prepared a sweet milk, as a supposed peace offering, in which he had dissolved sleeping pills. Her mother found her lifeless body the next morning. She had been strangled. The day after, July 17, Waseem was arrested, alongside a cousin and two other men. Under Sharia Law, the family of a victim of an honor killing could exonerate a perpetrator for blood money, but her parents refused to excuse their son, as they were too traumatized by the death of their brave daughter.

"You're going to miss me when I'm gone," Qandeel posted. "You're so terrible, with your double standards. You like to watch me, and then you like to say: 'Why don't you just die?'"[34]

As for Kim, Kanye had helped elevate her from vacuous reality TV star to bona fide fashion icon. He introduced her to cutting-edge designers, helped her earn approval from Anna Wintour, editor of *Vogue*, and invites to the Met Gala for the first time, although when she arrived heavily pregnant and in a floral Givenchy dress the critics weren't kind. Yet each year, she chose to push boundaries. In 2019 she appeared as if she was soaking wet in a Thierry Mugler dress, two years later she arrived completely covered head-to-toe in black Balenciaga. In 2022 she sparked a worldwide scandal by wearing the Marilyn dress, and then again in 2024 for squeezing into a corset to achieve a painfully tiny waist.

As she shifted and adapted her look, she was often accused of appropriating other cultures, and "blackfishing," such as when she sported braids in her hair. Kim's mixed heritage, of being half-Armenian, had given her the curvaceous figure and dark hair and skin, yet her critics said she was profiting from an aesthetic that Black women had previously been condemned for.

The accusation of blackfishing originated on social media in 2018. "They've been called out for cultural appropriation for a decade plus now, and it's no secret that they've adopted many styles that Black women or

Black culture have created and made them more palatable," said a 2021 article in *Time*. "Now people think they're copying the Kardashian-Jenners when they dress or do their hair or tan their skin a certain way."[35]

The accusations would peak in 2019 when she announced her plans for her own shapewear business, under the name "Kimono." It was met with a huge outcry over her disrespect to Japanese culture. A #KimOhNo twitter hashtag gathered pace, and seeing the negativity trending, she was forced to back down—changing her branding to SKIMS.

With the nude fabric coming in a variety of different skin tones, Kim's shapewear would not only become a bestseller and lead in its diversity, but also would change aesthetics as stretchy, flesh-colored fabrics became the look on social media. There were countless TikTok videos of women opening their bounty from SKIMS and trying the pieces on for themselves.

Kardashian had a desire to be taken seriously, and in a May 2019 *Vogue* cover story, she revealed her plans to train to be a lawyer and was studying to take the "baby bar" exam. She was asked in an interview whether the awakening of her activism came from her now being the mother of four African American children, and she conceded it "definitely has a lot to do with it. I want my children to have a fair life."[36]

Scrolling through Twitter she came across a call to help an inmate, Alice Marie Johnson, fight for clemency after having been given a life sentence without parole for a nonviolent drug offense. Kim chose prison reform as her cause, and it brought her to the White House as she met face-to-face with President Donald Trump. As the reality television president, he spoke the language of celebrity, and with Kim's influence he agreed to grant Johnson clemency.

She had begun the decade as a famous-for-being-famous celebrity, an "It" girl who lived every aspect of her life under the lens. She reinvented the American Dream as the best friend of a "celebutante," who became the breakout star. She refused to be shamed for her sexuality, she ushered in a complete shift in beauty standards, and reinvented the way people did their makeup, wore their clothes, and posed in their selfies.

As Sarah Ditum wrote in her book *Toxic*, "By accepting the commodification of her private life, her relationships, even her body, Kim was able to travel all the way from a sex tape to the White House. Kim was the one who made it, and in the process, she remade what beauty meant in the Upskirt Decade."[37]

Thanks to Kim, new "It" girls, whatever their background, could commodify their lifestyle, and make a living, through social media. All they needed was an infectious personality, a unique image, the skills to edit their photos and amass followers through algorithms, and a willingness to co-opt every aspect of their lives for their followers. It was now a democracy of celebrity—where the only "right" place to be was on TikTok and Instagram.

As Kim reflected in 2019, "I have always felt that with my show starting off on regular television and then transcending into the social-media world, it was the perfect magic of old-school media with new-school media all happening at the same time. I do think that there will be something else that will be big and just as amazing, but it won't be the same."[38]

17

K-pop "It" Girls

Fashion and Pop Perfection

Jennie Kim on the front row at Chanel during Paris Fashion Week in March 2022. *Zabulon Laurent/ABACA/Shutterstock.*

At Paris Fashion Week in October 2023 the Kardashians were soaking up the attention of the paparazzi for their appearances at the Victoria Beckham and Schiaparelli shows. But on the last day, Jennie Kim caused a sensation when she rocked up to the Chanel show, claiming a prominent seat in the front row. Jennie, the de facto leader of girl group Blackpink, was one of the new generation of "It" girls of K-pop who had Instagram accounts reaching tens of millions, and were courted and signed up by major fashion brands. As fashion ambassadors, not only would they tap into the lucrative Asian market, but they also held a crossover appeal for their unique, edgy style.

The other three members of Blackpink were equally coveted. Lisa represented Celine, Rosé was the ambassador for Saint Laurent, and Jisoo for Dior, and their presence at these prestigious shows created a spectacle for K-pop enthusiasts. They gathered outside the fashion week venues for a glimpse of their favorites and shared their fan-made Jennie content on TikTok, praising her dimples and rounded cheeks, and her dance moves.[1]

The K-pop domination in fashion is part of a much bigger wave of Korean ascendancy. Known by the Chinese term "Hallyu," over the last decade this sweep of Korean pop culture dominated music, film, and television. Blackpink and boy band BTS topped charts, Bong Joon-ho's *Parasite* won the Academy Award for Best Picture in 2020, and Netflix's *Squid Game* broke viewership records as the series to watch during the pandemic. It also turned one of its actors, former model Jung Ho-yeon, into an overnight star, with *Vulture* naming her as "the world's current 'It' girl."[2]

K-pop is a kitschy, upbeat, highly produced musical hybrid of pop, hip-hop, and EDM, performed by young, beautiful singers who, in vibrant music videos, execute skillful, energetic dance routines. The K-pop stars like Jennie and her bandmates are known in Korea as "idols," and they have a loyal, switched-on fanbase who follow their every move on social media and online platforms, share memes with fan artwork with one another, copy their looks and dance moves on TikTok, and can respond as a critical mass to defend or chastise them.

The new "It" girls of K-pop were not expected to imbue the same chaos as the ones who came before. Rather than champagne-swilling on yachts in the south of France, nightclub-hopping in Los Angeles, and navigating sex scandals, they lived under a weight of expectations to be polished and clean-living. Instead, they were fashion "It" girls, admired for their eclectic style that mixed streetwear with luxury high-end fashion. Before Blackpink, Irene of Red Velvet and Bae Suzy were coveted by beauty and fashion brands. New generations, including "teen crush" band NewJeans, whose Korean-Australian member Danielle Marsh was signed as the face of Burberry and Chanel, are also being sought. Their coveted lifestyle was about being constantly on the move; flying on private jets, staying in top hotels for Paris Fashion Week or in New York for the Met Gala, where Jennie wore a vintage Chanel dress from 1990 for her first time in 2023. But it was a tough road to get there.

Like the Hollywood studio system of the forties and fifties, in K-pop, young hopefuls are molded and shaped to be the stars of the future by entertainment agencies who pluck them from auditions, sign them to seven-year contracts and place them on a rigorous training program, which can take years.

Just as young stars like Judy Garland were expected to follow a morality clause and their love lives were heavily controlled, in Korea, the idols are banned from having boyfriends or girlfriends for fear of putting off their young fans. And if they are found to have contravened these rules, they face being slut-shamed and mocked by an army of anonymous trolls.[3] As colorful and poptastic as it is, Hallyu has a darker side that raises questions about the country's attitudes toward mental health, sexual assault, and exploitation, especially of women. While South Korea is one of the most innovative, technically advanced countries in the world, there is an economic disparity that touches all lives, and conservative notions that hark back to its troubled history.

Throughout the twentieth century, Korea was torn apart by colonialism, war, and division. After being freed from Japanese occupation in 1945 it was split in half, with the North controlled by the Soviets, and the South by the US military. It became the focus of the American fight against communism in the fifties and after a prolonged war, South Korea was placed under military rule and US occupation. The 1988 Seoul Olympics marked its hopeful return from dictatorship, and its people fought for a path for economic and cultural revival. The booming electronics industry was a major export and in 1998, in a further drive to lift the country out of poverty, the government developed a policy to support, rather than interfere with cultural content. To help dramas and pop music thrive, they introduced tax breaks and promoted Korean culture overseas through the foreign ministry and their embassies around the world.[4]

K-dramas and K-pop were initially popular in China, Japan, and southeast Asia, and by 2011, Hallyu contributed more than £2.3 billion to the South Korean economy. In November 2012 Psy's "Gangnam Style" topped the charts around the world for the viral dance moves, the addictive beats, and the simplicity of its lyrics flecked with English expressions like "Hey, sexy lady." It was kitschy, it was fun, and it became one of the most watched YouTube videos of all time. It shone an international light on K-pop, which had at that point already spread its wings through Asia. Korean culture was placed as a challenger to American dominance, and as K-pop, K-beauty, fashion, movies, and television thrived, all aspects of Korean culture became trendy. Corn dogs, jars of kimchi, and bao buns became international favorites, driving new street food menus at festivals and in "hipster" enclaves, and championed by health influencers like Gwyneth Paltrow.

"Gangnam Style" made South Korea hot, but until then most people hadn't heard of the ritzy district of Seoul where fashion and pop flourish. It's home to designer brands, American coffee chains, plastic surgery clinics, and to K-pop's biggest production companies.

Psy became the first Korean artist to gain household-name status outside of Asia, and while he was more of a one-hit wonder internationally, Girls' Generation, a nine-member Korean girl group, made real headway in the States. They released their first English-language album on Lady Gaga's label Interscope, and made their American debut on the *Late Show with David Letterman* in 2012.[5] They were followed by the phenomenon of BTS, the clean-cut boy band who dominated charts around the world, embarked on sold-out world tours, and whose army of loyal, devoted fans could be galvanized for a cause. The significance of Hallyu was demonstrated through the introduction of a K-pop category at the MTV Video Music Awards in 2019.

As for Blackpink, by 2023 they were considered the most successful girl group in the world, the first K-pop act to perform at Coachella, and as the number one pop act on YouTube, they had more subscribers than Taylor Swift. All four girls came from across the Asia-Pacific region to crack the industry as teenagers. Jennie Kim grew up in Seoul and New Zealand, Lisa Manobal from Thailand, Rosé (Roseanne) Park was born in New Zealand and grew up in Australia, and Jisoo Kim is from Gunpo, Korea.

After being signed up by YG Entertainment, the same label as Psy, they underwent extensive training at the glittering Seoul headquarters, where they practiced for twelve hours a day to perfect their vocals and dance moves. Jennie spent six years as a trainee while Rosé joined in 2012 when she was fifteen, after beating out 700 contestants at an audition in Sydney.[6]

They shared an apartment at YG headquarters, and the four girls bonded together as they jammed all night around the kitchen table, until the sun was rising the next morning.[7] All these hopefuls could think about was making their "debut," the term for being released on the public with an introduction to the music press and a first single, but they had no idea when they would be deemed ready. Sometimes the training was so intense, and they missed their families so much, that they thought about quitting, made harder by the monthly auditions to check whether they had progressed enough to continue in the program.

"We were on survival mode," Jennie told *Rolling Stone*. "Every month, our friends were forced to leave, go home. Getting stressed? Having it rough? Those feelings were a luxury. What mattered was debuting."[8]

They were also expected to follow the morality rules of no dating, drinking, or driving, which would continue even after the band was successful. They received mental health advice and therapy, but they preferred to talk to one another about their shared problems. "We just endured," said Jennie.[9]

Once they made their debut in 2016 their rise to fame was lightning fast as their debut single album *Square One* helped cement them as the biggest girl group on the planet. With the bombastic EDM beats and hip-hop influence, they were styled like swaggering dystopian icons who threatened to give "all the guys nosebleeds," and bragged about their status as independent women. Their choreography was designed to inspire viral dance trends, but rather than perform prettily, they rapped and played guitar. The opening line to their singles, "Blackpink in your area," was their calling card and a nod to the production style of many big-name American hip-hop and EDM acts.

For the first three years of success, they worked nonstop without proper rest and by the time they'd finished the world tour in 2020, Jennie said she was sick, mentally and physically, with her immune system destroyed, and she had to learn how to take care of herself.[10]

Jennie was one of the shyest of the members. "I wasn't bright and bubbling with energy," she said, but she forced herself to come out of her shell for fear of being accused of looking "pissed." She created the Blackpink persona: a character who is "Someone really forceful. Someone really solid. Aggressive, in a good way."[11]

As the stand-out "It" girl, she was the first member to go solo in 2018, and was signed up as a brand ambassador for Chanel, Adidas, and Calvin Klein.[12] In 2023 she crossed into international television with a role on HBO's *The Idol*, which was more provocative than what K-pop stars would usually appear in.

Blackpink made it look easy, but the glamor and perfected choreography came at a price. Not only did they combine the fashion photoshoots and promotional films with grueling rehearsals and public appearances, but Blackpink also faced enormous pressure around rumors they had plastic surgery, with discussions and analysis on YouTube, TikTok, and Reddit to compare before and after photos on whether Jisoo underwent rhinoplasty.

K-pop stars are expected to look a certain way. They can dye their hair crazy colors—Jung Ho-yeon made a striking impression walking the runways of Paris and Milan for her vivid red hair—but their skin is expected to be clear and shining, and tattoo-free. K-pop's "It" girls brought K-beauty to the forefront, transforming it into a $6.5 billion export industry and was even hailed by US congresswoman Alexandria Ocasio-Cortez when she shared her skincare routine in 2019. K-beauty brands are all about using effective ingredients in skincare for glowing skin, yet the stars did sometimes use plastic surgery to perfect their image, such as tweaking the eyelids to create a double-fold, and this had a knock-on effect for the fans who wished to emulate them. A Gallup Korea poll found that one in three South Korean women underwent cosmetic surgery between the ages of nineteen and twenty-nine to try to emulate the K-pop beauty standards.[13] In a pair of 2017 music videos called "Becoming Prettier," members of the K-pop group Six Bomb went to a plastic surgeon and then revealed their before and after looks.[14]

Blackpink were often condemned for the slightest transgressions. This included cuddling a panda cub at a South Korean zoo without wearing the correct masks and gloves, for their online reality show, *24/365 With Blackpink*. Chinese media accused the band of potentially exposing the cub to harmful infections, and on Weibo, China's version of Twitter, commentators attacked them for wearing makeup while doing so. The criticism was so intense they took down the teaser clip from YouTube. In India, they were similarly rounded on for insulting Hinduism in a music video by featuring an image of the Hindu god Ganesha.[15]

They were also attacked for being overtly sexual. They were forced to re-edit a video when Jennie was criticized for wearing a nurse's uniform and heels in the music video for "Lovesick Girls" in late 2020. It was said she was trivializing and sexualizing the profession at a time when the Covid-19 pandemic was still a threat.[16]

In Korean culture there's an intense pressure to be perfect, and success is measured by the caliber of education, work, wealth, and appearance, known as "specs" or "specifications."[17] Women are expected to be attractive yet modest in their dress and manners, and while the pressure to be perfect is difficult for ordinary Koreans, it's even more intense for K-pop idols, and high competitiveness, jealousy, and cyberbullying have led to devastatingly tragic consequences. In 2019, two idols, Sulli and Goo Hara, close friends who bonded over their shared trauma under the spotlight, killed themselves.

South Korea has the highest suicide rate of the world's wealthiest nations, due to high unemployment, a lack of affordable housing, and high levels of depression which often go untreated.[18] This disaffection has been explored in Korean movies including *Parasite*.

Female stars are also exposed to the double standards and are expected to be self-effacing despite their celebrity. As Ho-yeon told *GQ* in 2023: "In Korea, we have a saying: as rice ripens, it bows its head. It means that even as you succeed, you really have to continue to stay humble."[19]

If they deviate from what they are supposed to wear, and how they are supposed to behave, then they are targeted by relentless trolling and doxing from anonymous male "anti-fans" and "anti-feminists" who harass and target women who step out of line.

Sulli had always been a rebellious figure in the K-pop movement. As she spoke openly about mental health, cyberbullying, and women's rights, she didn't fit in with the conservative parameters of Korea, particularly as an unashamed member of the "no-bra" feminist movement.[20]

Sulli, whose real name was Choi Jin-ri, was eleven when she was signed up to the SM Entertainment training program in 2005. She'd had a lonely childhood. "Mom's absences. Too many to count," she said in an interview that would be released after her death as a documentary, *Dear Jinri*. "I don't have many memories of my dad. I remember him always lying on his side." She had one strong memory of being given a Barbie doll by a colleague of her dad's, and while she was pleased with an expensive gift, she tore it apart limb by limb and colored it red. "My mom never bought me dolls again."

In 2009, she was included in the five-piece girl group f(x), whose debut album *Pinocchio* topped the Korean charts. After Girls' Generation, they were one of the first K-pop groups to gain international followers, even appearing at the South by Southwest festival in 2013. They were considered more "hard-hitting" and rebellious in their music and stylings, sparking an edgy, female empowerment sub-genre known as "girl crush," which Blackpink and Red Velvet fall under.[21]

Sulli had been one of the standout stars from the group, but in 2014 SM Entertainment released a statement that she was "suffering physically and mentally from malicious and untrue rumors spreading about her." These rumors, that she was secretly pregnant, were sparked by her admission to an emergency hospital for severe stomach pain, and gained traction after it was revealed the nineteen-year-old was dating rapper Choiza, who was fourteen years older.

She eventually quit the group to concentrate on acting, and in 2019 she released a solo debut EP *Goblin*.[22] Sulli was a free spirit who believed women should be free to dress as they wanted, and by choosing not to wear a bra in public and showing visible nipples on social media, she was further targeted by "anti-feminists." In 2019 she became a regular on the television show *The Night of Hate Comments*, in which she read out and laughed off the mean online judgments. She used it as a chance to refute some of the rumors, that she was using drugs because of her dilated pupils and that she was going braless just for attention. Yet the relentless pressure was triggering the anxiety she had felt since she was abandoned by her parents as a child. In an Instagram video in 2018, she confessed to the panic disorders she had been suffering at a young age. "Even close people left me. I was hurt by them and felt there was nobody who understands me, which made me fall apart," she said.[23]

She brought awareness to the conveyor-belt production of girl and boybands, and how the restrictions on their private lives, such as bans on dating, mobile phone restrictions, and grueling schedules had a major impact on mental health. "Being a K-Pop idol is the worst," she said in the *Dear Jinri* interview, in which she was cautious in her words and cried as she talked about the pressure. "I don't feel people think celebrities are humans. They don't see us as humans. . . . We were basically puppets. Who cares if I'm exhausted? The only time I felt in control was when I was giving myself pain." She had asked, on several occasions, for help from SM Entertainment to combat cyberbullying, but she felt they didn't do enough.

One afternoon in October 2019, Sulli's brother, who was also her manager, entered her home and discovered her body hanging. Her death was ruled a suicide and the police revealed she was suffering from severe depression.[24]

Sulli's death shocked the Korean entertainment industry, and it was further rocked by the death of another K-pop star, twenty-eight-year-old Goo Hara, just over a month later. Goo Hara also found fame as a means of escaping a painful childhood. Growing up in Gwangju, a city in the southwest of the country, her mother abandoned the family when Hara was eight, and with her father traveling the country for work, Hara and her brother were sent to stay with different relatives, where they felt like a burden.[25] The siblings had always enjoyed performing and dancing together, and so Hara joined a local dance school for young K-pop hopefuls. She was completely dedicated to her practice, sometimes working until eleven at night. "I went to classes even when I was sick and had nosebleeds," she said. "If I didn't practice, I got nervous."[26]

When their father finally returned from his itinerant life, he took his children to Seoul to live with him and his new wife. After spending two years going to rounds of auditions, Hara was finally signed to an entertainment agency at the age of seventeen, and she was trained up to join the five-piece girl's group, Kara, in 2008, following the departure of a previous member.[27] They were one of the fastest-selling acts in Japan, with their bubble-gum appearance and sound. As K-pop cross-pollinated other media, she became a fixture on reality shows where she competed against other stars. This included the *Invincible Youth* in 2009, a version of *The Simple Life* in which K-pop girls learned about farming and agriculture. She also got her own reality show, *Hara On & Off: The Gossip*, in 2014.

While appearing on a talk show in 2010, Hara confessed to having had surgery on her eyelids, and she was bombarded with messages that she had looked better before. Hara struggled with self-esteem, likely to have been compounded by the feelings of rejection when her mother left her, and it made it particularly painful to deal with the harsh social media comments.[28] When Kara broke up in 2016, Hara worked hard to launch her own solo career, having already released her debut EP, *Alohara (Can You Feel It?)*, the year before.

"Her work as a K-pop star got a lot of love and attention from fans," Goo Ho-in, her older brother, told the *New York Times*. After going solo, "she worked less and less and she spent more and more time alone at home. So she received less and less love and attention from other people and she struggled, because she is someone who needs a lot of love and attention."[29]

She also struggled with her relationship issues. She met celebrity hairstylist Choi Jong-bum on her beauty show *My Mad Beauty Diary* in 2018 and the two started dating. Their breakup in September of that year was horrifically acrimonious. Entering her apartment late at night, Jong-bum woke her up and their arguments led to a violent assault. They both posted their injuries online, blaming the other for starting it, and Hara revealed that he had threatened to release a video of the two of them having sex.

In 2018, K-pop had been rocked by a scandal in which some of their most beloved stars were exposed as having secretly filmed themselves having sex with women. It highlighted a spycam epidemic targeting women, known in Korea as "Molka." Jung Joon-young was a popular star who also owned a Seoul nightclub called Burning Sun, where, through chat messages on his phone, it was discovered he and his friends raped unconscious women and then shared videos and gloated about it afterward. For these supposedly clean-cut stars to engage in this behavior was shocking, and the case high-lighted the rampant misogyny within the entertainment industry, and how it seeped into ordinary life. In 2018, there were around 6,800 cases reported to the supreme prosecutors' office, with some in women's public toilets and motel rooms, and others as revenge porn by partners.[30]

The BBC's podcast *Burning Sun* offers an in-depth exploration of the scandal, and reveals the years of debilitating harassment that female report-ers were subjected to from anonymous trolls after exposing it. Hara had con-tacted one of the reporters to offer her help, given her own experiences with a trusted boyfriend having secretly filmed her.

When news reached the press about the existence of the sex tape, it was Hara who was criticized and shamed for having had sex. She bravely sued Choi for threatening to release it without her consent. But the pressure proved too much, and just before she was due to testify, she was found unconscious after a suicide attempt. After her recovery, Hara apologized to her fans for her own distress. In a statement she wrote, "I'm truly sorry for causing concern due to the recent event. I am currently recovering my health. I was feeling distressed due to various incidents that piled up. I will try my best to show a healthy side of myself by having a stronger mindset."[31]

Choi was acquitted of filming the tape without permission, but he was convicted of assault, destroying property, and of threatening to release the tape, and after an appeal, in 2020 he was sentenced to a year in prison.

On November 23, 2019, having returned to Seoul from touring Japan, she posted on Instagram a photo of herself in bed with the caption "Good night." She was found dead the next day at the age of twenty-eight.

Before her death, Sulli had completed a short film, *Clean Island*, as part of a series called "Persona," and when it was released posthumously, it seemed even more prescient. She played a character called Four, which in Korean is associated with death, who works in a pig abattoir. These pigs that go to slaughter are much like the young stars who are placed on the conveyor belt, and are then sent to "Clean Island," where they can erase all their "pain and guilt." Her character wears a red dress, also associated with death, as she thinks back to being in a car crash that killed her mother, and is symbolic of Sulli's own feelings of abandonment. On Clean Island the pigs, a symbol of wealth and prestige in Korea, have passed through an "advanced cleaning system," just as idols are manufactured into becoming a star, and are sold to the public as a product. In the documentary *Dear Jinri* Sulli said she would always remember the words she had been told when she was first starting out. "You are a product. You need to exist as the finest, top-quality product."[32]

They may have been exhausted at times, but Blackpink also adored their position as one of the biggest bands in the world, and unable to imagine a future without it, they thought they might follow the trajectory of the Spice Girls, getting married and going solo, but still coming back for reunion shows.[33]

In their Netflix documentary *Blackpink: Light up the Sky*, Lisa was reflective of the future. "It doesn't matter if we grow old and get replaced by a new younger generation. As long as there is still someone talking about us. Because they will still remember how we shone so bright."

Conclusion

In April 2024, fifty-nine years after her death, Clara Bow hit the headlines once again when the final track on Taylor Swift's eleventh studio album, *The Tortured Poets Department*, was named after the original "It" girl. Given that her much-anticipated release broke streaming records, and with every lyric poured over in album reviews, op-eds, and on social media, there was a huge amount of speculation as to why Taylor chose Clara as an inspiration.

The track, "Clara Bow," was an exploration of the fickle nature of fame, of a star who burns bright for a short time, but with plenty of other girls waiting in the wings, she is destined to be replaced. The subject of the lyrics dreams of the bright lights of Manhattan from the narrow confines of her small town, and professes that she would die if she was able to see them for herself.

After being plucked like a rose, she arrives in the big city with a determination to give everything she possesses to dazzle and shine, but to be a star in heaven is to suffer a hell on earth in the fakery of the industry, as they demand more and more of her, until she's replaced. There is always a new "It" girl of the moment, a "girl of the year," and no matter her talents, eventually her sparkle will dim and she will be cast aside.

Taylor had previously explored the theme of fame, and the uniquely female concerns around being replaced, in "Nothing New," a duet with Phoebe Bridgers from the album *Red (Taylor's Version)*. Written in her early twenties, when her unjaded optimism should have been at its peak, she reveals a savvy awareness of how young, famous women are treated. Those who initially soar with naïve enthusiasm are quickly brought down to earth by criticism and condemnation. Once her novelty fades, she wonders, what will become of her?

For Clara Bow, the original "It" girl, the one for whom the name was invented, her burnout was crushing, and yet she was only twenty-eight when she quit the industry. Having suffered a traumatic childhood of extreme poverty and abuse, she achieved a rare celebrity, always with the hope that the global adulation and acceptance would heal her. All the while Clara's fizzing personality made her fans think she was having the time of her life, she was struggling. The sex scandals, the drinking, and the gambling turned people away, and with the Great Depression relegating the hedonism of the flapper and the "It" girl to the decadent past, Clara vanished.

Exhausted by Hollywood, she thought marriage and children would be the key to her happiness. Again, the childhood trauma that she had never fully dealt with came back to haunt her. After undergoing shock treatment in 1949 in an attempt to cure her chronic insomnia, she spent her final days in a Culver City bungalow separated from her family, living as a recluse. One can imagine her in the dim light of her living room, flicking through the pages of *Life* magazine to admire the photo spreads of Marilyn Monroe—her worthy, sparklingly beautiful and damaged successor.

As I've explored in the pages of this book, "It" girls are novel because of their youthfulness, and by the time they reach their thirties, they are faced with a potential downward spiral into irrelevancy. They may have succeeded because of their skills as actresses and singers, but they are judged on their beauty, and as they get older, they are so often derided and dismissed as being washed-up, ravaged by time, and desperate. Some found a new career, like Georgian mistress Mary Robinson, who reinvented herself as an esteemed novelist and social commentator. But for Edie Sedgwick and Jean Seberg, Mabel Normand and Lizzie Siddal, they were destroyed by the pressures of fame, the temptations of easy-to-come-by narcotics, and by forces that sought to use them as scapegoats, to undermine them and damage their reputations.

The "It" girl may not have been fully formed until novelist Elinor Glyn's presence in the movie colony served up a priceless publicity opportunity for a popular movie star, but she had predecessors. An actress and king's mistress whose portraits were copied and sold as mezzotints, and a courtesan of the Georgian-era who set silken fashion trends with every whim. She was the "Stunner" discovered by the pre-Raphaelite painter who elevated her as a glorified, tragic creature with every stroke of his brush.

After the "It" girl moniker faded with Clara's crash to earth, Brenda Frazier was the celebutante of the thirties whose all-night coming-out party and doughnut-dunking antics dominated headlines, Betty Grable and Marilyn Monroe were the pin-ups who decorated G.I. lockers and garage walls, and by the sixties, as the youthquakers shook up the conventions of the generation before, there was the "girl of the year." She was as much an invention of Andy Warhol's Factory as the Campbell's soup cans, Brillo pad boxes, and Marilyn screenprints, the disposable symbols of marketing and consumerism.

They were provocative in their novel sex appeal and youth; from Edie to Twiggy, Jean Shrimpton to Jane Birkin. As their star blazed as the girl of the moment, the spidery eyelashes, the leotards and tights, the miniskirts and straw baskets, were symbols not just of their status, but of the year they were made. Studio 54 became the center of hedonistic celebrity, where queens of the scene came into focus under the glitter and strobe lights. Margaux Hemingway grinning and laughing, Brooke Shields revealing a maturity beyond her age despite being exposed to the uneasy sexual mores of the seventies.

It wasn't until the 1990s that the "It" girl came full circle and the Roaring Twenties moniker was revived by *Tatler* magazine as a label for the famous-for-being-famous socialites who swilled champagne on super-yachts and whose effervescent presence at an opening night was guaranteed to be splashed in the papers the next day.

The noughties was the decade of the all-access "It" girl, of Paris and Britney, who single-handedly boosted the bank accounts of bitchy online bloggers and paparazzi as they recorded every antic and every low point. These women were an industry. The designer bags that dangled from their arms became cult items and the impossible glamor of their lifestyles set the dreams of brazen teenagers who wanted it for themselves. It was emulation culture, but it was also peak cruelty. Young and beautiful female celebrities were pushed to breaking point. The photos of Britney shaving her head and of being carried off on a stretcher are now horrific to see, and the neon headlines, the awful captions, the circles of shame, are a particular form of misogyny, a psychological warfare, that specifically targeted young women to keep them in their place.

There was a glee to the reporting of their destruction, which was also laced with puritanical outrage. The message was that women who were too hot, too successful, who were having too much of a good time, having sex and dating, deserved to be knocked down to size. Sienna Miller's famous relationships and "It" girl status as boho icon had triggered an unlivable circus around her. Her life was a tabloid hell, and she stood up to the press by suing those that targeted her. She effectively changed the law in England to protect her privacy and to ensure that new measures would dampen the feeding frenzy for other young starlets.

With a thousand names all given the "It" girl moniker in countless magazine articles and columns, there are far too many to have featured them all in this book, and the criteria for who earns the title is not set in stone. I chose to feature some women who are not necessarily considered pure "It" girls but who helped define a look and a mood for their era. The tragedy of their lives was that fame also proved to be a poisoned chalice for many, or a way to paint over the cracks of a painful childhood.

In today's media landscape, where lives are played out online, "It" girls are expected to be more polished and less destructive. For the Kardashians, everything about them is airbrushed to perfection; they don't drunkenly stumble out of clubs or reveal their greasy hair and spots. Rather they operate in a very controlled way to promote the idea of hard work to earn a billion-dollar fortune. As Kim Kardashian controversially chastised in *Variety* in March 2022: "I have the best advice for women in business. Get your fucking ass up and work."

The world of celebrity in the 2020s is entwined with social media influencing and the hustle of endorsement deals, and who is defined as an "It" girl is a contentious subject. In 2021, *Tatler* unveiled a list of modern "It" girls, including Fry's Chocolate Cream heiress March Fry, and splashed Ella Richards, granddaughter of Rolling Stone Keith Richards, as the "It" girl cover star for March 2023, but their names don't register much beyond the pages of fashion magazines. "It" girls were once created by column inches, but now that they can be made on TikTok, young women with a million followers can generate generous sponsorship deals, making it difficult to determine who is the true modern incarnation.

There's even more competition to achieve the status, as influencers, paparazzi magnets, fashion icons, nepo babies, and party girls are interchangeably labeled with the title. Whoever the next "It" girl is, no matter how rich and famous and hot she is, it will be a full-time job to manage the social media accounts, the sponsorships, the orchestrated public events. But whatever her background, she must possess that charisma, the X factor and the "It," that gets everyone talking.

Notes

INTRODUCTION

1. Rudyard Kipling, *Mrs. Bathurst and Other Stories* (Oxford Paperbacks, 1991).
2. David Stenn, *Clara Bow: Runnin' Wild* (Rowman & Littlefield, 2000).
3. Hilary Lynn, "What Is This Thing Called 'X'?," *Photoplay*, April 1933.
4. *Chicago Tribune*, "Ann Sheridan Voted Leading 'Oomph' Girl by Jury of Twenty-five Men," March 18, 1939.
5. Thomas Moore, *Letters and Journals of Lord Byron: With Notices of His Life, Volume 1* (J & J Harper, 1830–1831).
6. Fremont Power, "She Wasn't Just a Plain Jayne," *Indianapolis News*, July 3, 1967.
7. Sharon Marcus, *The Drama of Celebrity* (Princeton University Press, 2019).
8. Adela Rogers St. Johns, "Clara Bow: My Life Story," *Photoplay*, February 1928.
9. Elisabeth Goldbeck, "The Real Clara Bow," *Motion Picture*, September 1930.
10. Lois Shirley, "Empty Hearted," *Photoplay*, October 1929.

CHAPTER 1

1. John Wilmot, *Earl of Rochester: Complete Poetical Works* (Delphi Classics, 2014).
2. John Downe, *Roscius Anglicanus: An Historical Review of the Stage* (J. W. Jarvis & Son, 1886).
3. Charles Beauclerk, *Nell Gwyn: A Biography* (Grove Press, 2006).
4. Samuel Pepys, *Diary of Samuel Pepys* (Legare Street Press, 2022).
5. John Downes, *Roscius Anglicanus* (1886).
6. Beauclerk, *Nell Gwyn.*
7. Linda Porter, *Mistresses: Sex and Scandal at the Court of Charles II* (Picador, 2020).
8. Antonia Fraser, *King Charles II* (Orion, 2011).
9. Porter, *Mistresses.*
10. Porter, *Mistresses.*
11. Royal Collection Trust, Charles II: Art & Power exhibition – The Circulation of Images, The circulation of images (rct.uk).

12. Porter, *Mistresses*.
13. Virginia Woolf, *A Room of One's Own* (e-artnow ebooks, 2013).
14. Clarissa Hyman, *Oranges: A Global History* (Reaktion Books, 2013).
15. John Seymour, *Memoirs of the Life of Eleanor Gwinn: A Celebrated Courtesan in the Reign of King Charles II and Mistress to the Monarch* (E. Stamper, 1752).
16. Pepys, *Diary*.
17. Beauclerk, *Nell Gwyn*.
18. Julia Novak, "'Rais'd from a Dunghill, to a King's Embrace': Restoration Verse Satires on Nell Gwyn as Life-Writing," *Life Writing*, 2016.
19. Peter Cunningham, *The Story of Nell Gwyn and the Sayings of Charles II* (Henry Benjamin Wheatley, 1896).
20. Beauclerk, *Nell Gwyn*.
21. Cunningham, *The Story of Nell Gwyn*.
22. Beauclerk, *Nell Gwyn*.
23. Don Jordan and Michael Walsh, *The King's Bed: Sex, Power and the Court of Charles II* (Little Brown, 2015).

CHAPTER 2

1. Mike Rendell, *Georgian Harlots & Whores: Fame, Fashion & Fortune* (Pen & Sword, 2022).
2. Rendell, *Georgian Harlots*.
3. Alice Loxton, *UPROAR!: Satire, Scandal and Printmakers in Georgian London* (Icon Books, 2023).
4. Greg Jenner, *Dead Famous: An Unexpected History of Celebrity from Bronze Age to Silver Screen* (Weidenfeld & Nicolson, 2020).
5. Loxton, *UPROAR!*.
6. Jenner, *Dead Famous*.
7. Gretchen Gerzina, *Black England: A Forgotten Georgian History* (John Murray, 2022).
8. Rendell, *Georgian Harlots*.
9. Rendell, *Georgian Harlots*.
10. Giacomo Casanova, *History of My Life* (Johns Hopkins University Press, 1997).
11. Rendell, *Georgian Harlots*.
12. Paula Byrne, *Perdita: The Life of Mary Robinson* (Harper Press, 2012).
13. Mary Robinson and J. Fitzgerald Molloy, ed., *Memoirs of Mary Robinson, "Perdita"* (Gibbings and Company, Ltd., 1895).
14. Byrne, *Perdita*.
15. Robinson and Molloy, *Memoirs of Mary Robinson*.
16. Mary Robinson, *The Memoirs of Perdita* (G. Lister, 1784).
17. Rendell, *Georgian Harlots*.
18. Kimberly Chrisman-Campbell, *Fashion Victims* (Yale University Press, 2014).
19. Antonia Fraser, *Marie Antoinette* (Weidenfeld & Nicolson, 2010).

20. Sarah Gristwood, *Perdita: Royal Mistress, Writer, Romantic* (Bantam Press, 2005).

21. Byrne, *Perdita*.

CHAPTER 3

1. Lucinda Hawksley, *Lizzie Siddal: The Tragedy of a Pre-Raphaelite Supermodel* (Andre Deutsch, 2013).

2. Franny Moyle, *Desperate Romantics* (John Murray, 2009).

3. Henrietta Garnett, *Wives and Stunners: The Pre-Raphaelites and Their Muses* (Macmillan, 2012).

4. Hawksley, *Lizzie Siddal*.

5. William Holman Hunt, *Pre-Raphaelitism and the Pre-Raphaelite Brotherhood, vol. I* (1905).

6. Hunt, *Pre-Raphaelitism*.

7. Hawksley, *Lizzie Siddal*.

8. Hawksley, *Lizzie Siddal*.

9. Moyle, *Desperate Romantics*.

10. John Chapple, *Elizabeth Gaskell: A Portrait in Letters* (Manchester University Press, 2007).

11. Hawksley, *Lizzie Siddal*.

12. Judith Watt, "Flaming Libertines: Dante Gabriel Rossetti and His Muse," *The Telegraph*, March 22, 2011.

13. William Michael Rossetti, *Ruskin, Rossetti, Preraphaelitism: Papers, 1864 to 1862* (Dodd, Mead and Company, 1899).

14. Kirsty Stonell Walker, *Stunner: The Rise and Fall of Fanny Cornforth* (Unicorn, 2022).

15. Suzanne Fagence Cooper, *How We Might Live: At Home with Jane and William Morris* (Quercus, 2022).

16. Henrietta Garnett, *Wives and Stunners: The Pre-Raphaelites and Their Muses* (Macmillan, 2012).

17. Fagence Cooper, *How We Might Live*.

18. National Trust, Who Was William Morris?, https://www.nationaltrust.org.uk/discover/history/people/who-was-william-morris.

19. Garnett, *Wives and Stunners*.

20. Garnett, *Wives and Stunners*.

21. Hawksley, *Lizzie Siddal*.

22. Fagence Cooper, *How We Might Live*.

CHAPTER 4

1. Richard Ellmann, *Oscar Wilde* (Vintage, 1988).

2. Beatty Laura, *Lillie Langtry: Manners, Masks and Morals* (Vintage, 2000).

3. Laura, *Lillie Langtry*.

4. Lillie Langtry, *The Days I Knew* (Panoply Productions, 2012).

5. Sarah Bernhardt, *My Double Life* (State University of New York Press, 1999).

6. Robert Gottlieb, *Sarah: The Life of Sarah Bernhardt* (Yale University Press, 2010).

7. Gottlieb, *Sarah*.

8. Gottlieb, *Sarah*.

9. Kim Willsher, "Paris Exhibition to Tell Story of Eccentric Acting Pioneer Sarah Bernhardt," *The Guardian*, April 9, 2023.

10. Holly Williams, "Sarah Bernhardt: Was She the First 'A-list' Actress?," BBC Culture, The It Girls, December 15, 2017.

11. Willsher, "Paris Exhibition."

12. Olivia Laing, "Sarah: The Life of Sarah Bernhardt by Robert Gottlieb—review," *The Guardian*, *The Observer*, October 24, 2010.

13. *Boston Post*, New Items, December 25, 1875.

14. Bernhardt, *My Double Life*.

15. Greg Jenner, *Dead Famous: An Unexpected History of Celebrity from Bronze Age to Silver Screen* (Weidenfeld & Nicolson, 2020).

16. Langtry, *The Days I Knew*.

17. Laura, *Lillie Langtry*.

18. Langtry, *The Days I Knew*.

19. Laura, *Lillie Langtry*.

20. Mrs. George Cornwallis-West, *The Reminiscences of Lady Randolph Churchill* (Edward Arnold, 1908).

21. Langtry, *The Days I Knew*.

22. Langtry, *The Days I Knew*.

23. Langtry, *The Days I Knew*.

24. Gottlieb, *Sarah*.

25. Langtry, *The Days I Knew*.

26. Langtry, *The Days I Knew*.

27. Margot Asquith, *An Autobiography: Volumes I and II* (Outlook Verlag, 2019).

28. Langtry, *The Days I Knew*.

29. *New York Times*, "Scenes of Life in London: Reigning Beauties," July 15, 1878.

30. Gottlieb, *Sarah*.

31. Sharon Marcus, "The First Modern Celebrity Was Born 175 Years Ago," *Vox*, June 26, 2019.

32. Gottlieb, *Sarah*.

33. Langtry, *The Days I Knew*.

34. Laura, *Lillie Langtry*.

35. Marcus, "The First Modern Celebrity."

36. Langtry, *The Days I Knew*.

37. Willsher, "Paris Exhibition."

38. "'She Is My Wife'—declaration made by Edward Langtry," *Boston Globe*, June 16, 1897.

39. *Sunday Chronicle*, February 1928.

40. Willsher, "Paris Exhibition."

41. *The Guardian*, "A Reigning Beauty: Death of Lily Langtry," February 13, 1929.

42. *Reno Gazette-Journal*, "What Woman Knows," April 8, 1911.

CHAPTER 5

1. A. Scott Berg, *Goldwyn: A Biography* (Simon & Schuster, 2013).

2. Frederick James Smith, "Mabel in a Hurry," *Motion Picture Magazine*, November 1918.

3. Smith, "Mabel in a Hurry."

4. Mabel Norman as told to Chandler Sprague, "Mabel Normand's Own Life Story!" *Los Angeles Examiner*, February 17, 1924.

5. Nichi Hodgson, *The Curious History of Dating From Jane Austen to Tinder* (Robinson, 2017).

6. S. J. Woolf, "The Gibson Girl Is Still With Us," *The New York Times*, September 20, 1942.

7. Paula Uruburu, *American Eve* (Riverhead Books, 2008).

8. Irene Gammel, *Looking for Anne of Green Gables: The Story of L. M. Montgomery and Her Literary Classic* (St. Martin's Press, July 2008).

9. Deborah Paul, *Tragic Beauty: The Lost 1914 Memoirs of Evelyn Nesbit* (Lulu.com, 2006).

10. Greg Jenner, *Dead Famous: An Unexpected History of Celebrity from Bronze Age to Silver Screen* (Weidenfeld & Nicolson, 2020).

11. *The Baltimore Sun*, "Leads Quiet Life: Young Wife of Harry Thaw Thoroughly Secluded," January 5, 1907.

12. Seymour Korman, "Gibson Girl Evelyn Nesbit Thaw Dies: Central Figure in 1906 Love Slaying Trial," *Chicago Tribune*, January 19, 1967.

13. Normand and Sprague, "Mabel Normand's Own Life Story!"

14. Normand and Sprague, "Mabel Normand's Own Life Story!"

15. *Motion Picture Magazine*, June 1913.

16. *Fort Wayne Sentinel*, "'Mabel of the Movies' Calls Herself the Airman's Hoo Doo, Gertrude Price," March 15, 1913.

17. Berg, *Goldwyn*.

18. *Salt Lake Telegram*, "Mabel Normand: Fun Girl of Film," September 18, 1916.

19. Don Schneifer interview with Minta Durfee, July 21, 1974.

20. Timothy Dean Lefler, *Mabel Normand: The Life and Career of a Hollywood Madcap* (McFarland, November 2023).

21. Edwin Schallert, "Ritzy People Are Out," *Los Angeles Times*, November 27, 1921.

22. Betty Harper Fussell, *Mabel: Hollywood's First I-Don't-Care-Girl* (Ticknor & Fields, 1982).

23. William J. Mann, *Tinseltown: Murder, Morphine, and Madness at the Dawn of Hollywood* (Harper, 2014).

24. Lefler, *Mabel Normand.*

25. Mann, *Tinseltown.*

26. Mann, *Tinseltown.*

27. Normand and Sprague, "Mabel Normand's Own Life Story!"

28. Normand and Sprague, "Mabel Normand's Own Life Story!"

29. *Evening Journal*, "Mabel Normand Films under Ban," January 5, 1924.

30. Cynthia Grey, "Motion Picture Censors Would Best Spend Their Time Barring Society Films," *Seattle Star*, January 16, 1924.

31. Lefler, *Mabel Normand.*

CHAPTER 6

1. Bill Egan, *Florence Mills: Harlem Jazz Queen* (Scarecrow Press, 2004).

2. Egan, *Florence Mills.*

3. Egan *Florence Mills.*

4. Egan, *Florence Mills.*

5. Manning Marable and Leith Mullings, *Let Nobody Turn Us Around: Voices of Resistance, Reform and Renewal* (Rowman & Littlefield, 2003).

6. Graham White and Shane White, *Stylin': African American Expressive Culture* (Cornell University Press, 1999).

7. *Oregon Daily Journal*, "'Shuffle Along' Is a 'Lol' With 'NYawk Aghast,'" August 21, 1921.

8. Lester A. Walton, "Shuffle Along Is in Its Six Month Run," *New York Age*, October 15, 1921.

9. Egan, *Florence Mills.*

10. "Florence Mills: Broadway Sensation of the 1920s," Susan Johnson, March 24, 1920 at The Museum of the City of New York (mcny.org).

11. *Pittsburgh Courier*, "Early Days Desperate, says 'Flo,'" February 28, 1925.

12. *Pittsburgh Courier*, "Early Days Desperate."

13. Langston Hughes, *The Big Sea: An Autobiography* (Hill & Wang Inc., 1993).

14. Langston Hughes, "The Negro Artist and the Racial Mountain," *Nation*, June 23, 1926.

15. *Brooklyn Citizen*, "'Plantation Revue' Is Well Received," July 18, 1922.

16. *Pittsburgh Courier*, "Early Days Desperate."

17. *Pittsburgh Courier*, "Early Days Desperate."

18. *New Pittsburgh Courier*, "Florence Mills to Head an All-Colored Revue as Permanent Institution," May 9, 1925.

19. *The Northwestern Bulletin-Appeal*, "Florence Mills Hailed a Genius by NY Critics," November 8, 1924.

20. *Vanity Fair*, "Florence Mills Leads a Harlemquinade on Broadway," February 1925.

21. A. E. Hotchner, *Papa Hemingway: A Personal Memoir* (Open Road Media, 2018).

22. Lauren Michele Jackson, "Josephine Baker Was the Star France Wanted—and the Spy It Needed," *The New Yorker*, August 8, 2022.

23. Jean-Claude Baker, *Josephine Baker: The Hungry Heart* (Cooper Square Press, 2001).

24. Baker, *Josephine Baker*.

25. Baker, *Josephine Baker*.

26. Maurice Rochambeau, "The Life Story of Josephine Baker," *Kansas City American*, December 12, 1929.

27. *Brooklyn Daily Eagle*, Stage Notes, May 28, 1922.

28. Judith Mackrell, *Flappers: Six Women of a Dangerous Generation* (Pan, 2014).

29. Jackson, "Josephine Baker Was the Star France Wanted."

30. Mackrell, *Flappers*.

31. Mackrell, *Flappers*.

32. Mackrell, *Flappers*.

33. *The Times*, "Blackbirds," September 13, 1926.

34. Caroline Bressey and Gemma Romain, "Staging Race: Florence Mills, Celebrity, Identity and Performance in 1920s Britain," *Women's History Review*, Volume 28, Issue 3, 2019.

35. Jon Savage, *Teenage: The Creation of Youth 1875 to 1945* (Chatto and Windus, 2007).

36. *The New York Age*, "150,000 Throng Harlem to Pay Last Tribute and Honor to Dainty Star, Florence Mills," November 12, 1927.

37. Mackrell, *Flappers*.

38. Jackson, "Josephine Baker Was the Star France Wanted."

39. Baker, *Josephine Baker*.

40. Jackson, "Josephine Baker Was the Star France Wanted."

41. St. Louis LGBT History Project, 1952 Josephine Baker Event—stlouislgbthistory.com/timeline/1900-1960s/1952-josephine-baker-event.htm.

CHAPTER 7

1. David Stenn, *Clara Bow: Runnin' Wild* (Cooper Square Press, 2000).

2. *Photoplay*, "Clara Bow: My Life Story," as told to Adela Rogers St. Johns, February 1928.

3. Stenn, *Clara Bow*.

4. *Photoplay*, "Clara Bow: My Life Story."

5. Stenn, *Clara Bow*.

6. Judith Mackrell, *Flappers: Six Women of a Dangerous Generation* (Pan, 2014).

7. *Photoplay*, "Clara Bow: My Life Story."

8. *Photoplay*, "Clara Bow: My Life Story."

9. *Motion Picture Magazine*, "The New Star," January 1922.

10. *Photoplay*, "Clara Bow: My Life Story."

11. *Photoplay*, "Clara Bow: My Life Story."

12. *San Francisco Examiner*, "They'll Shine at Film Frolic Here," January 2, 1924.

13. Stenn, *Clara Bow*.

14. *Omaha Daily News*, "Clara Bow; Newly Made Flapper Star, in Black Oxen," January 3, 1924.

15. Deborah Nadoolman-Landis, *Dressed: A Century of Hollywood Costume Design* (Harper Collins, 2006).

16. *Motion Picture Magazine*, "Has the Flapper Changed?" Margaret Reid, July 1927.

17. *Los Angeles Times*, "Colleen Away from Flappers," May 18, 1924.

18. *New York Times*, "Those Hectic Youngsters," July 19, 1926.

19. Pamel Hutchinson, "Clara Bow: The Hard-Partying Jazz-Baby Airbrushed from Hollywood History," *The Guardian*, June 21, 2016.

20. Stenn, *Clara Bow*.

21. Stenn, *Clara Bow*.

22. Lois Shirley, "Empty Hearted," *Photoplay*, October 1929.

23. *Daily News*, "Daisy Tells of Paying Clara's Rum Bills," January 17, 1931.

24. *Wichita Eagle*, "Clara Vows Titian Tresses Are Real," January 18, 1931.

25. Stenn, *Clara Bow*.

CHAPTER 8

1. *Oklahoma News*, "No 1 Debutante—She Likes Them All," December 4, 1938.

2. Greg Jenner, *Dead Famous: An Unexpected History of Celebrity from Bronze Age to Silver Screen* (Weidenfeld & Nicolson, 2020).

3. Karen Heller, "Brenda Frazier: Truly Miserably Rich," *St. Louis Post-Dispatch*, June 11, 1987.

4. Helen Worden, "My Debut—a Horror, Brenda Frazier," *Life* magazine, December 6, 1963.

5. Kristen Richardson, *The Season: A Social History of the Debutante* (W.W. Norton & Company, 2020).

6. Worden, "My Debut—a Horror, Brenda Frazier."

7. Worden, "My Debut—a Horror, Brenda Frazier."

8. Richardson, *The Season*.

9. Richardson, *The Season*.

10. Worden, "My Debut—a Horror, Brenda Frazier."

11. *San Francisco Examiner*, "Cholly Knickerbocker Observes," December 4, 1938.

12. *Life* magazine, "The Debutante," November 14, 1938.

13. *Oklahoma News*, "No 1 Debutante."

14. Worden, "My Debut—a Horror, Brenda Frazier."

15. Joan Durham, "Brenda Frazier Leads Season's Glamour Girls," *The Dispatch*, October 29, 1938.

16. *San Francisco Examiner*, "Cholly Knickerbocker Observes."

17. *Oklahoma News*, "No 1 Debutante."

18. Richardson, *The Season*.

19. Associated Press, "AP Cameramen Take Top Prizes at Press Photo Show," January 23, 1939.

20. Raquel Laneri, "The Sensational Debut and Fall of the World's First 'Celebutante,'" *New York Post*, November 16, 2019.

21. Worden, "My Debut—a Horror, Brenda Frazier."

22. Richardson, *The Season*.

23. Worden, "My Debut—a Horror, Brenda Frazier."

24. Worden, "My Debut—a Horror, Brenda Frazier."

25. Worden, "My Debut—a Horror, Brenda Frazier."

26. Morgan Baila, "How Kim Kardashian Reinvented the Socialite," *Refinery 29*, October 21, 2016.

27. Worden, "My Debut—a Horror, Brenda Frazier."

28. Worden, "My Debut—a Horror, Brenda Frazier."

CHAPTER 9

1. *Daily Herald-Tribune*, "Grable Pin-up Photog Is Dead," June 28, 1986.

2. *Los Angeles Times*, "Snapped Famed WWII Betty Grable Pinup: Photographer Frank Powolny Dies at 84," January 11, 1986.

3. Maria Elena Buzek, "War Goddess: The Varga Girls, WW2 and Feminism," in *n.paradoxa*, Issue 6, March 1998.

4. Kirtley Baskette, "A High Kick and a Hot Lick," *Modern Screen*, March 1945.

5. Doug Warren, *Betty Grable: The Reluctant Movie Queen* (Crossroad Press, 2016).

6. Homer Bassford, "Betty Grable's Star Beginning to Twinkle," *St. Louis Star and Times*, August 19, 1935.

7. Warren, *Betty Grable*.

8. *Life* magazine, "Betty Grable's Legs," June 7, 1943.

9. Warren, *Betty Grable*.

10. Greg Jenner, *Dead Famous: An Unexpected History of Celebrity from Bronze Age to Silver Screen* (Weidenfeld & Nicolson, 2020).

11. Patrick Agan, "Rita's Real-life Drama," *Minneapolis Star*, August 5, 1980.

12. *Chicago Tribune*, "Cinderella Girl of '41," February 22, 1941.

13. *Life* magazine, "Veronica Lake's Hair: It Is a Cinema Property of World Influence," November 24, 1941.

14. *Chicago Tribune*, "Cinderella Girl."

15. Veronica Lake, *Veronica: The Autobiography of Veronica Lake* (Dean Street Press, 2020).

16. Lake, *Veronica.*

CHAPTER 10

1. Betty Friedan, *The Feminine Mystique: The Classic that Sparked a Feminist Revolution* (Thread, 2021).

2. Sarah Churchwell, *The Many Lives of Marilyn Monroe* (Bloomsbury Publishing, 2019).

3. Charles Casillo, *Marilyn Monroe: The Private Life of a Public Icon* (St. Martin's Press, 2018).

4. Donald Spoto, *Marilyn Monroe: The Biography* (Dansker Press, 2014).

5. Casillo, *Marilyn Monroe.*

6. Richard Meryman, "Last Talk With a Lonely Girl: Marilyn Monroe," *Life* magazine, August 17, 1962.

7. Casillo, *Marilyn Monroe.*

8. Peter Bogdanovich, *Who the Hell's in It: Conversations with Hollywood's Legendary Actors* (Random House, 2005).

9. Casillo, *Marilyn Monroe.*

10. Aline Mosby, "Marilyn Admits it's She on that Calendar," United Press, March 13, 1952.

11. *Playboy*, "Sweetheart of the Month: Marilyn Monroe," December 1953.

12. *Life* magazine, "Hollywood Topic A-Plus: Whole Town's Talking about Marilyn Monroe," April 7, 1952.

13. Lowell E. Redelings, "The Hollywood Scene," *Los Angeles Evening Citizen*, June 10, 1953.

14. Churchwell, *The Many Lives of Marilyn Monroe.*

15. Casillo, *Marilyn Monroe.*

16. Casillo, *Marilyn Monroe.*

17. Spoto, *Marilyn Monroe.*

18. Casillo, *Marilyn Monroe.*

19. Elizabeth Winder, *Marilyn in Manhattan: Her Year of Joy* (Flatiron Books, 2017).

20. Lydia Lane, "Never Catty, Says Jayne Mansfield," *Los Angeles Times*, November 11, 1956.

21. Raymond Strait, *The Tragic Secret Life of Jayne Mansfield* (Crossroad Press, 2016).

22. Strait, *Jayne Mansfield.*

23. Daws, *Bombshells.*

24. Daws, *Bombshells.*

25. Daws, *Bombshells.*

26. Strait, *Jayne Mansfield.*

27. Daws, *Bombshells*.

28. Robert Wahls, "Scripter for Sexpots," *Daily News*, January 31, 1965.

29. Daws, *Bombshells*.

30. Daws, *Bombshells*.

31. Bosley Crowther, "Screen," *New York Times*, September 12, 1957.

32. Strait, *Jayne Mansfield*.

33. Lane, "Never Catty."

34. Lynn Peril, *Pink Think: Becoming a Woman in Many Uneasy Lessons* (W. W. Norton & Company, 2002.

35. Lane, "Never Catty."

36. Peril, *Pink Think*.

37. Peril, *Pink Think*.

38. May Mann, *Jayne Mansfield: A Biography* (Abelard-Schuman, 1974).

39. Meryman, "Last Talk With a Lonely Girl."

40. Casillo, *Marilyn Monroe*.

41. *Variety*, "Film review: Some Like it Hot," February 24, 1954.

42. Hedda Hopper, "Don't Drink, it Won't Bring Back Your Baby," *Motion Picture*, July 1960.

43. Daws, *Bombshells*.

44. Casillo, *Marilyn Monroe*.

45. Daws, *Bombshells*.

46. Janine Henni, "Marilyn Monroe's Estate Says Icon Would Approve of Kim Kardashian's Met Gala Dress Moment," *People*, May 4, 2022.

47. *Photoplay*, "Marilyn Poses Nude Again—Why Did She Do it?" September 1962.

48. Casillo, *Marilyn Monroe*.

49. Casillo, *Marilyn Monroe*.

50. *New York Times*, "Jayne Mansfield in 'Bus Stop,'" April 16, 1964.

51. Strait, *Jayne Mansfield*.

52. Strait, *Jayne Mansfield*.

53. *Daily News*, "Jayne Mansfield: Death on the Highway," June 30, 1967.

CHAPTER 11

1. Daniel P. Finney, "Jean Seberg Revisited," *Des Moines Register*, October 30, 2011.

2. Lee Grany, "Jean Seberg: Did Gossip Kill Her?" *Los Angeles Times*, September 23, 1979.

3. A. H. Weiler, "The Screen: Saint Joan, Preminger's Version of Shaw Play Bows," *New York Times*, June 27, 1957.

4. Weiler, "The Screen: Saint Joan."

5. Finney, "Jean Seberg Revisited."

6. Lloyd Shearer, "What Failure Has Done to Jean Seberg? It's Made Her Bigger and Better Than Ever," *Chattanooga Daily Times*, July 7, 1963.

7. Shearer, "What Failure Has Done to Jean Seberg?"

8. Shearer, "What Failure Has Done to Jean Seberg?"

9. Shearer, "What Failure Has Done to Jean Seberg?"

10. Rex Reed, "Some of the Folks in Iowa Think She's a Lost Woman," *New York Times*, August 11, 1968.

11. Shearer, "What Failure Has Done to Jean Seberg?"

12. Alice Sedgwick Wohl, *As It Turns Out: Thinking about Edie and Andy* (Fleet, 2023).

13. Jean Stein, *Edie: An American Biography* (Random House, 1988).

14. Andrew Wilson, "Edie Sedgwick: The It Girl Who Was Inspiration to Dylan and Warhol," *The Independent*, February 5, 2006.

15. Stein, *Edie*.

16. Melissa Painter, *Edie: Girl on Fire* (Chronicle Books, 2006).

17. Stein, *Edie*.

18. Matthew Schneier, "What Was (and Is) the 'It' Girl? An Investigation," *The Cut*, August 7, 2023.

19. Lili Anolik, "Andy Warhol and Edie Sedgwick: A Brief, White Hot and Totally Doomed Romance," *Vanity Fair*, December 6, 2017.

20. Andy Warhol and Pat Hackett, *Popism: The Warhol Sixties* (Penguin Classics, 2007).

21. Warhol and Hackett, *Popism*.

22. Anolik, *Andy Warhol and Edie Sedgwick*.

23. Stein, *Edie*.

24. *Life*, "Fashion: The Girl with the Black Tights," November 26, 1965.

25. John P. Corr, "Andy Warhol Pops in to Show Off Picture of Dollar Bills, Elvis," *Philadelphia Inquirer*, October 8, 1965.

26. Harry Harris, "Screening TV," *The Philadelphia Inquirer*, October 14, 1965.

27. Stein, *Edie*.

28. Stein, *Edie*.

29. Stein, *Edie*.

30. Reed, "Folks in Iowa."

31. Reed, "Folks in Iowa."

32. Eleanor Ringel, "After a Flicker, Actress' Star Fell Fast," *Atlantic Constitution*, May 3, 1996.

33. Grany, "Jean Seberg."

34. Grany, "Jean Seberg."

35. Grany, "Jean Seberg."

36. Finney, "Jean Seberg Revisited."

37. Helen Dudar, "Edie Sedgwick: Where the Road Led," *New York Post*, May 2, 1968.

38. Stein, *Edie*.

39. David Leacock, "Edie Sedgwick, 28, Andy Warhol Film Star," *Boston Globe*, November 28, 1971.

40. Alexandra Jacobs, "A Sister's Remembrance of Edie," *New York Times*, August 17, 2022.

41. Grany, "Jean Seberg."

42. David Richards, *Played Out: The Jean Seberg Story* (Random House, 1981).

43. Richards, *Played Out.*

44. Grany, "Jean Seberg."

45. Finney, "Jean Seberg Revisited."

46. Grany, "Jean Seberg."

CHAPTER 12

1. Twiggy Lawson, *In Black and White: An Autobiography* (Simon & Schuster, 1997).

2. *Time*, "The Swinging City," April 15, 1966.

3. Mary Quant, *Mary Quant: My Autobiography* (Headline, 2012).

4. Mark Donnelly, *Sixties Britain: Culture, Society and Politics* (Taylor & Francis, 2014).

5. Quant, *Mary Quant.*

6. Jean Shrimpton, *The Truth about Modelling* (V & Fashion Perspectives) (V & A Publishing, 2019).

7. *Family Weekly*, "The Girl Behind the World's Most Beautiful Face," January 8, 1967.

8. Shrimpton, *The Truth about Modelling.*

9. *Family Weekly*, "The Girl Behind."

10. Jessica Bumpus, "The Shrimpton Story," *British Vogue*, March 3, 2010.

11. Bumpus, "The Shrimpton Story."

12. Alex Wade, "The Saturday Interview: Jean Shrimpton," *The Guardian*, April 30, 2011.

13. Wade, "Jean Shrimpton."

14. Wade, "Jean Shrimpton."

15. Emine Saner, "Twiggy: I Don't Think High Fashion Will Ever Move Completely Away from Slimness," *The Guardian*, May 12, 2020.

16. Lawson, *In Black and White.*

17. Saner, "Twiggy: I Don't Think High Fashion."

18. *Life*, "The Arrival of Twiggy," February 3, 1967.

19. *Life*, "The Arrival of Twiggy."

20. Inez Robb, "Teenager, 5'7", 93 Pounds, Is Newest Queen of Models," *The Gazette*, November 30, 1966.

21. Charlotte Curtis, "Twiggy: She's Harlow, and the Boy Next Door," *New York Times*, March 21, 1967.

22. Oliver Lalanne, "From the Archive: When Jane Birkin Confided in Vogue," *French Vogue*, July 16, 2023.

23. Lalanne, "When Jane Birkin Confided."

24. Jane Birkin, *Munkey Diaries: The Extraordinary Early Years of an International Icon* (W & N, 2021).

25. Birkin, *Munkey Diaries.*

26. Birkin, *Munkey Diaries*.
27. *San Francisco Examiner*, "William Otterburn-Hall," November 23, 1969.
28. Birkin, *Munkey Diaries*.
29. Jack Gee, "For Bardot Read Birkin," *Sunday People*, February 8, 1970.
30. Lalanne, "When Jane Birkin Confided."
31. Lalanne, "When Jane Birkin Confided."
32. Lalanne, "When Jane Birkin Confided."
33. Rebecca Morehouse, "English 'Sex Symbol' Says a Sense of Humor Is Vital," *Asbury Park Press*, April 11, 1970.
34. Birkin, *Munkey Diaries*.
35. Birkin, *Munkey Diaries*.
36. Rachel Tashjian, "Jane Birkin Made Simple Things Feel Luxurious," *Washington Post*, July 16, 2023.
37. Wade, "Jean Shrimpton."
38. Wade, "Jean Shrimpton."

CHAPTER 13

1. Karen Schneider, "A Life Eclipsed," *People*, July 15, 1996.
2. Lynette Holloway, "Margaux Hemingway Is Dead; Model and Actress Was 41," *New York Times*, July 3, 1996.
3. James Rainey, "Margaux Hemingway's Death Ruled a Suicide," *Los Angeles Times*, August 21, 1996.
4. Holloway, "Margaux Hemingway Is Dead."
5. *Running from Crazy* documentary.
6. Marian Christy, "Hemingway's Girl," *Cincinnati Post*, January 24, 1975.
7. Rosemary McCracken, "Margaux Hemingway: Faberge's Star Barnstorms," *Montreal Star*, April 21, 1976.
8. *Daily Telegraph*, "Margaux Hemingway," July 3, 1996.
9. Associated Press, "Hot-Dog Skier Turns Million Dollar Cover Girl," June 4, 1975.
10. Rachel Campbell Johnston, "Bob Colacello: 'Andy Would Have Loved AI,'" *The Times*, June 1, 2023.
11. Maureen Callahan, *Champagne Supernovas: Kate Moss, Marc Jacobs, Alexander McQueen, and the 90s Renegades Who Remade Fashion* (Simon & Schuster, 2014).
12. *People*, "Beauty and the Bottle," February 8, 1988.
13. Pat Cleveland, *Walking with the Muses: A Memoir* (37 Ink, 2017).
14. Alice Drake, *The Beautiful Fall: Fashion, Genius and Glorious Excess in 1970s Paris* (Bloomsbury, 2007).
15. Cleveland, *Walking with the Muses*.
16. Tamara Sturtz-Filby, *Behind the Gloss* (Welbeck, 2023).
17. Sturtz-Filby, *Behind the Gloss*.
18. *The Observer*, "Studio 54 in Pictures," March 14, 2015.

19. Judy Klemesrud, "And Now, Make Room for the Berenson Sisters," *New York Times*, April 19, 1973.

20. Tom Ford, "Marisa Berenson," *Interview*, August 20, 2011.

21. Emine Saner, "I Did the First Nude in Vogue: Marisa Berenson on Being a Blazing Star of the 70s and Beyond," *The Guardian*, August 30, 2019.

22. Brooke Shields, *There Was a Little Girl: The Real Story of My Mother and Me* (Plume, 2014).

23. Jim Hanchett, "People," *New York Daily News*, June 4, 1978.

24. Shields, *There Was a Little Girl*.

25. *Philadelphia Inquirer*, Newsmakers, "Mother Tries to Suppress Photographs of a Nude Brooke Shields Taken at Age 10," September 27, 1981.

26. Shields, *There Was a Little Girl*.

27. Marian Christy, "A New Margaux—But Is It Real?" *Boston Globe*, August 24, 1979.

28. Schneider, "A Life Eclipsed."

29. Mariel Hemingway, *Finding My Balance: A Memoir* (Simon & Schuster, 2004).

30. Schneider, "A Life Eclipsed."

31. Schneider, "A Life Eclipsed."

32. *The Guardian*, "America's First Babe," July 3, 1996.

33. Saner, "I Did the First Nude in Vogue."

34. Shields, *There Was a Little Girl*.

35. *Primetime Live with Diane Sawyer*, Britney Spears, November 13, 2003.

CHAPTER 14

1. *The Daily Mail*, "Could Tara Be Trying a Little Too Hard?" December 17, 1998.

2. Shane Watson, "The Day I Met Kate Moss, Johnny Depp Was Upstairs," *The Times*, January 15, 2024.

3. Penny Wark, "The Rolex Rentacrowd," *Sunday Times,* May 26, 1996.

4. Phoebe McDowell and Megan Agnew, "At Home with Kate Moss: Crystals, Moonbathing and a Vegetable Patch," *Sunday Times*, September 23, 2023.

5. Watson, "The Day I Met Kate Moss."

6. James Fox, "The Riddle of Kate Moss," *Vanity Fair*, December 2012.

7. Liam Kelly, "Kate Moss Sets the Record Straight on Depp, Teenage Nudity and Drug Taking," *The Times*, July 24, 2022.

8. Maureen Callahan, *Champagne Supernovas: Kate Moss, Marc Jacobs, Alexander McQueen, and the 90s Renegades Who Remade Fashion* (Simon & Schuster, 2014).

9. Kelly, "Kate Moss Sets the Record Straight."

10. Callahan, *Champagne Supernovas*.

11. Fox, "The Riddle of Kate Moss."

12. BBC Radio 4, Desert Island Discs, Kate Moss, July 29, 2022.

13. Elizabeth Kaye, "So Weak, So Powerful," *New York Times*, June 6, 1993.

14. Brid Costello, "Kate Moss: The Waif that Roared," *WWD*, November 13, 2009.

15. Callahan, *Champagne Supernovas*.

16. Fox, "The Riddle of Kate Moss."

17. Wendy Holden, "Tara: Crazy Queen of the Party Scene," *The Times*, February 12, 2017.

18. Penny Wark, "Girls Just Want to Have Funds," *Sunday Times*, December 10, 1995.

19. *Daily Mirror*, "Charles' Pal Tara Is Held after B-test Steve Atkinson," July 8, 1995.

20. Gordon F. Sander, "Out There: London; She Without Whom No Party Is Complete," *New York Times*, May 2, 1999.

21. Victoria Mather, "A Frail Bunny Run to the Ground," *Evening Standard*, April 29, 1999.

22. Wark, "Girls Just Want to Have Funds."

23. Sophie Laybourne, "Tara-ra-boom-der-e!," *Daily Telegraph*, December 21, 1995.

24. *The Sun*, "Royal Boost for Ski Pal's Lover," January 5, 1996.

25. *The Times*, "Obituary: Tara Palmer-Tomkinson," February 9, 2017.

26. Wark, "Girls Just Want to Have Funds."

27. *The Times*, "Obituary: Tara Palmer-Tomkinson."

28. Polly Vernon, "From Our Archive: An Interview with Tara Palmer-Tomkinson, Who Has Died Aged 45," *The Times*, March 2012.

29. Holden, "Tara."

30. Sander, "Out There: London; She Without Whom."

31. Holden, "Tara."

32. Holden, "Tara."

33. Mather, "A Frail Bunny."

34. Holden, "Tara."

35. Sander, "Out There: London; She Without Whom."

36. Holden, "Tara."

37. Holden, "Tara."

38. Mather, "A Frail Bunny."

39. Fox, "The Riddle of Kate Moss."

40. Laura Collins, "Hooked on Hedonism . . . Inside the Dark and Disturbing World of Kate Moss—By the People Who Really Know Her," *Daily Mail*, October 13, 2008.

41. Collins, "Hooked on Hedonism."

42. *The Independent*, "Kate Moss More Damned than Beautiful?" December 26, 2004.

43. Collins, "Hooked on Hedonism."

44. Kelly, "Kate Moss Sets the Record Straight."

45. Polly Vernon, "The Fall and Rise of Kate Moss," *The Guardian*, May 14, 2006.

46. Kelly, "Kate Moss Sets the Record Straight."

47. Vernon, "An interview with Tara Palmer-Tomkinson."

48. Vernon, "An interview with Tara Palmer-Tomkinson."

49. Emily Maddick, "Goodbye Tara: The Original It Girl," *Grazia*, February 15, 2017.

50. Vernon, "An interview with Tara Palmer-Tomkinson."

51. Vernon, "An interview with Tara Palmer-Tomkinson."

52. Maddick, "Goodbye Tara."

53. Vernon, "An interview with Tara Palmer-Tomkinson."

CHAPTER 15

1. Sarah Ditum, *Toxic* (Fleet 2023).

2. Paris Hilton, *Paris: The Memoir* (HQ, 2023).

3. Michelle Gotthelf, "Debutantes They Ain't Hot Young Heiresses Partying Up a Storm," *New York Post*, October 15, 2000.

4. Bob Morris, "Next Generation: The Hilton Sisters," *The New Yorker*, October 10, 1999.

5. Hilton, *Paris*.

6. Hilton, *Paris*.

7. Nancy Jo Sales, "Hip-Hop Debs," *Vanity Fair*, September 1, 2000.

8. Hilton, *Paris*.

9. Ariel Levy, *Female Chauvinist Pigs: Women and the Rise of Raunch Culture* (Simon & Schuster, 2006).

10. Ditum, *Toxic*.

11. Dalton Narine, "People," *Miami Herald*, March 29, 2001.

12. Britney Spears, *The Woman in Me* (Gallery UK, 2023).

13. Krista Smith, "The Inescapable Paris," *Vanity Fair*, October 2005.

14. Hugo Rifkind, "Paris by Paris Hilton Review—Famous for Nothing: The Rise of the Original Influencer," *The Times*, March 11, 2023.

15. Jennifer Otter Bickerdike, *Being Britney: Pieces of a Modern Icon* (Nine Eight Books, 2021).

16. Hilton, *Paris*.

17. Jonah E. Bromwich, "Paris Said She Invented the Selfie. We Set Out to Find the Truth," *New York Times*, November 20, 2007.

18. Spears, *The Woman in Me*.

19. *Primetime Live with Diane Sawyer*, Britney Spears, November 13, 2003.

20. Spears, *The Woman in Me*.

21. Spears, *The Woman in Me*.

22. Otter Bickerdike, *Being Britney*.

23. Smith, "The Inescapable Paris."

24. Nancy Jo Sales, "The Suspects Wore Louboutins," *Vanity Fair*, March 2010.

25. Sales, "The Suspects Wore Louboutins."

26. Emma Brockes, "Sienna Miller on Taking on the Tabloids: 'It Was So Toxic What Women Were Subjected To,'" *The Guardian*, April 23, 2022.

27. Brockes, "Sienna Miller on Taking on the Tabloids."

28. Barbara Davies, "Magic and Mischief: The Rise of Sienna the New Hipchick," *Daily Mirror*, July 31, 2004.

29. Katie Rosseinsky, "The Reinvention of Sienna Miller," *Evening Standard*, April 14, 2022.

30. Louisa Pritchard, "Jude Law Falls for His Alfie Girl," *The Mail on Sunday*, September 28, 2003.

31. Emily Sheffield, "The Vogue Interview: Sienna Miller," *British Vogue*, October 26, 2015.

32. Claudia Croft, "Wardrobe Mistress—Letters," *The Sunday Times*, August 1, 2004.

33. Emily Cronin, "Sienna Miller on Turning 40," *The Telegraph*, August 28, 2021.

34. Erica Davies, "Sienna Is the New Kate Moss (and Kate's mighty miffed about it)," *The Sun*, July 8, 2004.

35. Brockes, "Sienna Miller on Taking on the Tabloids."

36. Simon Hattenstone, "I Always End Up Putting My Big Fat Foot in It," *The Guardian*, March 3, 2007.

37. Hattenstone, "I Always End Up."

38. Hattenstone, "I Always End Up."

39. Brockes, "Sienna Miller on Taking on the Tabloids."

40. Sheffield, "Vogue Interview: Sienna Miller."

41. *The Times*, "Sienna Miller: I Was Hounded and Spat at by Photographers," November 25, 2011.

42. Hilton, *Paris*.

CHAPTER 16

1. Emma Brockes, "Kim Kardashian: My Life as a Brand," *The Guardian*, September 7, 2012.

2. *The Tonight Show with Jimmy Fallon*, Kim Kardashian West, September 11, 2019.

3. *E! News*, 2006 Throwback: Watch Kim Kardashian's First-Ever E! Interview, Allison Crist, March 13, 2021.

4. Oli Coleman, "The Kim Kardashian Sex Tape: An Oral History," *Page Six*, March 27, 2017.

5. Coleman, "The Kim Kardashian Sex Tape."

6. Christi Carras, "Ray J Slams Kris Jenner for Denying She Helped Kim Kardashian Release Sex Tape," *Los Angeles Times*, September 12, 2022.

7. Brockes, "Kim Kardashian."

8. Aly Semigran, "Jon Hamm Kim Kardashian Dispute," *Entertainment Weekly*, March 13, 2012.

9. Brockes, "Kim Kardashian."

10. Caity Weaver, "Kim Kardashian West on Kanye and Taylor Swift, What's in O.J.'s Bag, and Understanding Caitlyn," *GQ*, June 16, 2016.

11. Jonathan Van Meter, "In the 2010s, Fame Went Multi-Platform Kim Kardashian West on Life as a Brand and Her Political Awakening," *The Cut*, November 25, 2019.

12. Sarah Frier, *No Filter: The Inside Story of Instagram* (Random House Business, 2020).

13. Van Meter, "In the 2010s, Fame Went Multi-Platform."

14. Paris Hilton, *Paris: The Memoir* (HQ, 2023).

15. Frier, *No Filter*.

16. Weaver, "Kim Kardashian West on Kanye and Taylor Swift."

17. Van Meter, "In the 2010s, Fame Went Multi-Platform."

18. Todd Martens, "Name of the Game Is Fame," *Chicago Tribune*, August 12, 2014.

19. *The Cut*, "'It' Girl Inflation: You're an 'It' girl! You're an 'It' girl! Everyone's an 'It' girl!," April 24, 2023.

20. Frier, *No Filter*.

21. Jia Tolentino, "The Age of Instagram Face," *The New Yorker*, December 12, 2019.

22. Frier, *No Filter*.

23. 2022 American Society of Plastic Surgeons Statistics Report.

24. Tolentino, "The Age of Instagram Face."

25. Emily Ratajkowski, *My Body* (Quercus, 2021).

26. Sophie Gilbert, "The Problem with Emily Ratajkowski's *My Body*," *The Atlantic*, November 11, 2021.

27. Eva Wiseman, "*My Body* by Emily Ratajkowski Review—Revelatory Essays," *The Guardian,* November 14, 2021.

28. Wiseman, "*My Body* by Emily Ratajkowski Review."

29. Jon Boone, "'She Feared No One': The Life and Death of Qandeel Baloch," *The Guardian*, September 22, 2017.

30. Boone, "'She Feared No One.'"

31. *Indian Express*, "Qandeel Baloch murder," July 22, 2016.

32. *Indian Express*, "Qandeel Baloch murder."

33. Boone, "'She Feared No One.'"

34. Boone, "'She Feared No One.'"

35. Cady Lang, "*Keeping Up with the Kardashians* Is Ending. But Their Exploitation of Black Women's Aesthetics Continues," *Time*, June 10, 2021.

36. Jonathan Van Meter, "The Interview: Kim Kardashian West on Craving Fame and Family Life with Kanye," *The Times*, December 22, 2019.

37. Sarah Ditum, *Toxic* (Fleet 2023).

38. Van Meter, "In the 2010s, Fame Went Multi-Platform."

CHAPTER 17

1. Ashley Ogawa Clarke, Emi Kameoka, Yui Sugiyama, Masayo Ugawa, "Into the Jennieverse: An Exclusive Interview with Blackpink's Jennie," *Vogue Japan*, May 30, 2023.

2. K-Ci Williams, "Jung Ho-yeon Says Squid Game 'Changed Me for the Better,'" *Vulture*, October 12, 2021.

3. Richard Lloyd Parry, "Demands of Fame Crush K-pop Stars," *The Times*, April 24, 2023.

4. Justin McCurry, "The Myeongdong Neighbourhood in Seoul at Night," *The Guardian*, March 6, 2024.

5. Crystal Tai, "Exploding the Myths behind K-pop," *The Observer*, March 29, 2020.

6. Haeryun Kang, "How Blackpink Went from Strangers to Sisters to Pop Supernovas," *Rolling Stone*, May 23, 2022.

7. Kang, "How Blackpink Went from Strangers."

8. Kang, "How Blackpink Went from Strangers."

9. Kang, "How Blackpink Went from Strangers."

10. Kang, "How Blackpink Went from Strangers."

11. Kang, "How Blackpink Went from Strangers."

12. Ashleigh Carter, "Blackpink's Jennie Wore a Lace LBD in New Chanel Promo," *Teen Vogue*, February 3, 2024.

13. Tiffany May, "Calling K-Pop Stars 'Identical,' South Korea Tries to Limit Their Influence," *New York Times*, February 20, 2019.

14. BBC News, "K-pop Band Six Bomb 'Celebrate' Plastic Surgery with Before and After Videos," March 17, 2017.

15. Yan Zhuang, "Blackpink Cuddled a Baby Panda. Not Cute, the Chinese Internet Said," *New York Times*, November 12, 2020.

16. Jessica Norton, "Blackpink's Jennie Criticized for Nurse Costume Worn in 'Lovesick Girls' Video, YG Entertainment Responds," *Pop Crush*, October 6, 2020.

17. Tai, "Exploding the Myths behind K-pop."

18. Parry, "Demands of Fame Crush K-pop Stars."

19. Yang-Yi Goh, "How Squid Game's Hoyeon Became a New Kind of Megastar," *GQ*, April 5, 2023.

20. Yvette Tan and Wonsang Kim, "Sulli: The Woman Who Rebelled against the K-pop World," BBC, October 18, 2019.

21. BBC, "K-pop Star Sulli Found Dead Aged 25," October 14, 2019.

22. Tan and Kim, "Sulli."

23. *The Korea Times*, "K-pop Star Sulli Reveals Her Struggles with Panic Disorder," October 18, 2018.

24. Justin McCurry in Tokyo, "K-pop Under Scrutiny over 'Toxic Fandom' after Death of Sulli," *The Guardian*, October 18, 2019.

25. Motoko Rich and John Yoon, "A K-Pop Star's Lonely Downward Spiral," *New York Times*, February 28, 2024.

26. Rich and Yoon, "A K-Pop Star's Lonely Downward Spiral."

27. Rich and Yoon, "A K-Pop Star's Lonely Downward Spiral."

28. Rich and Yoon, "A K-Pop Star's Lonely Downward Spiral."

29. Rich and Yoon, "A K-Pop Star's Lonely Downward Spiral."

30. Tai, "Exploding the Myths behind K-pop."

31. *The Vancouver Sun*, "Hara Sorry for Suicide Attempt," June 4, 2019.

32. Soo Kim, "Persona: Sulli—Hidden Symbols in K-Pop Star's Posthumous Netflix Series," *Newsweek*, November 16, 2023.

33. Kang, "How Blackpink Went from Strangers."

Bibliography

BOOKS

Asquith, Margot, *An Autobiography: Volumes I and II* (Outlook Verlag, 2019).

Baker, Jean-Claude, *Josephine Baker: The Hungry Heart* (Cooper Square Press, 2001).

Beatty, Laura, *Lillie Langtry: Manners, Masks and Morals* (Vintage, 2000).

Beauclerk, Charles, *Nell Gwyn: A Biography* (Grove Press, 2006).

Berg, A. Scott, *Goldwyn: A Biography* (Simon & Schuster, 2013).

Bernhardt, Sarah, *My Double Life* (State University of New York Press, 1999).

Birkin, Jane, *Munkey Diaries: The Extraordinary Early Years of an International Icon* (W & N, 2021).

Bogdanovich, Peter, *Who the Hell's in It: Conversations with Hollywood's Legendary Actors* (Random House, 2005).

Byrne, Paula, *Perdita: The Life of Mary Robinson* (Harper Press, 2012).

Callahan, Maureen, *Champagne Supernovas: Kate Moss, Marc Jacobs, Alexander McQueen, and the 90s Renegades Who Remade Fashion* (Simon & Schuster, 2014).

Casanova, Giacomo, *History of My Life* (Johns Hopkins University Press, 1997).

Casillo, Charles, *Marilyn Monroe: The Private Life of a Public Icon* (St. Martin's Press, 2018).

Chapple, John, *Elizabeth Gaskell: A Portrait in Letters* (Manchester University Press, 2007).

Chrisman-Campbell, Kimberly, *Fashion Victims* (Yale University Press, 2014).

Churchwell, Sarah, *The Many Lives of Marilyn Monroe* (Bloomsbury Publishing, 2019).

Cleveland, Pat, *Walking with the Muses: A Memoir* (37 Ink, 2017).

Cornwallis-West, Mrs. George, *The Reminiscences of Lady Randolph Churchill* (Edward Arnold, 1908).

Cunningham, Peter, *The Story of Nell Gwyn and the Sayings of Charles II* (Henry Benjamin Wheatley, 1896).

Daws, Shar, *Bombshells: Five Women Who Set the Fifties on Fire* (History Press, 2020)

Ditum, Sarah, *Toxic* (Fleet 2023).

Donnelly, Mark, *Sixties Britain: Culture, Society and Politics* (Taylor & Francis, 2014).

Downes, John, *Roscius Anglicanus: An Historical Review of the Stage* (J. W. Jarvis & Son, 1886).

Drake, Alice, *The Beautiful Fall: Fashion, Genius and Glorious Excess in 1970s Paris* (Bloomsbury, 2007).

Egan, Bill, *Florence Mills: Harlem Jazz Queen* (Scarecrow Press, 2004).

Ellmann, Richard, *Oscar Wilde* (Vintage, 1988).

Fagence Cooper, Suzanne, *How We Might Live: At Home with Jane and William Morris* (Quercus, 2022).

Fraser, Antonia, *King Charles II* (Orion, 2011).

Fraser, Antonia, *Marie Antoinette* (Weidenfeld & Nicolson, 2010).

Friedan, Betty, *The Feminine Mystique: The Classic that Sparked a Feminist Revolution* (Thread, 2021).

Frier, Sarah, *No Filter: The Inside Story of Instagram* (Random House Business, 2020).

Fussell, Betty Harper, *Mabel: Hollywood's First I-Don't-Care-Girl* (Ticknor & Fields, 1982).

Gammel, Irene, *Looking for Anne of Green Gables: The Story of L.M. Montgomery and Her Literary Classic* (St. Martin's Press, July 2008).

Garnett, Henrietta, *Wives and Stunners: The Pre-Raphaelites and Their Muses* (Macmillan, 2012).

Gerzina, Gretchen, *Black England: A Forgotten Georgian History* (John Murray, 2022).

Gottlieb, Robert, *Sarah: The Life of Sarah Bernhardt* (Yale University Press, 2010).

Gristwood, Sarah, *Perdita: Royal Mistress, Writer, Romantic* (Bantam Press, 2005).

Hawksley, Lucinda, *Lizzie Siddal: The Tragedy of a Pre-Raphaelite Supermodel* (Andre Deutsch, 2013).

Hemingway, Mariel, *Finding My Balance: A Memoir* (Simon & Schuster, 2004).

Hilton, Paris, *Paris: The Memoir* (HQ, 2023).

Hodgson, Nichi, *The Curious History of Dating from Jane Austen to Tinder* (Robinson, 2017).

Hotchner, A. E., *Papa Hemingway: A Personal Memoir* (Open Road Media, 2018).

Hughes, Langston, *The Big Sea: An Autobiography* (Hill & Wang Inc., 1993).

Hyman, Clarissa, *Oranges: A Global History* (Reaktion Books, 2013).

Jenner, Greg, *Dead Famous: An Unexpected History of Celebrity from Bronze Age to Silver Screen* (Weidenfeld & Nicolson, 2020).

John Wilmot, *Earl of Rochester: Complete Poetical Works* (Delphi Classics, 2014).

Jordan, Don, and Michael Walsh, *The King's Bed: Sex, Power and the Court of Charles II* (Little Brown, 2015).

Kipling, Rudyard, *Mrs. Bathurst and Other Stories* (Oxford Paperbacks, 1991).

Lake, Veronica, *Veronica: The Autobiography of Veronica Lake* (Dean Street Press, 2020).

Langtry, Lillie, *The Days I Knew* (Panoply Productions, 2012).

Lawson, Twiggy, *In Black and White: An Autobiography* (Simon & Schuster, 1997).

Lefler, Timothy Dean, *Mabel Normand: The Life and Career of a Hollywood Madcap* (McFarland, November 2023).

Levy, Ariel, *Female Chauvinist Pigs: Woman and the Rise of Raunch Culture* (Simon & Schuster, 2006).

Loxton, Alice, *UPROAR!: Satire, Scandal and Printmakers in Georgian London* (Icon Books, 2023).

Mackrell, Judith, *Flappers: Six Women of a Dangerous Generation* (Pan, 2014).

Mann, May, *Jayne Mansfield: A Biography* (Abelard-Schuman, 1974).

Mann, William J., *Tinseltown: Murder, Morphine, and Madness at the Dawn of Hollywood* (Harper, 2014).

Marable, Manning, and Leith Mullings, *Let Nobody Turn Us Around: Voices of Resistance, Reform and Renewal* (Rowman & Littlefield, 2003).

Marcus, Sharon, *The Drama of Celebrity* (Princeton University Press, 2019).

Moore, Thomas, *Letters and Journals of Lord Byron: With Notices of His Life, Volume 1* (J & J Harper, 1830–1831).

Moyle, Franny, *Desperate Romantics* (John Murray, 2009).

Nadoolman-Landis, Deborah, *Dressed: A Century of Hollywood Costume Design* (Harper Collins, 2006).

Otter Bickerdike, Jennifer, *Being Britney: Pieces of a Modern Icon* (Nine Eight Books, 2021).

Painter, Melissa, *Edie: Girl on Fire* (Chronicle Books, 2006).

Paul, Deborah, *Tragic Beauty: The Lost 1914 Memoirs of Evelyn Nesbit* (Lulu.com, 2006).

Pepys, Samuel, *Diary of Samuel Pepys* (Legare Street Press, October 2022).

Peril, Lynn, *Pink Think: Becoming a Woman in Many Uneasy Lessons* (W. W. Norton & Company, 2002).

Porter, Linda, *Mistresses: Sex and Scandal at the Court of Charles II* (Picador, 2020).

Quant, Mary, *Mary Quant: My Autobiography* (Headline, 2012).

Ratajkowski, Emily, *My Body* (Quercus, 2021).

Rendell, Mike, *Georgian Harlots & Whores: Fame, Fashion & Fortune* (Pen & Sword, 2022).

Richards, David, *Played Out: The Jean Seberg Story* (Random House, 1981).

Richardson, Kristen, *The Season: A Social History of the Debutante* (W.W. Norton & Company, 2020).

Robinson, Mary, *The Memoirs of Perdita* (G. Lister, 1784).

Robinson, Mary, and J. Fitzgerald Molloy, ed., *Memoirs of Mary Robinson "Perdita"* (Gibbings and Company, Ltd., 1895).

Rossetti, William Michael, *Ruskin, Rossetti, Preraphaelitism: Papers, 1864 to 1862* (Dodd, Mead and Company, 1899).

Savage, Jon, *Teenage: The Creation of Youth 1875 to 1945* (Chatto and Windus, 2007).

Seymour, John, *Memoirs of the Life of Eleanor Gwinn: A Celebrated Courtesan in the Reign of King Charles II and Mistress to the Monarch* (E. Stamper, 1752).

Shields, Brooke, *There Was a Little Girl: The Real Story of My Mother and Me* (Plume, 2014).

Shrimpton, Jean, *The Truth About Modelling* (V & Fashion Perspectives) (V & A Publishing, 2019).

Spears, Britney, *The Woman in Me* (Gallery UK, 2023).

Spoto, Donald, *Marilyn Monroe: The Biography* (Dansker Press, 2014).

Stein, Jean, *Edie: An American Biography* (Random House, 1988).

Stenn, David, *Clara Bow: Runnin' Wild* (Rowman & Littlefield, 2000).

Strait, Raymond, *The Tragic Secret Life of Jayne Mansfield* (Crossroad Press, 2016).

Sturtz-Filby, Tamara, *Behind the Gloss* (Welbeck, 2023).

Uruburu, Paula, *American Eve* (Riverhead Books, 2008).

Walker, Kirsty Stonell, *Stunner: The Rise and Fall of Fanny Cornforth* (Unicorn, 2022).

Warhol, Andy, and Pat Hackett, *POPism: The Warhol '60s* (Penguin Classics, 2007).

Warren, Doug, *Betty Grable: The Reluctant Movie Queen* (Crossroad Press, 2016).

White, Graham, and Shane White, *Stylin': African American Expressive Culture* (Cornell University Press, 1999).

William Holman Hunt, *Pre-Raphaelitism and the Pre-Raphaelite Brotherhood, vol. 1* (1905).

Winder, Elizabeth, *Marilyn in Manhattan: Her Year of Joy* (Flatiron Books, 2017).

Wohl, Alice Sedgwick, *As It Turns Out* (Fleet, 2023).

Woolf, Virginia, *A Room of One's Own* (e-artnow ebooks, 2013).

MAGAZINE AND NEWSPAPER ARTICLES

Asbury Park Press, English "Sex Symbol" Says a Sense of Humor Is Vital, Rebecca Morehouse, April 11, 1970.

Associated Press, AP Cameraman Take Top Prizes at Press Photo Show, January 23, 1939.

Associated Press, Hot-Dog Skier Turns Million Dollar Cover Girl, June 4, 1975.

The Atlantic, The Problem with Emily Ratajkowski's *My Body*, Sophie Gilbert, November 11, 2021.

The Atlantic Constitution, After a Flicker, Actress' Star Fell Fast, Eleanor Ringel, May 3, 1996.

The Baltimore Sun, Leads Quiet Life: Young Wife of Harry Thaw Thoroughly Secluded, January 5, 1907.

BBC Culture, The It Girls, Sarah Bernhardt: Was She the First "A-list" Actress?, Holly Williams, December 15, 2017.

BBC News, K-Pop Band Six Bomb "Celebrate" Plastic Surgery with Before and After Videos, March 17, 2017.

BBC Radio 4, Desert Island Discs, Kate Moss, July 29, 2022.

BBC, K-pop Star Sulli Found Dead Aged 25, October 14, 2019.

BBC, Sulli: The Woman Who Rebelled against the K-pop World, Yvette Tan and Wonsang Kim, October 18, 2019.

The Boston Globe, A New Margaux—But Is It Real? Marian Christy, August 24, 1979.

The Boston Globe, Edie Sedgwick, 28, Andy Warhol Film Star, David Leacock, November 28, 1971.

Boston Post, New Items, December 25, 1875.

British Vogue, The Shrimpton Story, Jessica Bumpus, March 3, 2010.

British Vogue, The Vogue Interview: Sienna Miller, Emily Sheffield, October 26, 2015.

The Brooklyn Citizen, "Plantation Revue" Is Well Received, July 18, 1922.

The Brooklyn Daily Eagle, Stage Notes, May 28, 1922.

Chattanooga Daily Times, What Failure Has Done to Jean Seberg? It's Made Her Bigger and Better Than Ever, Lloyd Shearer, July 7, 1963.

Chicago Tribune, Ann Sheridan Voted Leading "Oomph" Girl by Jury of 25 Men, March 18, 1939.

Chicago Tribune, Cinderella Girl of '41, February 22, 1941.

Chicago Tribune, Gibson Girl Evelyn Nesbit Thaw Dies: Central Figure in 1906 Love Slaying Trial, Seymour Korman, January 19, 1967.

Chicago Tribune, Name of the Game Is Fame, Todd Martens, August 12, 2014.

The Cincinnati Post, Hemingway's Girl, Marian Christy, January 24, 1975.

The Cut, "It" Girl Inflation: You're an "It" Girl! You're an "It" Girl! Everyone's an "It" Girl!, April 24, 2023.

The Cut, In the 2010s, Fame Went Multi-platform Kim Kardashian West on Life as a Brand and Her Political Awakening, Jonathan Van Meter, November 25, 2019.

The Cut, What Was (and Is) the "It" Girl? An Investigation, Matthew Schneier, August 7, 2023.

The Daily Herald-Tribune, Grable Pin-up Photog Is Dead, June 28, 1986.

The Daily Mail, Could Tara Be Trying a Little too Hard? December 17, 1998.

The Daily Mail, Hooked on Hedonism . . . Inside the Dark and Disturbing World of Kate Moss—By the People Who Really Know Her, Laura Collins, October 13, 2008.

Daily Mirror, Charles' Pal Tara Is Held after B-test Steve Atkinson, July 8, 1995.

Daily Mirror, Magic and Mischief: The Rise of Sienna the New Hipchick, Barbara Davies, July 31, 2004.

Daily News, Daisy Tells of Paying Clara's Rum Bills, January 17, 1931.

Daily News, Jayne Mansfield: Death on the Highway, June 30, 1967.

Daily News, Scripter for Sexpots, Robert Wahls, January 31, 1965.

The Daily Telegraph, Margaux Hemingway, July 3, 1996.

The Daily Telegraph, Tara-ra-boom-der-e!, Sophie Laybourne, December 21, 1995.

The Des Moines Register, Jean Seberg Revisited, Daniel P. Finney, October 30, 2011.

The Dispatch, Brenda Frazier Leads Season's Glamour Girls, Joan Durham, October 29, 1938.

E! News, 2006 Throwback: Watch Kim Kardashian's First-Ever E! Interview, Allison Crist, March 13, 2021.

Entertainment Weekly, Jon Hamm Kim Kardashian Dispute, Aly Semigran, March 13, 2012.

Evening Journal, Mabel Normand Films Under Ban, January 5, 1924.

Evening Standard, A Frail Bunny Run to the Ground, Victoria Mather, April 29, 1999.

Evening Standard, The Reinvention of Sienna Miller, Katie Rosseinsky, April 14, 2022.

Family Weekly, The Girl behind the World's Most Beautiful Face, January 8, 1967.

Florence Mills: Broadway Sensation of the 1920s, Susan Johnson, March 24, 1920 at The Museum of the City of New York (mcny.org).

Fort Wayne Sentinel, "Mabel of the Movies" Calls Herself the Airman's Hoo Doo, Gertrude Price, March 15, 1913.

French Vogue, From the Archive: When Jane Birkin Confided in *Vogue*, Oliver Lalanne, July 16, 2023.

The Gazette, Teenager, 5'7", 93 pounds, Is Newest Queen of Models, Inez Robb, November 30, 1966.

GQ, How Squid Game's Hoyeon Became a New Kind of Megastar, Yang-Yi Goh, April 5, 2023.

GQ, Kim Kardashian West on Kanye and Taylor Swift, What's in O.J.'s Bag, and Understanding Caitlyn, Caity Weaver, June 16, 2016.

Grazia, Goodbye Tara: The Original It Girl, Emily Maddick, February 15, 2017.

The Guardian, "She Feared No One": The Life and Death of Qandeel Baloch, Jon Boone, September 22, 2017.

The Guardian, A Reigning Beauty: Death of Lily Langtry, February 13, 1929.

The Guardian, America's First Babe, July 3, 1996.

The Guardian, Clara Bow: The Hard-Partying Jazz-Baby Airbrushed from Hollywood History, Pamel Hutchinson, June 21, 2016.

The Guardian, I Did the First Nude in *Vogue*: Marisa Berenson on Being a Blazing Star of the 70s and Beyond, Emine Saner, August 30, 2019.

The Guardian, Kim Kardashian: My Life as a Brand, Emma Brockes, September 7, 2012.

The Guardian, K-pop under Scrutiny over "Toxic Fandom" after Death of Sulli, Justin McCurry in Tokyo, October 18, 2019.

The Guardian, *My Body* by Emily Ratajkowski Review—Revelatory Essays. Eva Wiseman, November 14, 2021.

The Guardian, Paris Exhibition to Tell Story of Eccentric Acting Pioneer Sarah Bernhardt, Kim Willsher, April 9, 2023.

The Guardian, Sienna Miller on Taking on the Tabloids: "It Was So Toxic—What Women Were Subjected to," Emma Brockes, April 23, 2022.

The Guardian, Simon Hattenstone, "I Always End Up Putting My Big Fat Foot in it," March 3, 2007.

The Guardian, The Fall and Rise of Kate Moss, Polly Vernon, May 14, 2006.

The Guardian, The Myeongdong Neighbourhood in Seoul at Night, Justin McCurry, March 6, 2024.

The Guardian, The Observer, Sarah: The Life of Sarah Bernhardt by Robert Gottlieb—Review, Olivia Laing, October 24, 2010.

The Guardian, The Saturday Interview: Jean Shrimpton, Alex Wade, April 30, 2011.

The Guardian, Twiggy: I Don't Think High Fashion Will Ever Move Completely Away from Slimness, Emine Saner, May 12, 2020.

The Independent, Edie Sedgwick: The It Girl Who Was Inspiration to Dylan and Warhol, Andrew Wilson, February 5, 2006.

The Independent, Kate Moss More Damned Than Beautiful? December 26, 2004.

The Indianapolis News, She Wasn't just a Plain Jayne, Fremont Power, July 3, 1967.

Indian Express, Qandeel Baloch Murder, July 22, 2016.

Interview, Marisa Berenson, Tom Ford, August 20, 2011.

The Kansas City American, The Life Story of Josephine Baker, Maurice Rochambeau, December 12, 1929.

The Korea Times, K-pop Star Sulli Reveals Her Struggles with Panic Disorder, October 18, 2018.

Life magazine, Betty Grable's Legs, June 7, 1943.

Life magazine, Helen Worden, My Debut—a Horror, Brenda Frazier, December 6, 1963.

Life magazine, Hollywood Topic A-Plus: Whole Town's Talking about Marilyn Monroe, April 7, 1952.

Life magazine, Last Talk with a Lonely Girl: Marilyn Monroe, Richard Meryman, August 17, 1962.

Life magazine, The Debutante, November 14, 1938.

Life magazine, Veronica Lake's Hair: It Is a Cinema Property of World Influence, November 24, 1941.

Life, Fashion: The Girl with the Black Tights, November 26, 1965.

Life, The Arrival of Twiggy, February 3, 1967.

Los Angeles Evening Citizen, The Hollywood Scene, Lowell E. Redelings, June 10, 1953.

Los Angeles Examiner, Mabel Normand's Own Life Story! Mabel Normand as told to Chandler Sprague, February 17, 1924.

The Los Angeles Times, Colleen Away from Flappers, May 18, 1924.

The Los Angeles Times, Jean Seberg: Did Gossip Kill Her? Lee Grany, September 23, 1979.

The Los Angeles Times, Margaux Hemingway's Death Ruled a Suicide, James Rainey, August 21, 1996.

The Los Angeles Times, Never Catty, Says Jayne Mansfield, Lydia Lane, November 11, 1956.

The Los Angeles Times, Ray J Slams Kris Jenner for Denying She Helped Kim Kardashian Release Sex Tape, Christi Carras, September 12, 2022.

The Los Angeles Times, Ritzy People Are Out, Edwin Schallert, November 27, 1921.

The Los Angeles Times, Snapped Famed WWII Betty Grable Pinup: Photographer Frank Powolny Dies at 84, January 11, 1986.

The Mail on Sunday, Jude Law Falls for His Alfie Girl, Louisa Pritchard, September 28, 2003.

The Miami Herald, People: Dalton Narine, March 29, 2001.

The Minneapolis Star, Rita's Real-life Drama, Patrick Agan, August 5, 1980.

Modern Screen, Kirtley Baskette, A High Kick and a Hot Lick, March 1945.

The Montreal Star, Margaux Hemingway: Faberge's Star Barnstorms, Rosemary McCracken, April 21, 1976.

Motion Picture Magazine, Has the Flapper Changed? Margaret Reid, July 1927.

Motion Picture Magazine, Mabel in a Hurry, Frederick James Smith, November 1918.

Motion Picture Magazine, The New Star, January 1922.

Motion Picture, Don't Drink, It Won't Bring Back Your Baby, Hedda Hopper, July 1960.

Motion Picture, The Real Clara Bow, Elisabeth Goldbeck, September 1930.

Nation, The Negro Artist and the Racial Mountain, Langston Hughes, June 23, 1926.

New Pittsburgh Courier, Florence Mills to Head an All-colored Revue as Permanent Institution, May 9, 1925.

New York Daily News, People, Jim Hanchett, June 4, 1978.

The New Yorker, The Age of Instagram Face, Jia Tolentino, December 12, 2019.

The New Yorker, Josephine Baker Was the Star France Wanted—and the Spy It Needed, Lauren Michele Jackson, August 8, 2022.

The New Yorker, Next Generation: The Hilton Sisters, Bob Morris, October 10, 1999.

New York Post, Debutantes They Ain't Hot Young Heiresses Partying Up a Storm, Michelle Gotthelf, October 15, 2000.

New York Post, Edie Sedgwick: Where the Road Led, Helen Dudar, May 2, 1968.

New York Post, The Sensational Debut and Fall of the World's First "Celebutante," Raquel Laneri.

The New York Age, 150,000 Throng Harlem to Pay Last Tribute and Honor to Dainty Star, Florence Mills, November 12, 1927.

The New York Age, Shuffle Along Is in Its Six Month Run, Lester A. Walton, October 15, 1921.

The New York Times, A K-Pop Star's Lonely Downward Spiral, Motoko Rich and John Yoon, February 28, 2024.

The New York Times, Alexandra Jacobs, A Sister's Remembrance of Edie, August 17, 2022.

The New York Times, And Now, Make Room for the Berenson Sisters, Judy Klemesrud, April 19, 1973.

The New York Times, Blackpink Cuddled a Baby Panda. Not Cute, the Chinese Internet Said, Yan Zhuang, November 12, 2020.

The New York Times, Calling K-Pop Stars "Identical," South Korea Tries to Limit Their Influence, Tiffany May, February 20, 2019.

The New York Times, Jayne Mansfield in "Bus Stop," April 16, 1964.

The New York Times, Margaux Hemingway Is Dead; Model and Actress Was 41, Lynette Holloway, July 3, 1996.

The New York Times, Out There: London: She Without Whom No Party Is Complete, Gordon F. Sander, May 2, 1999.

The New York Times, Paris Said She Invented the Selfie. We Set Out to Find the Truth, Jonah E. Bromwich, November 20, 2007.

The New York Times, Scenes of Life in London: Reigning Beauties, July 15, 1878.

The New York Times, Screen, Bosley Crowther, September 12, 1957.

The New York Times, So Weak, So Powerful, Elizabeth Kaye, June 6, 1993.

The New York Times, Some of the Folks in Iowa Think She's a Lost Woman, Rex Reed, August 11, 1968.

The New York Times, The Gibson Girl Is Still with Us, S. J. Woolf, September 20, 1942.

The New York Times, The Screen: Saint Joan, Preminger's Version of Shaw Play Bows, A. H. Weiler, June 27, 1957.

The New York Times, Those Hectic Youngsters, July 19, 1926.

The New York Times, Twiggy: She's Harlow, and the Boy Next Door, Charlotte Curtis, March 21, 1967.

Newsweek, Persona: Sulli—Hidden Symbols in K-Pop Star's Posthumous Netflix Series, Soo Kim, November 16, 2023.

The Northwestern Bulletin-Appeal, Florence Mills Hailed a Genius by NY Critics, November 8, 1924.

n.paradoxa, Maria Elena Buzek, War Goddess: The Varga Girls, WW2 and Feminism, edited by Katy Deepwell, March 1998.

The Observer, Exploding the Myths behind K-pop, Crystal Tai, March 29, 2020.

The Observer, Studio 54 in Pictures, March 14, 2015.

The Oklahoma News, No 1 Debutante—She Likes Them All, December 4, 1938.

The Omaha Daily News, Clara Bow; Newly Made Flapper Star, in Black Oxen, January 3, 1924.

The Oregon Daily Journal, "Shuffle Along" Is a "Lol" with "NYawk Aghast," August 21, 1921.

Page Six, The Kim Kardashian Sex Tape: An Oral History, Oli Coleman, March 27, 2017.

People, A Life Eclipsed, Karen Schneider, July 15, 1996.

People, Beauty and the Bottle, February 8, 1988.

People, Janine Henni, Marilyn Monroe's Estate Says Icon Would Approve of Kim Kardashian's Met Gala Dress Moment, May 4, 2022.

The Philadelphia Inquirer, Andy Warhol Pops in to Show Off Picture of Dollar Bills, Elvis, John P. Corr, October 8, 1965.

The Philadelphia Inquirer, Newsmakers, Mother Tries to Suppress Photographs of a Nude Brooke Shields Taken at Age 10, September 27, 1981.

The Philadelphia Inquirer, Screening TV, Harry Harris, October 14, 1965.

Photoplay, Clara Bow: My Life Story Part 1, as Told to Adela Rogers St. Johns, February 1928.

Photoplay, Clara Bow: My Life Story Part 2, as Told to Adela Rogers St. Johns, March 1928.

Photoplay, Empty Hearted, Lois Shirley, October 1929.

Photoplay, Marilyn Poses Nude Again—Why Did She Do It? September 1962.

Photoplay, What Is This Thing Called "X"?, Hilary Lynn, April 1933.

The Pittsburgh Courier, Early Days Desperate, Says "Flo," February 28, 1925.

Playboy, Sweetheart of the Month: Marilyn Monroe, December 1953.

Pop Crush, Blackpink's Jennie Criticized for Nurse Costume Worn in "Lovesick Girls" Video, YG Entertainment Responds, Jessica Norton, October 6, 2020.

Refinery 29, How Kim Kardashian Reinvented the Socialite, Morgan Baila, October 21, 2016.

Reno Gazette-Journal, What Woman Knows, April 8, 1911.

Rolling Stone, How Blackpink Went from Strangers to Sisters to Pop Supernovas, Haeryun Kang, May 23, 2022.

Salt Lake Telegram, Mabel Normand: Fun Girl of Film, September 18, 1916.

The San Francisco Examiner, Cholly Knickerbocker Observes, December 4, 1938.

The San Francisco Examiner, They'll Shine at Film Frolic Here, January 2, 1924.

The San Francisco Examiner, William Otterburn-Hall, November 23, 1969.

The Seattle Star, Motion Picture Censors Would Best Spend Their Time Barring Society Films, Cynthia Grey, January 16, 1924.

St. Louis Post-Dispatch, Brenda Frazier: Truly Miserably Rich, Karen Heller, June 11, 1987.

The St. Louis Star and Times, Betty Grable's Star Beginning to Twinkle, Homer Bassford, 19 August 1935.

The Sun, Royal Boost for Ski Pal's Lover, January 5, 1996.

The Sun, Sienna Is the New Kate Moss (and Kate's mighty miffed about it), Erica Davies, July 8, 2004.

The Sunday People, For Bardot Read Birkin, Jack Gee, February 8, 1970.

The Sunday Times, At Home with Kate Moss: Crystals, Moonbathing and a Vegetable Patch, Phoebe McDowell and Megan Agnew, September 23 2023.

The Sunday Times, Girls Just Want to Have Funds, Penny Wark, December 10, 1995.

The Sunday Times, The Rolex Rentacrowd, Penny Wark, May 26, 1996.

The Sunday Times, Wardrobe Mistress—Letters, Claudia Croft, August 1, 2004.

Teen Vogue, Blackpink's Jennie Wore a Lace LBD in New Chanel Promo, Ashleigh Carter, February 3, 2024.

The Telegraph, Flaming Libertines: Dante Gabriel Rossetti and His Muse, Judith Watt, March 22, 2011.

The Telegraph, Sienna Miller on Turning 40, Emily Cronin, August 28, 2021.

Time, Keeping Up with the Kardashians Is Ending. But Their Exploitation of Black Women's Aesthetics Continues, Cady Lang, June 10, 2021.

Time, The Swinging City, April 15, 1966.

The Times, Blackbirds, September 13, 1926.

The Times, Bob Colacello: "Andy Would Have Loved AI," Rachel Campbell Johnston, June 1, 2023.

The Times, Demands of Fame Crush K-pop Stars, Richard Lloyd Parry, April 24, 2023.

The Times, From our Archive: An Interview with Tara Palmer-Tomkinson, Who Has Died Aged 45, Polly Vernon, March 2012.

The Times, Kate Moss Sets the Record Straight on Depp, Teenage Nudity and Drug Taking, Liam Kelly, July 24, 2022.

The Times, Obituary: Tara Palmer-Tomkinson, February 9, 2017.

The Times, *Paris* by Paris Hilton Review—Famous for Nothing: The Rise of the Original Influencer, Hugo Rifkind, March 11, 2023.

The Times, Sienna Miller: I Was hounded and Spat at By Photographers, November 25, 2011.

The Times, Tara: Crazy Queen of the Party Scene, Wendy Holden, February 12 2017.

The Times, The Day I Met Kate Moss, Johnny Depp Was Upstairs, Shane Watson, January 15 2024.

The Times, The Interview: Kim Kardashian West on Craving Fame and Family Life with Kanye, Jonathan Van Meter, December 22, 2019.

United Press, Marilyn Admits It's She on that Calendar, Aline Mosby, March 13, 1952.

The Vancouver Sun, Hara Sorry for Suicide Attempt, June 4, 2019.

Vanity Fair, Andy Warhol and Edie Sedgwick: A Brief, White Hot and Totally Doomed Romance, Lili Anolik, December 6, 2017.

Vanity Fair, Florence Mills Leads a Harlemquinade on Broadway, February 1925.

Vanity Fair, Hip-Hop Debs, Nancy Jo Sales, September 1, 2000.

Vanity Fair, The Inescapable Paris, Krista Smith, October 2005.

Vanity Fair, The Riddle of Kate Moss, James Fox, December 2012.

Vanity Fair, The Suspects Wore Louboutins, Nancy Jo Sales, March 2010.

Variety, Film Review: Some Like It Hot, February 24, 1954.

Variety, "Money Always Matters": The Kardashians Tell All about Their New Reality TV Reign, Elizabeth Wagmeister, March 9, 2022.

Vogue Japan, Into the Jennieverse, Ashley Ogawa Clarke, Emi Kameoka, Yui Sugiyama, Masayo Ugawa, May 30, 2023.

Vox, The First Modern Celebrity Was Born 175 Years Ago, Sharon Marcus.

Vulture, Jung Ho-yeon Says Squid Game "Changed Me for the Better," K-Ci Williams, October 12, 2021.

Washington Post, Rachel Tashjian, Jane Birkin Made Simple Things Feel Luxurious, July 16, 2023.

The Wichita Eagle, Clara Vows Titian Tresses Are Real, January 18, 1931.

Women's History Review, Staging Race: Florence Mills, Celebrity, Identity and Performance in 1920s Britain, Caroline Bressey and Gemma Romain, Volume 28, Issue 3, 2019.

WWD, Kate Moss: The Waif that Roared, Brid Costello, November 13, 2009.

Index

"Golden Dreams" calendar, 14, 119, 190, 197, 206
Golden Globe Awards, 124, 143, 155
Goldsmith, Jemima, 180
Goldwyn, Samuel, 63–64, 109
Gone Girl, 2014 film, 215
Goo, Hara, 226, 228–230
Gosling, Ryan, 194
Goudar, Ange, 18
Goude, Jean-Paul, 211
GQ magazine 211, 226
Grable, Betty, *105*, 105–106, 108–111, 114, 116, 118, 133, 232
The Graces in a High Wind, 1810 print, 21
Grammy Awards, 211
Grauman's Chinese Theatre, Hollywood, 110
the Great Depression, 82, 97, 98, 103
the Great Fire of London, 1666, 7
The Great Gatsby, 1925 novel, 179
the Great Migration, 72
Gréco, Juliette, 134
The Greeks Had a Word for Them, 1932 film, 109
Green, Cora, 71
Greene, Graham, 157
Greene, Milton H., 122
Greenfield, Howard, 114
Greenson, Ralph, 128
Griffith, D.W., 60–61
Grimblat, Pierre, 158
Grit, 1924 film, 89
Gross, Garry, 169
Grunge movement, xiii, 176–180,
Guy-Blaché, Alice, 55
Gwyn, Ellen (Old Madam), 3, 6–7, 8, 10
Gwyn, Nell, xi, *1*, 1–3, 6–11, 15, 38,

Haas, Charles, 41
Haber, Joyce, 144
Hack, Jefferson, 184
Hadid, Bella, 214
Hadid, Gigi, 213

Hal Roach Studios, 67
Haley, Jack, 72, 108
Halston, 164–166
Hamlet, 1623 play, 27, 49, 141
Hamm, Jon, 210
Hammam, Imaan, 213
Hanna, Kathleen, 193
Hara On & Off: The Gossip, reality show, 228
Hardy, Thomas, 23
Hargitay, Mariska, 130
Hargitay, Mickey, 130
Harlem Renaissance, 69–70 72,
Harlow, Jean, 98, 117, 120, 155
Harper's Bazaar magazine, 56, 58, 152, 166, 177
Harrison, George, 167
Harry, Prince, Duke of Sussex, 179
Hart, Charles, 6–7
Hart, Roxie, 54
Hasni, Ahmed, 146
Haymarket Theatre, 48, 157
Hays Code (The Motion Picture Production Code), 88
Hays, William Harrison, 88
Hayworth, Rita, 108, 110–111
Hecht, Ben, 117
Hefner, Hugh, 114, 119
Hemingway, Ernest, 162–164
Hemingway, Jack, 162
Hemingway, Margaux, *161*, 161–165, 167, 170–171
Hemingway, Mariel, 162–163, 167–168, 170–171
Hennessy, Ed, 138
Henri, Prince de Ligne, 40
Her Awakening, 1911 short film, 61
Hermès, 160
Hills, Gillian, 157
The Hills, reality show, 201
Hilton, Barron, 196
Hilton, Conrad, 196
Hilton, Kathy, 192
Hilton, Nicky, 99, 191–192

About the Author

Caroline Young is an author from Edinburgh, Scotland, who specializes in film, fashion, and popular culture. Her previous works include *Hitchcock's Heroines*, *Living with Coco Chanel, Audrey in Paris*, *The Fabulous Frances Farquharson: The Colourful Life of an American in the Highlands*, and *Crazy Old Ladies: The Story of Hag Horror*, which was nominated for both a Rondo Hatton Award 2023 and the 2022 Richard Wall Memorial Award.